W9-AXQ-939

Switching Basics and Intermediate Routing

CCNA 3 Companion Guide

Wayne Lewis, Ph.D.

Cisco Press

800 East 96th Street

Indianapolis, Indiana 46240 USA

Switching Basics and Intermediate Routing

CCNA 3 Companion Guide

Wayne Lewis, Ph.D.

Copyright© 2006 Cisco Systems, Inc.

Published by:
Cisco Press
800 East 96th Street
Indianapolis, IN 46240 USA

Printed in the United States of America

Sixteenth Printing: February 2013

Library of Congress Cataloging-in-Publication Number: 2005934967

ISBN-10: 1-58713-170-6
ISBN-13: 978-1-58713-170-7

Warning and Disclaimer

This book is part of the Cisco Networking Academy® Program series from Cisco Press. The products in this series support and complement the Cisco Networking Academy Program curriculum. If you are using this book outside the Networking Academy program, then you are not preparing with a Cisco trained and authorized Networking Academy provider.

 CISCO SYSTEMS

For information on the Cisco Networking Academy Program or to locate a Networking Academy, please visit www.cisco.com/edu.

Publisher
Paul Boger

Cisco Representative
Anthony Wolfenden

Cisco Press Program Manager
Jeff Brady

Executive Editor
Mary Beth Ray

Production Manager
Patrick Kanouse

Development Editor
Andrew Cupp

Senior Project Editor
San Dee Phillips

Copy Editors
Sheri Cain
Karen Gill

Technical Editors
Robert Rummel
Michael Sthultz

Book and Cover Designer
Louisa Adair

Composition
Mark Shirar

Indexer
Tim Wright

Feedback Information

At Cisco Press, our goal is to create in-depth technical books of the highest quality and value. Each book is crafted with care and precision, undergoing rigorous development that involves the unique expertise of members from the professional technical community.

Readers' feedback is a natural continuation of this process. If you have any comments regarding how we could improve the quality of this book, or otherwise alter it to better suit your needs, you can contact us through e-mail at feedback@ciscopress.com. Please make sure to include the book title and ISBN in your message.

We greatly appreciate your assistance.

Trademark Acknowledgments

All terms mentioned in this book that are known to be trademarks or service marks have been appropriately capitalized. Cisco Press or Cisco Systems, Inc., cannot attest to the accuracy of this information. Use of a term in this book should not be regarded as affecting the validity of any trademark or service mark.

CISCO SYSTEMS

Corporate Headquarters
Cisco Systems, Inc.
170 West Tasman Drive
San Jose, CA 95134-1706
USA
www.cisco.com
Tel: 408 526-4000
    800 553-NETS (6387)
Fax: 408 526-4100

European Headquarters
Cisco Systems International BV
Haarlerbergpark
Haarlerbergweg 13-19
1101 CH Amsterdam
The Netherlands
www-europe.cisco.com
Tel: 31 0 20 357 1000
Fax: 31 0 20 357 1100

Americas Headquarters
Cisco Systems, Inc.
170 West Tasman Drive
San Jose, CA 95134-1706
USA
www.cisco.com
Tel: 408 526-7660
Fax: 408 527-0883

Asia Pacific Headquarters
Cisco Systems, Inc.
Capital Tower
168 Robinson Road
#22-01 to #29-01
Singapore 068912
www.cisco.com
Tel: +65 6317 7777
Fax: +65 6317 7799

Cisco Systems has more than 200 offices in the following countries and regions. Addresses, phone numbers, and fax numbers are listed on the
Cisco.com Web site at www.cisco.com/go/offices.

Argentina • Australia • Austria • Belgium • Brazil • Bulgaria • Canada • Chile • China PRC • Colombia • Costa Rica • Croatia • Czech Republic
Denmark • Dubai, UAE • Finland • France • Germany • Greece • Hong Kong SAR • Hungary • India • Indonesia • Ireland • Israel • Italy
Japan • Korea • Luxembourg • Malaysia • Mexico • The Netherlands • New Zealand • Norway • Peru • Philippines • Poland • Portugal
Puerto Rico • Romania • Russia • Saudi Arabia • Scotland • Singapore • Slovakia • Slovenia • South Africa • Spain • Sweden
Switzerland • Taiwan • Thailand • Turkey • Ukraine • United Kingdom • United States • Venezuela • Vietnam • Zimbabwe

About the Author

Wayne Lewis is the Cisco Networking Academy Program manager for the Pacific Center for Advanced Technology Training, based at Honolulu Community College. Since 1998, he has taught routing and switching, remote access, troubleshooting, network security, and wireless networking to instructors from universities, colleges, and high schools in Australia, Canada, Mexico, Central America, South America, China, Hong Kong, Indonesia, Korea, Singapore, Taiwan, and Japan, both on site and at Honolulu Community College.

Cisco Systems has sent Wayne to several countries to conduct inaugural Networking Academy teacher training sessions in networking to certify the initial cohorts of instructors for these countries. Before teaching networking, Wayne began teaching math at age 20 at Wichita State University, followed by the University of Hawaii and Honolulu Community College. In 1992, he received a Ph.D. in math, specializing in finite rank torsion-free modules over a Dedekind domain. He works as a contractor for Cisco Systems, performing project management for the development of network security curriculum and creating certification exam questions. He enjoys surfing the South Shore of Oahu in the summer and surfing big waves on the North Shore of Oahu in the winter.

About the Technical Reviewers

Robert Rummel, CCIE No. 9012, is a systems engineer for Cisco Systems on the federal Navy-Marine team. He has more than 16 years of networking and telecommunications experience. He has a diverse background, ranging from serving eight active-duty years in the Navy to operating a satellite teleport. He currently resides in San Diego with his wife, Vivian, and two children, Brittany and Jordan.

Michael Sthultz received his undergraduate education at Claremont Men's College (B.A.) and the University of California, Berkeley (B.S.E.E.). His M.S. in computer science was completed at the University of Nevada, Las Vegas (UNLV). He also holds industry certifications in A+, CCNP, CCAI, CEH, CLS, CLP, CNA, MCSE, and MCT. Michael has more than 40 years of industry experience in the areas of systems engineering (IBM), programming, network administration, management, consulting, and post-secondary education at both private and public colleges. He is professor and program director for the Cisco Networking Academy Program at Community College of Southern Nevada (CCSN), where he has also developed and taught several digital forensics courses. Michael is currently on a temporary leave of absence from CCSN to serve as associate director for the Identity Theft and Financial Fraud Research and Operations Center at UNLV. Michael has been a reviewer and technical editor for numerous college textbooks and has published several articles and books on computer security and forensics.

Dedications

To my wife and soul mate, Leslie, for always being there for me and enduring my eccentricity.

To my daughter, Christina, for setting high goals and always rising to the occasion.

To my daughter, Lenora, for bringing joy to her dad each day.

To my niece, Sunny, for setting a good example for her friends.

Acknowledgments

Don Bourassa, previous director for the Pacific Center for Advanced Technology Training (PCATT), was the best boss I ever had. He recently went back to being part of the physics faculty at Honolulu Community College (HCC). I would once again like to thank Don for being so supportive of me during the years I worked for him. He has a natural ability to lead faculty, who are not known for being easy to lead. He enabled me to grow and experiment, to succeed and to fail, and I am sure that PCATT and HCC have made very significant progress in the arena of technology education as a result.

Ramsey Pedersen, chancellor of Honolulu Community College, hired me in 1992 when he was but a dean. He has consistently encouraged me to strive to be my best while staying out of the way to allow that to happen. He has the professional confidence to permit his faculty to take risks so that our institution is able to keep up with the rapid pace of technology. As a result, HCC has been a continuing role model in the international arena of technology education.

Mary Beth Ray, executive editor for Cisco Press, has made this and several other projects possible for me. While writing books is extremely time consuming and takes away from quality time with family, it is truly a one in a million opportunity. I am very grateful to her for making this project possible for me.

Andrew Cupp, development editor for Cisco Press, worked with me over the last year on this project. I can't speak for other authors, but I think that writers tend to behave somewhat like the stereotypical artist and have trouble working within prescribed frameworks when it relates to their creative output. Drew was very patient with me when I did not meet certain timelines or carefully follow guidelines, and he always nudged me in a positive way to get me to do what needed to be done. I am very thankful for his guidance and assistance along the way.

Contents at a Glance

Contents

Icons Used in This Book

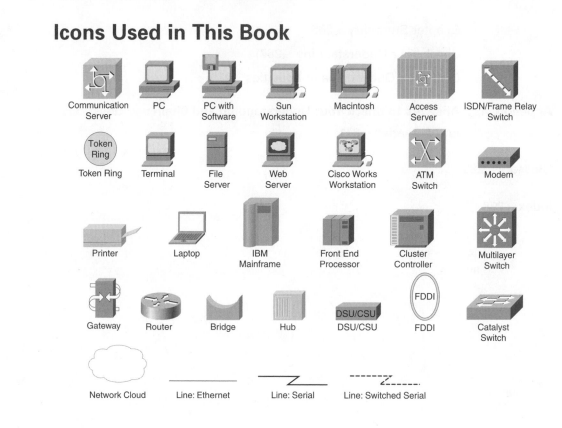

Command Syntax Conventions

The conventions used to present command syntax in this book are the same conventions used in the IOS Command Reference. The Command Reference describes these conventions as follows:

- **Boldface** indicates commands and keywords that are entered literally as shown. In actual configuration examples and output (not general command syntax), boldface indicates commands that the user manually inputs (such as a **show** command).

- *Italics* indicate arguments for which you supply actual values.

- Vertical bars (l) separate alternative, mutually exclusive elements.

- Square brackets [ ] indicate optional elements.

- Braces { } indicate a required choice.

- Braces within brackets [{ }] indicate a required choice within an optional element.

Introduction

The Cisco Networking Academy Program is a comprehensive e-learning program that provides students with Internet technology skills. A Networking Academy delivers web-based content, online assessment, student performance tracking, and hands-on labs to prepare students for industry-standard certifications. The CCNA curriculum includes four courses oriented around the topics on the Cisco Certified Network Associate (CCNA) certification.

Switching Basics and Intermediate Routing: CCNA 3 Companion Guide is the official supplemental textbook to use with v3.1.1 of the CCNA 3 online curriculum of the Cisco Networking Academy Program. As a textbook, this book provides a ready reference to explain the same networking concepts, technologies, protocols, and devices as the online curriculum.

This book goes beyond previous editions of the Cisco Press Companion Guides by providing many alternate explanations and examples as compared with the course. You can use the online curriculum as normal and use this Companion Guide's alternate examples to help solidify your understanding of all the topics.

Goal of This Book

First and foremost, by providing a fresh, complementary perspective of the online content, this book helps you learn all the required materials of the third course in the Networking Academy CCNA curriculum. As a secondary goal, individuals who do not always have Internet access can use this text as a mobile replacement for the online curriculum. In those cases, you can read the appropriate sections of this book, as directed by your instructor, and learn the same material that the online curriculum covers. Another secondary goal of this book is to serve as your offline study material to help you prepare for the CCNA exam.

Audience for This Book

This book's main audience is anyone taking the third CCNA course of the Networking Academy curriculum. Many Networking Academies use this textbook as a required tool in the course, while other Networking Academies recommend the Companion Guides as an additional source of study and practice materials.

This book's secondary audience includes people taking CCNA-related classes from professional training organizations and anyone wanting to read and learn the basics of switching and routing.

Book Features

All the features of this book are either new or improved to facilitate your full understanding of the course material. The educational features focus on supporting topic coverage, readability, and practice of the course material.

Topic Coverage

The following features give you a thorough overview of the topics covered in each chapter so that you can make constructive use of your study time:

- **Objectives**—Listed at the beginning of each chapter, the objectives reference the core concepts covered in the chapter. The objectives match the objectives stated in the corresponding modules of the online curriculum; however, the question format in the Companion Guide encourages you to think about finding the answers as you read the chapter.

- *NEW* **Additional topics of interest**—A few chapters of this book contain topics that cover more details about previous topics or related topics that are less important to the chapter's primary focus. The list at the beginning of the chapter lets you know that additional coverage can be found in the "Additional Topics of Interest" section at the end of the chapter.

- *NEW* **"How to" feature**—When this book covers a set of steps that you need to perform for certain tasks, this book lists the steps as a how-to list. When you are studying, the icon helps you easily refer to this feature as you skim through this book.

- **Notes, tips, cautions, and warnings**—Short sidebars listed in the margins of the page.

- **Chapter summaries**—At the end of each chapter is a summary of the chapter's key concepts. It provides a synopsis of the chapter and serves as a study aid.

How To

Readability

The author has completely rewritten the material so that it has a more conversational tone that follows a consistent and accessible reading level. In addition, the following features have been updated to assist your understanding of the networking vocabulary:

- *NEW* **Key Terms**—Each chapter begins with a list of key terms, along with a page number reference from inside the chapter. The terms are listed in the order in which they are explained inside the chapter. This handy reference allows you to find a term, flip to the page where the term appears, and see the term used in context. The Glossary defines all the key terms.

- *NEW* **Glossary**—This book contains an all-new Glossary with more than 250 terms. The Glossary defines not only the key terms from the chapters, but terms you might find helpful in working toward your CCNA certification.

Practice

Practice makes perfect. This new Companion Guide offers you ample opportunities to put what you learn to practice. You will find the following features valuable and effective in reinforcing the instruction that you receive:

- *NEW* **Check Your Understanding questions and answer key**—Updated review questions are presented at the end of each chapter as a self-assessment tool. These questions match the style of questions that you see on the online course assessments. Appendix A, "Answers to Check Your Understanding and Challenge Questions and Activities," provides an answer key to all the questions and includes an explanation of each answer.

- *NEW* **Challenge questions and activities**—Additional—and more challenging—review questions and activities are presented at the end of most chapters. These questions are purposefully designed to be similar to the more complex styles of questions you might see on the CCNA exam. This section might also include activities to help prepare you for the exams. Appendix A provides the answers.

- **Lab references**—This icon notes good places to stop and perform the related labs from the online curriculum. The supplementary book *Switching Basics and Intermediate Routing CCNA 3 Labs and Study Guide* by Cisco Press contains all the labs from the curriculum plus additional challenge labs and study guide material.

How This Book Is Organized

This book covers the major topic headings in the same sequence as the online curriculum for the CCNA 3 Cisco Networking Academy Program course. The online curriculum has nine modules for CCNA 3, so this book has nine chapters with the same numbers and similar names as the online course modules.

To make it easier to use this book as a companion to the course, inside each chapter, the major topic headings match the major sections of the online course modules (with Chapter 1 being a minor exception to that rule).

However, this *Companion Guide* presents many topics in slightly different ways than the online curriculum. As a result, students get more detailed explanations, a second set of examples, and different sequences of individual topics, all to aid the learning process. This new design, based on research into the needs of the Networking Academies, helps typical students lock in their understanding of all the course topics.

For people reading this book without being in the CCNA 3 class, or just using this book for self-study, the sequence of topics in each chapter provides a logical sequence for reading this book.

Chapters and Topics

The book has nine chapters and one appendix. Chapters 1 through 9 match the nine modules of the online curriculum in number and the topics covered, as described in this list:

- **Chapter 1, "Introduction to Classless Routing,"** provides a foundation in IP addressing using VLSM and CIDR. VLSM and CIDR are used in classless routing, which allows routing to occur independent of traditional classful routing boundaries. RIPv2 is introduced as a routing protocol that leverages VLSM.

- **Chapter 2, "Single-Area OSPF,"** explores link-state routing, in general, and the OSPF routing protocol, in particular. Link-state databases and the Dijkstra algorithm are the key elements in link-state routing. Distance vector concepts are compared to link-state concepts to differentiate the two types of routing protocols. OSPF is introduced as a link-state routing protocol, with a focus on configuring single-area OSPF, including cost, authentication, and network types.

- **Chapter 3, "EIGRP and Troubleshooting Routing Protocols,"** continues the exploration of classless routing protocols. EIGRP is a hybrid routing protocol, combining some of the features of distance vector and link-state routing protocols. EIGRP is relatively easy to configure compared to OSPF, so it provides a nice solution for campus networks comprised of Cisco routers and switches. This chapter concludes the look at routing protocols with an analysis of troubleshooting methods for RIP, OSPF, and EIGRP.

- **Chapter 4, "Switching Concepts,"** discusses Ethernet and the evolution of Ethernet/802.3. Collision domains, microsegmentation, and broadcast domains are introduced.

- **Chapter 5, "LAN Design and Switches,"** describes LAN design and the core-distribution-access LAN design model.

- **Chapter 6, "Catalyst Switch Configuration,"** shows how to configure Catalyst switches using the command-line interface: duplex and speed, managing the MAC address table, port security, password recovery, and upgrading images.

- **Chapter 7, "Spanning Tree Protocol,"** covers STP, which is a Layer 2 redundancy protocol that prevents physical loops from resulting in bridging loops and broadcast storms. A spanning tree is formed, with a root bridge serving as the key element in the spanning-tree topology. The original 802.1d Spanning Tree Protocol and the newer 802.1w Rapid Spanning Tree are explored.

- **Chapter 8, "Virtual LANs,"** covers VLANs, which are fundamental to LAN design and Catalyst switch configuration. All switching concepts relate to VLANs. VLANs provide a logical mechanism of segmenting campus switched networks. VLANs form broadcast domains and normally map in a one-to-one fashion with IP subnets. Configuration topics include adding, changing, and deleting VLANs, as well as verifying and troubleshooting VLAN configuration.

- **Chapter 9, "VLAN Trunking Protocol,"** introduces VLAN trunking with ISL and 802.1Q. VLAN trunks allow data from multiple VLANs to be transmitted and received over a single link. Basically, switches are connected by trunks to form the campus switched topology. VTP automates the population of VLANs throughout the switched topology. For data to flow between VLANs, inter-VLAN routing is required, and this is the final topic of this book.

- **Appendix A, "Answers to Check Your Understanding and Challenge Questions and Activities,"** provides the answers to the Check Your Understanding questions that you find at the end of each chapter. It also includes answers for the Challenge Questions and Activities that conclude most chapters.

- The Glossary provides a compiled list of all the key terms that appear throughout this book.

About the CD-ROM

The CD-ROM included with this book provides many useful tools:

- **Interactive media activities**—Activities from the online course that visually demonstrate some of the topics in the course. These tools can be particularly useful when your Networking Academy does not have the same cable or hardware, or when you use this book for self-study.

About the Cisco Press Website for This Book

Cisco Press provides additional content that can be accessed by registering your individual book at the ciscopress.com website. Becoming a member and registering is free, and you then gain access to exclusive deals on other resources from Cisco Press.

To register this book, go to http://www.ciscopress.com/bookstore/register.asp and enter this book's ISBN, which is located on the back cover. You are then prompted to log in or join ciscopress.com to continue registration.

After you register the book, a link to the supplemental content will be listed on your My Registered Books page. For this book, you will gain access to a PDF of Chapter 4, "Dynamic Routing Protocols," from *Routing TCP/IP*, Second Edition and a PDF of Chapter 3, "Information Technology: A Great Career," from *The IT Career Builder's Toolkit*. Also, take advantage of a coupon code for 35 percent off most Cisco Press titles.

About the CCNA Exam

The computing world has many different certifications available. Some of these certifications are sponsored by vendors and some by consortiums of different vendors. Regardless of the sponsor of the certifications, most IT professionals today recognize the need to become certified to prove their skills, prepare for new job searches, and learn new skills while at their existing job.

Over the years, the Cisco certification program has had a tremendous amount of success. The CCNA certification has become the most popular networking certification. Also, the CCIE certification has won numerous awards as the most prestigious certification in the computing industry. With well over 70 percent market share in the enterprise router and switch marketplace, having Cisco specific certifications on your resume is a great way to increase your chances of landing a new job, getting a promotion, or looking more qualified when representing your company on a consulting job.

How to Obtain Your CCNA Certification

Cisco Systems requires that you take one of two paths to get your CCNA certification. You can either take a single comprehensive exam or you can take two exams—with each exam covering a subset of the CCNA exam topics. Table I-1 lists these exams.

Table I-1   CCNA Exam Names and Numbers

Name	Exam	Comment
INTRO exam	640-821	Maps to Cisco Networking Academy Program CCNA 1 and 2
ICND exam	640-811	Maps to Cisco Networking Academy Program CCNA 3 and 4
CCNA exam	640-801	Covers all four courses

So, you could take the first two courses in the Academy Program, do some extra preparation for the exam, and take the INTRO exam. Then, you could take course 3 and 4, prepare for the ICND exam, and break up your study. Alternatively, you could take the CCNA exam at the end of all four courses.

How to Prepare to Pass the CCNA Exam(s)

The Cisco Networking Academy Program CCNA curriculum helps prepare you for CCNA certification by covering a superset of the topics on the CCNA exam. The four courses of the online curriculum, and the corresponding Cisco Press Companion Guides, cover many more introductory topics than the topics required for CCNA. The reason for this is that the curriculum is intended as a very first course in computing, not just networking. So, if you successfully complete all four semesters in the CCNA curriculum, you will learn the topics covered on the CCNA exam.

However, taking the CCNA curriculum does not mean that you will automatically pass the CCNA exam. In fact, Cisco purposefully attempts to make the CCNA exam questions prove that you know the material well by making you apply the concepts. The CCNA exam questions tend to be a fair amount more involved than the Cisco Networking Academy Program CCNA assessment questions. (For a deeper perspective on this point, refer to http://www.ciscopress.com/articles/article.asp?p=393075.) So, if you know all the concepts from the CCNA curriculum and *Companion Guides*, you have most of the factual knowledge you need for the exam. However, the exam requires that you apply that knowledge to different scenarios. So, many CCNA students need to study further to pass the exam(s).

Many resources exist to help you in your exam preparation. Some of these resources are books from Cisco Press and some are other online resources. The following list details some of the key tools:

- *CCNA Official Exam Certification Library*, **Second Edition (ISBN: 1-58720-169-0), by Wendell Odom**—This book covers the CCNA materials in more depth, with a large (more than 300) question bank of exam-realistic questions and many other tools to help in your study.

- *Cisco CCNA Network Simulator* **(ISBN: 1-58720-131-3), by Boson Software, Inc.**— This software tool is a router/switch/network simulator that you can use to practice hands-on skills on Cisco routers and switches without having a real lab available.

- **Cisco CCNA Prep Center (http://www.cisco.com/go/prepcenter)**—A free online resource from Cisco Systems. (You need a Cisco.com account to access this site, but registration is free.) It has discussion boards, interviews with experts, sample questions, and other resources to aid in your CCNA exam preparation.

Don't forget to register your copy of this book at ciscopress.com to receive a special offer on Cisco Press books.

What's on the CCNA Exams

Like any test, everyone wants to know what's on the exam. Thankfully, Cisco Systems publishes a list of exam topics for each exam to give candidates a better idea of what's on the exam. Unfortunately, those exam topics do not provide as much detail as most people want to see. However, the exam topics are a good starting point. To see the exam topics for the CCNA exams, follow these steps:

Step 1   Go to http://www.cisco.com/go/ccna.

Step 2   Click the text for the exam about which you want more information.

Step 3   On the next window, click the Exam Topics link.

Beyond that, the CCNA curriculum covers a superset of the CCNA exam topics. For example, the CCNA 1 curriculum covers much detail about the physics behind how bits can be transmitted over a cable. None of the CCNA exam topics comes close to referring to these details. However, the CCNA exams do cover the vast majority of the topics in the *CCNA Companion Guides*.

Some topics are certainly more important than others for the exams—exam topics that many people already know are more important. IP subnetting is probably the single most important topic because it is something that requires practice to master, and it can take time, and the exams are timed, of course. IP routing, LAN switching, and any hands-on skills covered in the curriculum are also important topics to know. Ironically, some of the topics that seem too basic to ever be on the exam just happen to be required to understand the more advanced topics. So, other than some of the extra details in Chapters 3 and 4 of this book, most of the rest of the topics in the curriculum and *Companion Guides* might be seen on the CCNA exam(s).

With a typical CCNA exam having only 45–55 questions, your individual exam cannot possibly cover all the topics in the CCNA curriculum. The comments listed here refer to the possible topics for the exams.

CHAPTER 1

Introduction to Classless Routing

Objectives

Upon completion of this chapter, you should be able to answer the following questions:

- What are the features and benefits of VLSM, CIDR, and route summarization?

- What is a classless routing protocol?

- What is meant by network summarization with a classless routing protocol?

- How do you calculate VLSM in a hierarchical network?

- How do you calculate a summary route?

- How do you compare and contrast RIPv1 and RIPv2?

- How do you configure, verify, and troubleshoot Routing Information Protocol (RIP)?

Key Terms

This chapter uses the following key terms. You can find the definitions in the Glossary:

variable-length subnet mask (VLSM)   *page 3*

prefix length   *page 3*

classless inter-domain routing (CIDR)   *page 9*

route summarization   *page 10*

route aggregation   *page 12*

supernetting   *page 13*

classful routing protocol   *page 14*

classless routing protocol   *page 14*

automatic summarization   *page 16*

fixed-length subnet masking (FLSM)   *page 17*

discontiguous subnets   *page 17*

default route   *page 18*

This chapter introduces classless IP addressing, classful routing, classless routing, VLSM, CIDR, RIP version 1 (RIPv1), and RIP version 2 (RIPv2).

Stable, scalable networks are designed; they are not a result of good luck. A key element of good network design is an IP addressing plan that optimizes the use of IP addresses and minimizes the size of the routing table.

As a network grows, the number of subnets and the volume of network addresses increase proportionally. Without IP addressing techniques, such as classless inter-domain routing (CIDR) and route summarization, the size of the routing table is increased, causing a variety of problems; for example, the network requires more CPU resources to acknowledge each topology change in a large routing table. In addition, large routing tables have greater potential for delays when the CPU resources sort and search for a match to a destination address. CIDR and route summarization mitigate these problems.

To effectively use CIDR and route summarization to control the size of routing tables, network administrators employ advanced IP addressing techniques, such as variable-length subnet masking (VLSM).

VLSM is a type of subnet masking used for hierarchical addressing. This advanced IP addressing technique allows the network administrator to subnet a previously subnetted address to make the best use of the available address space.

Another long-standing problem that network engineers must overcome is the exhaustion of available IP addresses caused by the increase in Internet use. The long-term solution is to migrate from the IP version 4 (IPv4) 32-bit address space to the IP version 6 (IPv6) 128-bit address space. However, the focus in this chapter is IP address conservation via CIDR and VLSM.

VLSM and CIDR are improvements to traditional classful IP addressing.

The first part of an IP address identifies the network on which the host resides, whereas the second part identifies the particular host on the given network. The network number field is called the network prefix. The prefix length is the number of bits in the first part of the IP address. All hosts on a given network share the same network prefix but must have a unique host number. In classful IP, the class of the address determines the boundary between the network prefix and the host number. In classless IP, the network engineer determines the boundary between the network prefix and the host number. As a result, classless IP addressing gives much more flexibility in IP network design.

With classless IP addressing, the router makes decisions based on the network prefix and the prefix length in IP address calculations. The high-order bits and the associated IP address class play no role.

This chapter looks first at using VLSM to optimize IP addressing design. Then it explores CIDR and route summarization. This chapter concludes with a discussion of RIPv2, which is an enhancement of RIPv1 and serves as the first example of a routing protocol that supports classless routing. You will learn to configure RIPv2, as well as to verify and troubleshoot RIPv2 configurations.

Note

Many times, when people discuss technical subject matter, terminology can get in the way of their understanding concepts. This is the case with classless IP addressing. You will see terms such as VLSM, CIDR, route summarization, route aggregation, and supernetting. Basically, all these acronyms and terms are focused on the same concept: abandoning the historical dependence of classful IP networking to optimize routing. You will find as you begin to master classless IP addressing that the terms are not that important, but the techniques used are. Relative to most subjects in science, networking is a relatively new field, so it is common to find conflicting usage of terms. You can see this with the terms associated with classless addressing and routing.

VLSM

Variable-length subnet masks were developed to allow multiple levels of subnetworked IP addresses within a single network. You can use this strategy only when the routing protocol in use, such as Open Shortest Path First (OSPF) or Enhanced Interior Gateway Routing Protocol (EIGRP), supports VLSM. VLSM is a key technology in large networks. Understanding its capabilities is important when planning large networks.

VLSM is a crucial component of an effective IP-addressing plan for a scalable network. This section introduces VLSM, provides examples, and discusses methods of determining the best subnet mask for a given address requirement.

Calculating a large enough subnet and determining the range of addresses for a given set of devices are imperative for implementing a scalable network. Understanding VLSM and how to implement it are fundamental to understanding route summarization and CIDR. After you implement VLSM, it is essential for configuring and troubleshooting advanced IP routing protocols and related routing tables.

Prefix Length

The *prefix length* is a shorthand way of expressing the subnet mask for a particular network. The use of the prefix length is key to relating hierarchical network implementations. The prefix length is the number of 1s in the binary representation of the subnet mask; it provides a concise but equivalent representation of the subnet mask.

A series of contiguous 1s from left to right in a subnet mask defines how many bits in the corresponding IP address belong to the network number. The series of contiguous 0s that follows represents the host bits in the corresponding IP address. When you add bits to the network part of an address to make the all-1s field longer, the number of bits in the host part of the address decreases. You create additional networks (subnets) at the expense of the number of host devices that can occupy each network segment.

The number of bits that you add to the default mask creates a counting range for subnets. Each count is a unique binary pattern. You can calculate the number of subnetworks created by using the 2^n formula, where n is the number of bits by which the default mask is extended. You must use the configuration commands in Cisco IOS Software Releases earlier than Software Release 12.0 to explicitly allow subnetwork 0. In Cisco IOS Software Release 12.0 and later, subnetwork 0 is enabled by default. Note that the all-1s subnet has always been allowed. This book assumes that IOS Software Release 12.0 or later is in effect.

The bits that are not allocated as the network part or the subnetwork part of the address form a counting range for hosts. Host addresses are selected from these remaining bits and must be numerically unique from all other hosts on the network. You can calculate the number of hosts created (per subnet) by using the formula $2^m - 2$, where m is the number of bits available in the host portion. In the host-counting range, the all-0s pattern is reserved as the subnet identifier, and the all-1s pattern is reserved as a broadcast address.

In the following example, a range of consecutive IP addresses illustrates these concepts:

Range of addresses: 192.168.1.64 through 192.168.1.79

This range has the first 28 bits in common, which is represented by a /28 prefix length. The 28 bits in common can also be represented in dotted decimal as 255.255.255.240.

In Table 1-1, binary 1s in the network mask represent network bits in the accompanying IP address; binary 0s represent host bits.

Table 1-1   Network Mask and IP Address for the Range 192.168.1.64 Through 192.168.1.79, with Host Bits Shaded

Network mask	11111111.11111111.11111111.11110000
IP address	11000000.10101000.00000001.0100xxxx

In the IP network number that accompanies the network mask, the following are true:

- When the host bits are all binary 0s, that address is the *beginning* of the address range.
- When the host bits are all binary 1s, that address is the *end* of the address range.

Table 1-2 shows the address range from beginning to end for this example, with the fourth octet in binary and the host bits shaded.

Table 1-2   Fourth Octet for the Range 192.168.1.64 Through 192.168.1.79

Fourth Octet in Decimal	Fourth Octet in Binary
64	01000000
65	01000001
66	01000010
67	01000011
68	01000100
69	01000101
70	01000110
71	01000111
72	01001000
73	01001001
74	01001010
75	01001011
76	01001100

Table 1-2   Fourth Octet for the Range 192.168.1.64 Through 192.168.1.79   *(continued)*

Fourth Octet in Decimal	Fourth Octet in Binary
77	01001101
78	01001110
79	01001111

If a PC has an IP address of 192.168.1.67 with a prefix length of 28 (or, equivalently, a mask of 255.255.255.240), it uses this value to determine which other devices with host addresses on the local connection have the first 28 bits in their IP address in common. A 28-bit prefix length for a subnet permits 14 hosts.

The PC uses ARP to find the corresponding MAC address if communication with any of these devices is necessary. The range of these local devices is 192.168.1.64 through 192.168.1.79. If the destination address is not in this range, the packet is forwarded to the default gateway.

A router behaves in a similar manner when it makes a routing decision. A packet arrives on the router and is passed to the routing table. The router compares the destination IP of the packet address to network entries in the routing table. These network entries have a prefix length associated with them. The router uses the prefix length to determine how many destination address bits must match to send the packet to the corresponding outbound interface that is associated with that network number in the routing table.

Consider the scenario in Example 1-1 in which an IP packet with a destination address of 192.168.1.67 is compared against the IP routing table of a router.

Example 1-1   Snippet of a Routing Table Displays the Subnets of 192.168.1.0

```
192.168.1.0 is subnetted, four subnets
O 192.168.1.16/28 [110/1800] via 172.16.1.1, 00:05:17, serial 0
C 192.168.1.32/28 is directly connected, Ethernet 0
O 192.168.1.64/28 [110,10] via 192.168.1.33, 00:05:17, Ethernet 0
O 192.168.1.80/28 [110/1800] via 172.16.2.1, 00:05:17, serial 1
```

Note

People often use the slash (/) notation as a shortcut to express a destination host or destination subnet. For example, you might see the IP address 192.168.1.67 with subnet mask 255.255.255.240 expressed as 192.168.1.67/28. Similarly, you might see subnet 192.168.1.64 with mask 255.255.255.240 expressed as 192.168.1.64/28; in fact, that is how Cisco routers express such a subnet in their routing tables. You normally use this slash notation with networks or subnets, but occasionally, people use it with hosts. If you use the slash notation with a network, be sure that all 0s follow the *n*th bit (where *n* is the prefix length).

In this example, the router determines where to send a packet that is destined for 192.168.1.67. The routing table has four entries for network 192.168.1.0. The router compares the destination address to each of the four entries for this network. The destination address matches the first 24 bits of each of these entries.

Notice that, in the list that follows (at the end of this section), the binary representation of the number 67 matches the first 25 bits of each network number (24 bits for the first three octets plus 1 bit in the displayed fourth octet). The number 67 does not match the first 26 bits for networks 16 and 32, but it does match the first 26 bits for 64 and 80. Address 192.168.1.67 matches all 28 bits of network address 192.168.1.64. If you want to use this network, the destination address needs to match the first 28 bits in the network number. The router forwards this packet to the next router (192.168.1.33) on the Ethernet 0 interface.

The destination address of 192.168.1.67 has the first three octets in common with all four entries in the routing table, but it is not clear by looking at the decimal representation which of those entries is the best match to route this packet. A router handles all packets in binary, not dotted-decimal, notation.

The following is the binary representation of the last octet for destination address 192.168.1.67 and the binary representation of the last octet for the four entries in the IP routing table. Because the prefix length is 28 and all four entries match to at least the first 24 bits of 192.168.1, the object is to find the routing table entry that matches the first four bits of the number 67. It is not important whether the last four bits match, so the target is 0100xxxx. (Note that the routing entry of 64, which has a value of 0100 in the first four bits, is the only one that matches this requirement.)

> 67: 01000011
>
> 16: 00010000
>
> 32: 00100000
>
> 64: 01000000
>
> 80: 01010000

Benefits of VLSM

VLSM allows more than one subnet mask to exist within a network allows subnetting of an already subnetted network address. VLSM offers the following benefits:

- **More efficient use of IP addresses**—Without the use of VLSM, companies must implement a single subnet mask within an entire Class A, B, or C network number.

  For example, consider the 172.16.0.0/16 network address divided into subnets using a 24-bit prefix length. One of the subnets in this range, 172.16.14.0/24, is further divided into smaller subnets with the /27 mask, as shown in Figure 1-1. These smaller subnets range from 172.16.14.0/27 to 172.16.14.224/27. In Figure 1-1, one of these smaller subnets, 172.16.14.128/27, is further divided with the /30 prefix, which creates subnets with only two hosts, to be used on the WAN links. The /30 subnets range from 172.16.14.128/30 to 172.16.14.156/30. In Figure 1-1, the WAN links used the 172.16.14.132/30, 172.16.14.136/30, and 172.16.14.140/30 subnets out of the range.

- **Greater capability to use route summarization**—VLSM allows more hierarchical levels within an addressing plan and thus allows better route summarization within routing tables. (Route summarization is discussed later in this chapter.) For example, in Figure 1-1, subnet 172.16.14.0/24 summarizes all the addresses that are further subnets of 172.16.14.0, including those from subnet 172.16.14.0/27 and from 172.16.14.128/30.

- **Isolation of topology changes from other routers**—Another advantage to using VLSM-enabled route summarization in a large, complex network is that it can isolate topology changes from other routers. For example, when a specific link in the 172.16.27.0/24 network is flapping (periodically going up and down because of intermittent interface failure), the summary route does not change. Therefore, no router that is external to the network needs to keep modifying its routing table because of this flapping activity.

Figure 1-1 VLSM Permits Flexible, Efficient IP Subnet Address Allocation

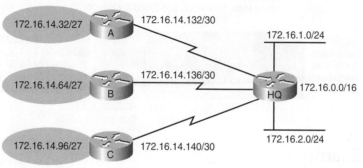

Subnet 172.16.14.0/24 is divided into smaller subnets.
  • Subnet with one mask (/27).
  • Then further subnet one of the unused /27 subnets into multiple /30 subnets.

VLSM Calculations

People commonly use VLSM to maximize the number of possible addresses available for a network. For example, because point-to-point serial lines require only two host addresses, using a /30 subnet does not waste scarce subnet IP addresses.

With VLSM, you can further subnet an already subnetted address. Consider, for example, that you have a subnet address 172.16.32.0/20 and that you need to assign addresses to a network that has ten hosts. With this subnet address, however, you have more than 4000 ($2^{12} - 2 = 4094$) host addresses, most of which will be wasted. With VLSM, you can further subnet address 172.16.32.0/20 to give you more network addresses and fewer hosts per network. If, for example, you subnet 172.16.32.0/20 to 172.16.32.0/26, you gain 64 (2^6) subnets, each of which can support 62 ($2^6 - 2$) hosts.

Use this procedure to further subnet 172.16.32.0/20 to 172.16.32.0/26:

How To

Step 1 Write 172.16.32.0 in binary form.

Step 2 Draw a vertical line between the twentieth and twenty-first bits, as shown in Figure 1-2. (/20 was the original subnet boundary.)

Step 3 Draw a vertical line between the twenty-sixth and twenty-seventh bits, as shown in Figure 1-2. (The original /20 subnet boundary is extended 6 bits to the right, becoming /26.)

Step 4 Calculate the 64 subnet addresses using the bits between the two vertical lines, from lowest to highest value. Figure 1-2 show the first five subnets available.

Figure 1-2   Further Subnetting 172.16.32.0/20 to /26 Prefixes

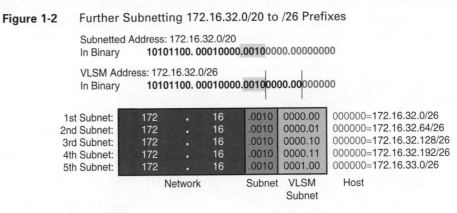

Subnetted Address: 172.16.32.0/20
In Binary   **10101100. 00010000.0010**0000.00000000

VLSM Address: 172.16.32.0/26
In Binary   **10101100. 00010000.0010**0000.00000000

	Network		Subnet	VLSM Subnet	Host
1st Subnet:	172 . 16	.0010	0000.00	000000=172.16.32.0/26
2nd Subnet:	172 . 16	.0010	0000.01	000000=172.16.32.64/26
3rd Subnet:	172 . 16	.0010	0000.10	000000=172.16.32.128/26
4th Subnet:	172 . 16	.0010	0000.11	000000=172.16.32.192/26
5th Subnet:	172 . 16	.0010	0001.00	000000=172.16.33.0/26

VLSM Example

In Figure 1-3, the subnet addresses that are used on the Ethernet segments are those generated from dividing the 172.16.32.0/20 subnet into multiple /26 subnets. (Note that 2^6, or 64, such subnets exist, with 172.16.47.192/26 being the last one.) Figure 1-3 illustrates where you can apply the subnet addresses, depending on the number of host requirements. For example, the WAN links use subnet addresses with a prefix of /30. This prefix allows for only two hosts, which is just enough for a point-to-point connection between a pair of routers.

Figure 1-3   VLSM Used to Define Subnets of 172.16.32.0/20 Across the Boundary Between Octets Three and Four

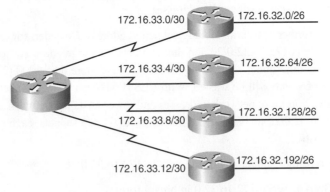

172.16.33.0/30   172.16.32.0/26

172.16.33.4/30   172.16.32.64/26

172.16.33.8/30   172.16.32.128/26

172.16.33.12/30   172.16.32.192/26

To calculate the subnet addresses that are used on the WAN links, further subnet one of the unused /26 subnets. In this example, 172.16.33.0/26 is further subnetted with a prefix of /30. This provides four more subnet bits and 16 (2^4) subnets for the WAN links.

Remember that you can only further subnet unused subnets. In other words, if you use addresses from a subnet, you cannot further subnet it. In the example, four subnet numbers are used on the LANs. Another unused subnet, 172.16.33.0/26, is further subnetted for use on the WANs.

Lab 1.1.4   Calculating VLSM Subnets

In this lab, you use VLSM to support more efficient use of the assigned IP addresses and to reduce the amount of routing information at the top level.

CIDR and Route Summarization

RFC 1519, "Classless Inter-Domain Routing (CIDR): An Address Assignment and Aggregation Strategy," was coauthored by Tony Li of Cisco Systems. This RFC and RFCs 1517, 1518, and 1520 define *classless inter-domain routing*.

Quoting from RFC 1519:

> The basic idea of the plan is to allocate one or more blocks of Class C network numbers to each network service provider. Organizations using the network service provider for Internet connectivity are allocated bitmask-oriented subsets of the provider's address space as required.
>
> It is also worthwhile to mention that once inter-domain protocols which support classless network destinations are widely deployed, the rules described by this plan generalize to permit arbitrary super/subnetting of the remaining Class A and Class B address space (the assumption being that classless inter-domain protocols will either allow for non-contiguous subnets to exist in the system or that all components of a sub-allocated Class A/B will be contained within a single routing domain). This will allow this plan to continue to be used in the event that the Class C space is exhausted before implementation of a long-term solution is deployed.

Because of the explosive growth of IP networks—most importantly, the global Internet—the available IP address space began shrinking, and the core Internet routers began running out of capacity. CIDR (pronounced "cider") was developed to address these problems.

CIDR replaced the process of assigning IP addresses based on Class A, B, and C addresses with a generalized network prefix. Instead of being limited to prefix lengths of 8, 16, or 24 bits, CIDR uses prefix lengths with bit counts ranging within the 32-bit continuum of IPv4 addresses. With CIDR, you can assign blocks of addresses to networks containing 32 hosts or to those with more than 500,000 hosts. This allows for address assignments that more closely fit the specific needs of an organization.

The concept of CIDR is focused on the allocation of blocks of IP addresses to organizations by those entities authorized to do so. The CIDR RFCs also go to some length describing how to do this block allocation to avoid conflicts within the routing tables of core Internet routers. For example, you should implement CIDR so that summarized routes do not black-hole traffic.

Route summarization is a term used to describe the representation by a single network of a group of contiguous networks. Route summarization is described in RFC 1518, "An Architecture for IP Address Allocation with CIDR." Although a consensus does not exist, the term *route summarization* often applies to summarizing within a classful boundary; on the other hand, CIDR almost always refers to combining several classful networks. With both CIDR and route summarization, the point is to optimize routing. To illustrate the difference between route summarization and CIDR, a network engineer can define a summary route on a Cisco router for a company's network, but this has nothing to do with allocating a block of addresses to a customer.

Figure 1-4 displays several subnets of 172.16.0.0/16.

Figure 1-4   Route Summarization of Contiguous Subnets of a Class B Network

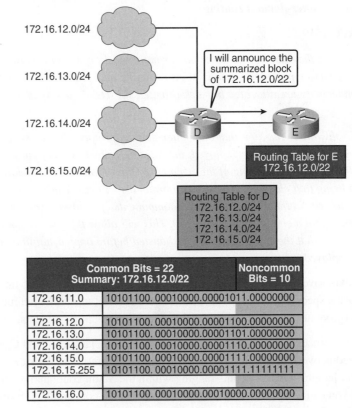

Common Bits = 22 Summary: 172.16.12.0/22		Noncommon Bits = 10
172.16.11.0	10101100. 00010000.00001011.00000000	
172.16.12.0	10101100. 00010000.00001100.00000000	
172.16.13.0	10101100. 00010000.00001101.00000000	
172.16.14.0	10101100. 00010000.00001110.00000000	
172.16.15.0	10101100. 00010000.00001111.00000000	
172.16.15.255	10101100. 00010000.00001111.11111111	
172.16.16.0	10101100. 00010000.00010000.00000000	

Router D has the following networks in its routing table. (You must summarize the networks before the router forwards them.)

- 172.16.12.0/24

- 172.16.13.0/24

- 172.16.14.0/24

- 172.16.15.0/24

Identifying the summary route requires finding the number of common bits shared among the IP addresses. To calculate the summary route, complete the following steps:

How To

Step 1 Find the number of highest-order bits that match in all the addresses, convert the addresses to binary format, and align them in a list.

Step 2 Locate where the common pattern of digits ends. (It might be helpful to draw a vertical line marking the last matching bit in the common pattern.)

Step 3 Count the number of common bits. This number is the prefix length of the summary route. It is represented at the end of the first IP address in the block and preceded by a slash. In Figure 1-4, the first 22 bits of the IP addresses from 172.16.12.0 through 172.16.15.255 are the same. Therefore, the best summary route is 172.16.12.0/22.

Follow these guidelines when calculating summary routes:

- Addresses that do not share the same number of bits as the prefix length of the summary route are not included in the summarization block.

- The IP addressing plan is hierarchical in nature to allow the router to aggregate the largest number of IP addresses into a single summary route. This approach is particularly important for VLSM.

- IP networks can only be summarized in contiguous groups of 2n networks (for some n) where the last octet of the first network in the sequence is divisible by 2n. If this is not the case, you can divide the IP networks into appropriate power-of-2-sized groups of networks and summarize the groups separately.

In the example network, router D can route to network 172.16.12.0/22 and all subnets of that network. However, if other subnets of 172.16.12.0/22 were elsewhere in the network (for example, if 172.16.15.0 was not physically contiguous), this summarization would be invalid.

Route Aggregation

By using a prefix length instead of an address class to determine the network portion of an address, CIDR allows routers to aggregate routing information. This shrinks the routing table of the router. In other words, just one address and mask combination can represent the routes to multiple networks.

The term *route aggregation* is used more loosely than CIDR. It typically describes the summarization of networks, where the summarized networks are classful networks or summaries of classful networks. Also, the term *aggregation* is used more frequently in the context of summarizing networks with Border Gateway Protocol (BGP). In addition, although it is unconventional, you can aggregate subnets of a classful network.

Without CIDR, a router must maintain individual entries for the Class B networks shown in Table 1-3. The shaded columns in Table 1-3 identify the 16 bits that, based on class rules, represent the network number. Classful routers are forced to handle Class B networks using these 16 bits. Because the first 16 bits of each of these eight network numbers are unique, a classful router sees eight unique networks and must create a routing table entry for each.

Table 1-3   CIDR Permits the Aggregation of Contiguous Class B Networks

Network Number	First Octet	Second Octet	Third Octet	Fourth Octet
172.24.0.0/16	10101100	00011000	00000000	00000000
172.25.0.0/16	10101100	00011001	00000000	00000000
172.26.0.0/16	10101100	00011010	00000000	00000000
172.27.0.0/16	10101100	00011011	00000000	00000000
172.28.0.0/16	10101100	00011100	00000000	00000000
172.29.0.0/16	10101100	00011101	00000000	00000000
172.30.0.0/16	10101100	00011110	00000000	00000000
172.31.0.0/16	10101100	00011111	00000000	00000000

However, these eight networks do have common bits, as shown by the shaded portion of Table 1-4. If the prefix defines the last common bit, which has been bolded in Table 1-3, the router can point to one common number representing many networks.

Table 1-4   Summarization Employs the Furthest-to-the-Right Match Principle

Network Number	First Octet	Second Octet	Third Octet	Fourth Octet
172.24.0.0/16	10101100	00011000	00000000	00000000
172.25.0.0/16	10101100	00011001	00000000	00000000
172.26.0.0/16	10101100	00011010	00000000	00000000
172.27.0.0/16	10101100	00011011	00000000	00000000
172.28.0.0/16	10101100	00011100	00000000	00000000
172.29.0.0/16	10101100	00011101	00000000	00000000
172.30.0.0/16	10101100	00011110	00000000	00000000
172.31.0.0/16	10101100	00011111	00000000	00000000

A CIDR-compliant router can summarize routes to these eight networks using a 13-bit prefix, which these eight networks (and only these networks) share: 10101100 00011.

To represent this prefix in decimal terms, the rest of the address is padded with 0s and then paired with a 13-bit subnet mask:

10101100 00011000 00000000 00000000 = 172.24.0.0

11111111 11111000 00000000 00000000 = 255.248.0.0

A single address and mask define a classless prefix that summarizes routes to the eight networks: 172.24.0.0/13.

Using a prefix address to summarize routes results in the following:

- More efficient routing

- A reduced number of CPU cycles when recalculating a routing table or when sorting through the routing table entries to find a match

- Reduced router memory requirements

Supernetting

Supernetting is the practice of using a summary network to group multiple classful networks into a single network address. Note that subnetting involves breaking down a classful network, whereas supernetting involves pasting together classful networks.

The Class A and Class B address space is virtually exhausted, leaving large organizations little choice but to request multiple Class C network addresses from their providers. If a company can acquire a block of contiguous Class C network addresses, supernetting can make the addresses appear as a single large network, or supernet.

You might have noticed the similarity between supernetting and route aggregation. Route aggregation is typically used in the context of summarizing routes with BGP. The term *supernetting* is most often applied when the summarized networks are under common administrative control, especially when the networks being summarized are classful networks. Unlike supernetting, there is no formal definition saying that you cannot apply the term *aggregation* to summarizing contiguous subnets of a classful network, such as "aggregating 192.168.1.0/25 and 192.168.1.128/25 into 192.168.1.0/24." In this case, the term *aggregation* is the same as route summarization. Recall that route summarization commonly refers to the combination of several subnets within a single classful boundary into a single network. However, be aware that many networking professionals use the terms route summarization and route aggregation interchangeably.

CIDR Example

In Figure 1-5, the ISP router receives routing updates for the Class C networks 192.168.8.0/24 through 192.168.15.0/24. When the ISP router advertises the networks toward the Internet, it summarizes them into one route. It does not advertise the eight Class C networks.

Figure 1-5   CIDR Permits the Aggregation of Several Classful Networks into a Single Route Advertisement

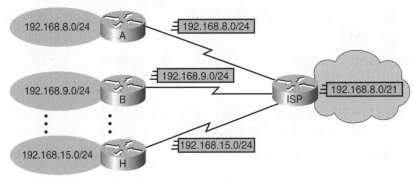

The ISP router advertises 192.168.8.0/21 so that other networks can reach destination addresses that match the first 21 bits of the address 192.168.8.0. At some other point in the internetwork, you can combine this summarized block into 192.168.0.0/16.

CIDR enables ISPs to hierarchically distribute and manage blocks of contiguous addresses so that the IPv4 address space is more efficiently allocated throughout the Internet.

Now you will begin to apply your knowledge of VLSM, CIDR, and route summarization to routing protocols. After that, this chapter explores RIPv2 and how it improves upon RIPv1; in particular, RIPv2 supports VLSM and CIDR.

Classful and Classless Routing

The behavior of *classful routing protocols*, such as RIPv1, on Cisco routers is distinctly limited compared to that of *classless routing protocols*, such as RIPv2. Classful routing protocols make routing decisions and send routing updates according to the Class A, Class B, and Class C constructs. Classless routing protocols work independently of Class A, B, and C. The world of networking is transitioning from classful routing protocols being considered relevant. In the near future, books will only discuss classful routing protocols to provide historical context. The reality is that organizations are running classless routing protocols almost without exception. The approach of this book is to avoid delving into the detail necessary to understand the intricacies of router theory and configuration required for optimal routing in networks employing classful routing protocols (that is, RIPv1 or IGRP) or combinations of classful and classless routing protocols.

First, this chapter looks at some general considerations for routing with classful routing protocols. It omits a significant set of material involving routing table population and interpretation pertaining to classful routing protocols. For more information, see *Cisco IP Routing: Packet Forwarding and Intra-Domain Routing Protocols* by Alex Zinin (Addison-Wesley Professional). Then, this chapter proceeds quickly to looking at principles of classless routing. This provides sufficient background to analyze RIPv2 on Cisco routers, which completes this chapter.

Classful Routing

RIPv1 and IGRP are the two classful IP routing protocols. It is extremely rare to see either of these protocols employed on routers today. For completion, this book provides some essential background on classful routing protocols.

When classful protocols were originally developed, networks were quite different from those used now. The best modem speed was 300 bps, the largest WAN line was 56 kbps, router memory was less than 640 KB, and processors were running in the kHz range. Routing updates had to be small enough not to monopolize the WAN link bandwidth. In addition, routers did not have the resources to maintain up-to-date information about every subnet.

A classful routing protocol does not include subnet mask information in its routing updates. Because no subnet mask information is known, when a classful router sends or receives routing updates, the router makes assumptions about the subnet mask that the networks listed in the update are using. These assumptions are based on IP address class. After a router that is running a classful routing protocol receives a routing update packet, it does one of the following to determine the network portion of the route:

- If the routing update information contains the same major network number as configured on the receiving interface, the router applies the subnet mask that is configured on the receiving interface.

- If the routing update information contains a different major network than the one configured on the receiving interface, the router applies the default classful mask by IP address class. The IP address classes and their default classful masks are as follows:

  — For Class A addresses, the default classful mask is 255.0.0.0.

  — For Class B addresses, the default classful mask is 255.255.0.0.

  — For Class C addresses, the default classful mask is 255.255.255.0.

All subnets of the same major network, Classes A, B, and C, must use the same mask when using a classful routing protocol. Otherwise, routers might assume incorrect subnet information.

Routers that are running a classful routing protocol perform automatic route summarization across network boundaries. Classful routing protocols make assumptions about networks based on their IP address class. These assumptions lead to automatic summarization of routes when routers send updates across major classful network boundaries.

Routers send update packets from their interfaces to other connected routers. The router sends the entire subnet address (without mask) when an update packet involves a subnet of the same classful network as the IP address of the transmitting interface. The router assumes that the network and the interface use the same subnet mask.

The router that receives the update also makes the same assumption. If that route was using a different subnet mask, the router would have incorrect information in its routing table. Thus, when using a classful routing protocol, it is important to use the same subnet mask on all interfaces belonging to the same classful network.

When a router that is using a classful routing protocol sends an update regarding a subnet of a classful network across an interface belonging to a different classful network, the router assumes that the remote router will use the default subnet mask for that class of IP address. Therefore, when the router sends the update, it does not include the subnet information. The update packet contains only the classful network information. This process is illustrated in Figure 1-6.

Figure 1-6   Automatic Summarization Occurs at Classful Network Boundaries with RIPv1 and IGRP

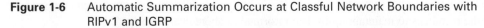

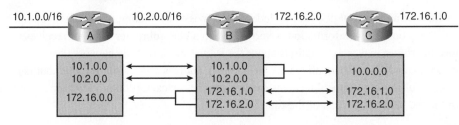

This process is *automatic summarization* across the network boundary. The router sends a summary of all the subnets in that network by sending only the major network information. Classful routing protocols automatically create a classful summary route at major network boundaries. Classful routing protocols do not allow summarization at other points within the major network address space.

The router that receives the update behaves in a similar fashion. When an update contains information about a different classful network than the one in use on its interface, the router applies the default classful mask to that update. The router must determine the correct subnet mask to apply because the update does not contain subnet mask information.

In Figure 1-6, router A advertises the 10.1.0.0 subnet to router B because the interface connecting them belongs to the same major classful 10.0.0.0 network. Router B uses a 16-bit subnet mask on the interface between itself and router A. When router B receives the update packet, it assumes that the 10.1.0.0 subnet uses the same 16-bit mask as the one used on its 10.2.0.0 subnet.

Routers B and C include the subnet information when they exchange information about the 172.16.0.0 network because the interface connecting them belongs to the same major classful

172.16.0.0 network. Therefore, the routing table of router B has information about all the sub-nets that are in use in the network.

However, router B summarizes 10.1.0.0 and 10.2.0.0 subnets to 10.0.0.0 before sending the routing information to router C. This summarization occurs because the update crosses a major network boundary. The update goes from a subnet of network 10.0.0.0, subnet 10.2.0.0, to a subnet of another major network, network 172.16.0.0.

Router B summarizes the 172.16.1.0 and 172.16.2.0 subnets to 172.16.0.0 before sending them to router A. Therefore, the routing table of router A contains summary information about only the 172.16.0.0 network. The routing table of router C contains summary information about only the 10.0.0.0 network.

When you are subnetting while using classful routing protocols, assign all subnets of the same major network to the same subnet mask. This technique is called *fixed-length subnet masking (FLSM)*. FLSM ensures consistency for correctly advertised subnetwork routes; however, the consistency of a subnet mask has a potential disadvantage from the standpoint of efficient address allocation.

For example, a 27-bit mask allocates the proper number of host addresses for an Ethernet seg-ment needing 30 hosts; however, 30 addresses are not used on a point-to-point serial link. A point-to-point serial link requires only two addresses. Therefore, 28 addresses are wasted.

Discontiguous Subnets

Figure 1-7 illustrates a classical problem with classful routing protocols. *Discontiguous subnets* occur when a different major network separates subnets of a major network. In Figure 1-7, router D has a subnet of the 10.0.0.0 network connected to it. It is important to notice the router C routing table. It has two summary routes to the 10.0.0.0 network: one through router B and one through router D. Because these paths have equal metrics, both of them are installed in the routing table. Router C attempts to perform load balancing over both paths.

Figure 1-7   Discontiguous Subnets Present a Problem with Classful Routing

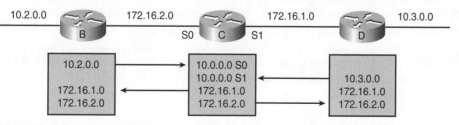

Traffic does not always reach its destination. Router C has a 50-50 chance of correctly routing the packets to a subnet of network 10.0.0.0. For example, router C would not know exactly which interface (serial 0 or serial 1) to use to reach the 10.2.0.0 and 10.3.0.0 subnets.

For this reason, do not permit discontiguous subnets when using classful routing protocols. All subnets of the same major network must be contiguous. Discontiguous subnets are not visible to each other because subnets are not advertised across the network boundary. A classful routing protocol assumes that it has knowledge of all existing subnets of a major classful network.

Default Routes

This chapter now takes a slight detour to discuss *default routes*. Default routes are used pervasively in routing, and this is as good a time as any to introduce (or reintroduce) them. Default routes are configured in conjunction with classful routing protocols just as frequently as with classless routing protocols. The method for configuring the default route depends somewhat on the routing protocol in play.

By default, routers learn paths to destinations in three different ways:

- The system administrator manually defines static routes via an attached interface or the next hop to a destination. These static hops are useful for security and for reduction in routing traffic.

- The network engineer manually defines default routes as the path to take when no known route exists to the destination. Default routes are essential to minimizing the size of a routing table. When an entry for a destination network does not exist in a routing table, the packet is sent via the route.

- Dynamic routing occurs when the router learns of paths to destinations by receiving routing updates from other routers via a routing protocol, such as RIP.

You can define a simple, static route by using the command shown in Example 1-2.

Example 1-2   Configuring a Static Route to a Destination Network

```
Router(config)#ip route 172.16.1.0 255.255.255.0 172.16.2.1
```

The **ip default-network** command establishes a candidate default route. If the referenced network is reachable, a gateway of last resort, or default route, is installed in the routing table. Example 1-3 illustrates the use of this command in a network running RIP, shown in Figure 1-8.

Example 1-3   Configuring a Default Network in Conjunction with Dynamic Routing

```
Router(config)#ip default-network 192.168.20.0
```

After you have configured the routing table with all the appropriate networks, it is useful to ensure that all packets not specified by one of the configured networks will go to a specific location, such as a router that connects to the Internet. A default route is the mechanism that routers use to ensure this function. All the packets that are not represented by a route in the routing table use the default route.

Figure 1-8 shows the default network where packets would be directed, as defined in Example 1-3. The **ip default-network** command is frequently used in conjunction with RIP and IGRP.

Figure 1-8   A Default Network Is Configured Pointing Toward the Internet

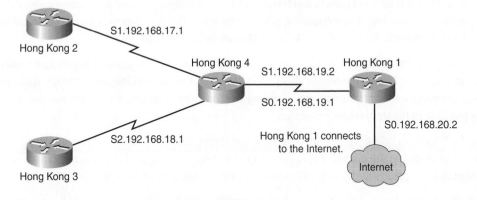

Example 1-4 shows the command to define a default route that you can use with either static or dynamic routing.

Example 1-4   Configuring a Default Route via a Next-Hop IP Address

```
Router(config)#ip route 0.0.0.0 0.0.0.0 192.168.20.2
```

In Figure 1-8, Hong Kong 2 and Hong Kong 3 use Hong Kong 4 as the default gateway. Hong Kong 4 uses Hong Kong 1's serial interface as its default gateway. Hong Kong 1 routes packets to the Internet for all internal hosts. To allow Hong Kong 1 to route these packets, you must configure a default route, as shown in Example 1-4.

The 0s represent any destination network with any mask. Default routes are often referred to as *quad-zero* routes. In Figure 1-8, Hong Kong 1 has only one way out to the Internet through the interface Serial 0.

The most common method for configuring default routes is illustrated in Example 1-4, especially when using EIGRP and OSPF.

Classful Routing Table

If a router is running a classful routing protocol, such as RIPv1 or IGRP, what does it do with an IP packet whose destination lies on an unknown subnet of a major network that does appear in the routing table?

By default, a classful routing protocol assumes that it knows about all subnets of a network in its routing table. It discards traffic routed to any unknown subnets, so the packet described in our question is discarded.

Well, this statement needs to be qualified a bit: It depends on whether the router has the command **ip classless** configured. If the command is *not* configured, the packet is dropped. The **ip classless** command is on by default in Cisco IOS Software Versions 12.0 and later.

The **ip classless** command causes a classful routing protocol to evaluate all packets using the longest-match criterion. The evaluation occurs even when the destination is an unknown subnet of a known network. It changes the default behavior of the classful protocol.

Instead of discarding traffic bound for unknown subnets of a known classful network, a router tries to match the largest number of bits possible against the route in its routing table. Routers using the longest-match criterion make routing decisions by matching the largest number of bits possible in the destination network.

A default route matches any destination. As a last resort, the router uses the default route instead of dropping the packet. Therefore, if **ip classless** is configured and a default route is configured, the packet in the original question is forwarded according to the default route.

Note that **ip classless** has no effect on routers running classless routing protocols because they already use the longest-match criterion to make routing decisions.

Classless Routing

All routing protocols except for RIPv1 and IGRP are classless routing protocols. RIPv2, OSPF, IS-IS, EIGRP, and BGPv4 are classless routing protocols that support VLSM and CIDR.

Classless routing protocols address some of the limitations of the earlier classful routing protocols. One of the most serious limitations in a classful network environment is that the subnet mask is not exchanged during the routing update process, thus requiring the same subnet mask to be used on all subnetworks within the same major network.

With classless routing protocols, different subnets within the same major network can have different subnet masks. Of course, the use of different subnet masks within the same major network is simply VLSM. With VLSM, you can customize the subnet mask to allow the appropriate number of hosts in a network.

If more than one entry in the routing table matches a particular destination, the longest prefix match in the routing table is used. For example, if a routing table has different paths to 172.16.0.0/16 and to 172.16.5.0/24, packets addressed to 172.16.5.99 are routed through the 172.16.5.0/24 path because that address has the longest match with the destination network.

Another limitation of the classful approach is the need to automatically summarize to the classful network boundary at major network boundaries. In the classless environment, you can control the route summarization process manually and invoke it at any bit position within the address. Because subnet routes are propagated throughout the routing domain, manual route summarization might be required to limit the size of the routing tables.

A routing protocol that is classless does not automatically advertise every subnet. By default, classless routing protocols, such as RIPv2, EIGRP, and BGP, perform automatic network summarization at classful boundaries, just like a classful protocol does. Automatic summarization enables RIPv2 and EIGRP to be backward compatible with their predecessors, RIPv1 and IGRP.

The difference between these protocols and their predecessors is that you can manually turn off automatic summarization. To do this, use the **no auto-summary** command under the routing process. You do not need this command when you are using OSPF or IS-IS because neither protocol performs automatic network summarization by default.

The automatic summarization behavior can cause problems in a network that has discontiguous subnets or if some of the summarized subnets are unreachable via the advertising router. If a summarized route indicates that certain subnets are reachable via a router, when in fact those subnets are discontiguous or unreachable via that router, the network might have problems similar to those that a classful protocol causes.

For example, in Figure 1-9, both router A and router B are advertising a summarized route to 172.16.0.0/16. Router C, therefore, receives two routes to 172.16.0.0/16 and cannot identify which subnets are attached to which router.

Figure 1-9   Discontiguous Subnets Presenting a Problem with Classless Routing

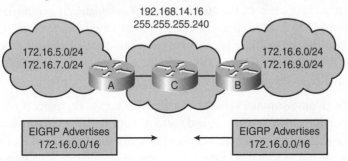

You can resolve this problem by disabling automatic summarization when you are running RIPv2, EIGRP, or BGP. Classless routers use the longest prefix match when selecting a route from the routing table. Therefore, if one of the routers advertises without summarizing, the other routers see subnet routes in addition to the summary route. The other routers can then select the longest prefix match and follow the correct path.

For example, in Figure 1-9, if router A continues to summarize to 172.16.0.0/16 and router B is configured not to summarize, router C receives explicit routes for 172.16.6.0/24 and 172.16.9.0/24 along with the summarized route to 172.16.0.0/16. All traffic for router B subnets is then sent to router B, and all other traffic for the 172.16.0.0 network is sent to router A. This treatment of traffic applies for any other classless protocol.

Effect of auto-summary and no auto-summary

Beginning with IOS Release 12.2(8)T, EIGRP and BGP had **auto-summary** disabled by default; prior to 12.2(8)T, EIGRP and BGP had **auto-summary** enabled by default. With RIPv2, **auto-summary** has always been and remains enabled by default.

In the RIPv2 network in Figure 1-10, router B is attached to subnet 172.16.1.0/24. Therefore, if router B recognizes any network on this interface that is also a subnet of the 172.16.0.0 network, it correctly applies the subnet mask of 255.255.255.0 to that recognized network.

Figure 1-10   Default Behavior of RIPv2 Is to Automatically Summarize at the Network Boundary

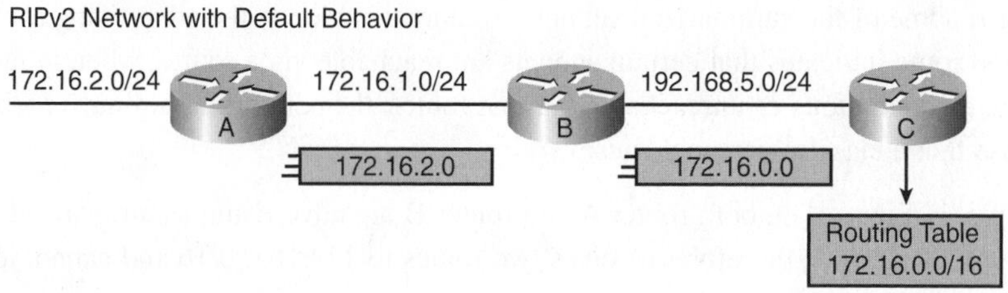

RIPv2 Network with Default Behavior

172.16.2.0/24   172.16.1.0/24   192.168.5.0/24

A   172.16.2.0   B   172.16.0.0   C

Routing Table
172.16.0.0/16

Notice how router C, which is attached to router B via the 192.168.5.0/24 network, handles routing information about network 172.16.0.0. Router B automatically summarized the 172.16.1.0/24 and 172.16.2.0/24 subnets to 172.16.0.0 before sending the route to router C because it was sent over an interface in a different network. Rather than using the subnet mask known to router B (/24), router C applied the default classful mask for a Class B address (/16) when it received information about 172.16.0.0.

In Figure 1-11, with **auto-summary** disabled in the RIPv2 network, router B passes the subnet and subnet mask information to router C, and router C puts the subnet details into its routing table. Router C does not need to use default classful masks for the received routing information because the subnet mask is included in the routing update, and RIPv2 with **auto-summary** disabled does not automatically summarize networks.

Figure 1-11   RIPv2 Supports VLSM with Automatic Summarization Disabled

RIPv2 Network with no auto-summary

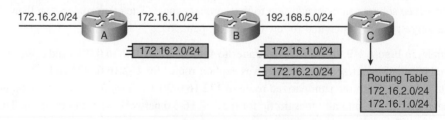

172.16.2.0/24   172.16.1.0/24   192.168.5.0/24

A   172.16.2.0/24   B   172.16.1.0/24
172.16.2.0/24   C

Routing Table
172.16.2.0/24
172.16.1.0/24

When automatic summarization is disabled, RIPv2, EIGRP, and BGP forward subnet information, even over interfaces belonging to different major networks. The behavior in Figure 1-11 would be identical for EIGRP or BGP with *no* **auto-summary** enabled. (This is the default behavior for these protocols after 12.2(8)T.)

To disable **auto-summary** in RIPv2, proceed as in Example 1-5.

Example 1-5   Disabling Automatic Summarization in RIP Version 2

```
Router(config)#router rip
Router(config-router)#version 2
Router(config-router)#no auto-summary
```

The remainder of this chapter analyzes RIPv1 and RIPv2 in particular. A study of the OSPF and EIGRP routing protocols follows in Chapter 2, "Single-Area OSPF," and Chapter 3, "EIGRP and Troubleshooting Routing Protocols."

RIP Version 2

RIPv2 provides a dramatic improvement to RIPv1. We first look at RIPv1 and then explore RIPv2, with a focus on the improvements. RIPv1 is a classful distance vector routing protocol defined in RFC 1058 (June 1988). Key characteristics of RIPv1 include the following:

- It uses the hop count as the metric for path selection.

- The maximum allowable hop count is 15, so infinite distance is equated with 16 hops.

- It uses hold-down timers to prevent routing loops with a default of 180 seconds.

- It employs split horizon to prevent routing loops.

- Failure to receive updates in a timely manner results in removal of routes previously learned from a neighbor.

- The administrative distance is 120.

- Routing updates are broadcast every 30 seconds by default.

- It is capable of load-balancing over as many as six equal-cost paths, with four paths being the default.

- It does not support authentication.

- It does not support VLSM because it is a classful routing protocol.

RIPv1 does not send the subnet mask in its updates. Also, it does not support VLSM.

RIPv2 is a classless distance vector routing protocol defined in RFC 1721 (November 1994), RFC 1722 (November 1994), and RFC 2453 (November 1998). The following are key characteristics of RIPv2:

- It uses the hop count as the metric for path selection.

- The maximum allowable hop count is 15, so infinite distance is equated with 16 hops.

- It uses hold-down timers to prevent routing loops with a default of 180 seconds.

- It employs split horizon to prevent routing loops.

- Failure to receive updates in a timely manner results in removal of routes previously learned from a neighbor.

- The administrative distance is 120.

- Routing updates are multicast every 30 seconds by default.

- It is capable of load-balancing over as many as six equal-cost paths, with four paths being the default.

- It supports clear text and Message Digest 5 (MD5) authentication.

- It supports VLSM by sending a mask in the update.

- It supports manual route summarization.

The major improvements with RIPv2 are the support of authentication, VLSM, sending subnet masks in routing updates, and the multicast of routing updates. RIPv2 also supports external route tags, which enable administrative control of route redistribution.

RIPv2 provides authentication in its updates. A set of keys can operate as an authentication check on an interface. RIPv2 allows a choice of the authentication type to be used in RIPv2 packets: clear text or MD5 encryption. Clear text is the default. You can use MD5 to authenticate the source of a routing update. You can also use MD5 to encrypt **enable secret** passwords; it is not reversible.

RIPv2 uses multicast addressing for more efficient periodic updating on each interface. RIPv2 uses the 224.0.0.9 multicast address to advertise to other RIPv2 routers. This approach is more efficient because when RIPv1 uses a 255.255.255.255 broadcast address, all devices, including PCs and servers, process this packet. They perform the checksum on the Layer 2 packet and pass it up their IP stack.

IP sends the packet to the User Datagram Protocol (UDP) process, and UDP checks whether RIP port 520 is available. Most PCs and servers do not have processes running on this port and discard the packet. However, RIP is sometimes used as a gateway discovery technique in

TCP/IP services, such as UNIX and Windows.

RIPv1 can fit up to 25 networks and subnets in each update, and updates are dispatched every 30 seconds. If the routing table had 1000 subnets, 40 packets would be dispatched every 30 seconds (80 packets a minute). With each packet being a broadcast, all devices must look at it; most of the devices will discard the packet.

The IP multicast address for RIPv2 has its own multicast MAC address: 0x0100.5e00.0009. Devices that can distinguish between a multicast and a broadcast at the MAC layer read the start of the Layer 2 frame and determine that the destination MAC address is not for them. They can then discard all these packets at the interface level and avoid using CPU resources or buffer memory for these unwanted packets.

Even on devices that cannot distinguish between broadcast and multicast at Layer 2, the worst that will happen is that the RIP updates will be discarded at the IP layer instead of being passed to UDP, because those devices are not using the 224.0.0.9 address.

RIPv2 Configuration

The **router rip** command starts a RIP routing process. The **network** command causes the implementation of the following three functions:

- Routing updates are multicast out an interface.

- Routing updates are processed if they enter that same interface.

- The subnet that is directly connected to that interface is advertised.

The **network** command is required because it allows the routing process to determine which interfaces participate in sending and receiving routing updates. The **network** command starts the routing protocol on all interfaces that the router has in the specified network. The **network** command also allows the router to advertise that network.

The **router rip** and **version 2** commands together specify RIPv2 as the routing protocol, whereas the **network** command identifies a participating attached network.

Referring to Figure 1-12, the router A configuration includes the following:

- **router rip**—Enables RIP as the routing protocol

- **version 2**—Identifies version 2 as the version of RIP being used

- **network 172.16.0.0**—Specifies a directly connected network

- **network 10.0.0.0**—Specifies a directly connected network

Figure 1-12   Sample Network and Configuration of RIPv2

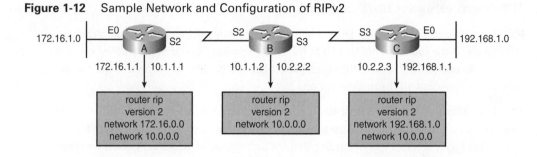

Router A interfaces that are connected to networks 172.16.0.0 and 10.0.0.0, or their subnets, send and receive RIPv2 updates. These routing updates allow the router to learn the network topology. Routers B and C have similar RIP configurations but different network numbers specified. Note that RIPv2 does not have an option to specify mask information in the definition of networks under the routing process. EIGRP and OSPF do permit this option, however. With RIPv1 or RIPv2, only classful networks are used with the **network** command.

Lab 1.2.3   Review of Basic Router Configuration with RIP

In this lab, you set up an IP addressing scheme using Class B networks and configure RIP on routers.

Lab 1.2.4   Converting RIPv1 to RIPv2

In this lab, you configure RIPv1 on the routers and then convert to RIPv2.

Verifying RIP Configuration

The most common commands used to verify a RIP configuration are **show ip protocols**, **show ip interface brief**, **show running-config**, and **show ip route**. Refer to the network in Figure 1-13.

Figure 1-13   Sample Network for Verifying RIP Configuration

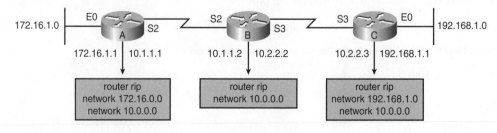

Router A interfaces that are connected to networks 172.16.0.0 and 10.0.0.0, or their subnets, send and receive RIP updates. These routing updates allow the routers to learn the network topology. Routers B and C have similar RIP configurations but different sets of attached networks.

The **show ip protocols** command output for router A is shown in Example 1-6. The output of this command displays parameters for routing protocols, including timer information associated with the router.

```
Example 1-6      show ip protocols Command
RouterA#show ip protocols
Routing Protocolis "rip"
  Sending updates every 30 seconds, next due in 12 seconds
  Invalid after 180 seconds, hold down 180, flushed after 240
  Outgoing update filter list for all interfaces is
  Incoming update filter list for all interfaces is
  Redistributing: rip
  Default version control: send version 1, receive any version
    Interface        Send  Recv  Triggered RIP  Key-chain
    Ethernet0          1     1 2
    Serial2            1     1 2
  Routing for Networks:
    10.0.0.0
    172.16.0.0
  Routing Information Sources:
    Gateway        Distance       Last Update
    (this router)       120       02:12:15
    10.1.1.2            120       01:09:01
  Distance: (default is 120)
```

A router sends RIP updates every 30 seconds. (The timer is configurable.) If a router that is running RIP does not receive an update from another router for 180 seconds or more, it marks the routes that are served by that router as being invalid. In Example 1-6, the hold-down timer is set to 180 seconds. As a result, an update to a route that was down and is now up stays in the hold-down (possibly down) state for at least 180 seconds. If there is still no update after 240 seconds (flush timer), the router removes the routing table entries from the router.

The router is injecting routes for the networks listed following the "Routing for Networks" line. The router is receiving routes from the neighboring RIP routers listed following the "Routing Information Sources" line. The default distance of 120 refers to the administrative distance set for any RIP route.

The **show ip interface brief** command can be useful when you are verifying a RIP configuration. It gives a summary of the IP information and status for all interfaces. You usually use the **show running-config** command when you want to ensure that the appropriate commands are configured for the RIP network.

The output of the **show ip route** command for router A is displayed in Example 1-7. It shows the contents of the IP routing table. The routing table contains entries for all known networks and subnetworks and a code that indicates how that information was learned. The output and function of key fields from this output are explained in Table 1-5.

Example 1-7   show ip route Command

```
RouterA#show ip route

Codes: C - connected, S - static, I - IGRP, R - RIP, M - mobile, B - BGP
       D - EIGRP, EX - EIGRP external, O - OSPF, IA - OSPF inter area
       N1 - OSPF NSSA external type 1, N2 - OSPF NSSA external type 2
       E1 - OSPF external type 1, E2 - OSPF external type 2, E - EGP
       I - IS-IS, L1 - IS-IS level-1, L2 - IS-IS level-2, * - candidate
       default, U - per-user static route, o - ODR, T - traffic engineered route

Gateway of last resort is not set

     172.16.0.0/24 is subnetted, 1 subnets
C       172.16.1.0 is directly connected, Ethernet0
     10.0.0.0/24 is subnetted, 2 subnets
R       10.2.2.0 [120/1] via 10.1.1.2, 00:00:07, Serial2
C       10.1.1.0 is directly connected, Serial2
R    192.168.1.0/24 [120/2] via 10.1.1.2, 00:00:07, Serial2
```

Table 1-5   Fields in the Routing Table Defined

Output	Description
R or C	This identifies the source of the route. For example, C indicates that the route came from a direct connection to a router interface. R indicates that RIP is the protocol that learned the route.
192.168.1.0 10.2.2.0	This indicates the address of the remote network.
120/1	The first number in the brackets is the administrative distance of the information source; the second number is the metric for the route. (Here, it is 1 hop.)
Via 10.1.1.2	This specifies the address of the next-hop router to the remote network.
00:00:07	This specifies the amount of time since the route was updated in hours:minutes:seconds. (Here, it is 7 seconds.)
Serial 2	This specifies the interface through which the specified network can be reached.

If routing information is not being exchanged (that is, if the **show ip route** command shows no entries that were learned from a routing protocol), use the **show running-config** or **show ip protocols** commands to check for a possible misconfigured routing protocol.

Lab 1.2.5   Verifying RIPv2 Configuration

In this lab, you configure RIPv1 and RIPv2 on routers and use **show** commands to verify RIPv2 operation.

Troubleshooting RIP Configuration

Although several **debug** command options exist for troubleshooting RIP, this chapter focuses on the **debug ip rip** command. Figure 1-14 shows a network running RIPv1.

Figure 1-14   Sample Network for Troubleshooting RIP Configuration

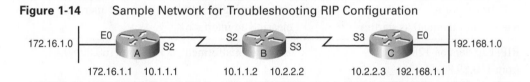

Example 1-8 shows typical output for **debug ip rip** for router A in Figure 1-14.

```
Example 1-8      debug ip rip Command
RouterA#debug ip rip
RIP protocol debugging is on
RouterA#
00:06:24: RIP: received v1 update from 10.1.1.2 on Serial2
00:06:24:        10.2.2.0 in 1 hops
00:06:24:        192.168.1.0 in 2 hops
00:06:33: RIP: sending v1 update to 255.255.255.255 via Ethernet0 (172.16.1.1)
00:06:34:        network 10.0.0.0, metric 1
00:06:34:        network 192.168.1.0, metric 3
00:06:34  RIP: sending v1 update to 255.255.255.255 via Serial2 (10.1.1.1)
00:06:34        network 172.16.0.0, metric 1
```

The **debug ip rip** command displays real-time RIP routing updates as they are sent and received. The command **no debug** all or **undebug all** (**u all** for short) turns off all debugging.

In Figure 1-14, router A has received updates from one router at source address 10.1.1.2. That router sent information about two destinations in the routing table update. Router A also sent updates, in both cases to broadcast address 255.255.255.255. The number in parentheses in Example 1-8 is the source address that is encapsulated in the IP header.

Other output that you might see from the **debug ip rip** command includes entries such as the following:

```
RIP: broadcasting general request on Ethernet 0
RIP: broadcasting general request on Ethernet 1
```

Entries like these can appear at startup when an event occurs, such as when an interface transitions or a user manually clears a routing table. The following entry is most likely caused by a malformed packet from the transmitter:

```
RIP: bad version 128 from 160.89.80.43
```

Table 1-6 describes sample output of the **debug ip rip** command.

Table 1-6   Sample **debug ip rip** Output

Output	Description
RIP: broadcasting general request on Ethernet0 as startup	Transitioning of interface, or a user manually clearing an interface
RIP: bad version 128 from 160.89.80.43	Indicates malformed packet from 160.89.80.43
RIP: received v2 update from 150.100.2.3 on Serial0	Shows version or RIP that 150.100.2.3 is sending
RIP: sending v1 update to 255.255.255.255 via Serial0 (150.100.2.2)	Shows that RIPv1 is configured on Serial0
RIP: ignored v1 packet from 150.100.2.2 (illegal version)	Shows that the router is not configured for RIPv1
RIP: sending v2 update to 224.0.0.9 via FastEthernet0 (150.100.3.1)	Shows that RIPv2 is configured and sending updates
RIP: build update entries 150.100.2.0/24 via 0.0.0.0, metric 1, tag0	Shows use of default route and tag

The **debug ip rip** command is extremely useful when troubleshooting problems with routing table population and route propagation with RIP.

This completes the analysis of RIP. This chapter compared the features of RIPv1 and RIPv2 and explored the configuration, verification, and debugging techniques for RIP.

 Lab 1.2.6   Troubleshooting RIPv2 Using debug

In this lab, you use **debug** commands to verify proper RIP operation and analyze data that is transmitted between routers.

Chapter Summary

Classless IP addressing is implemented with VLSM, CIDR, route summarization, route aggregation, and supernetting. VLSM is the ability to subnet a subnet and use different subnet masks with the same classful network. CIDR refers to the allocation of blocks of contiguous address space to customers by ISPs. Route summarization is a somewhat generic term that describes the use of a single network to represent a sequence of logically contiguous networks. People normally apply that term when the summarization is done within a traditional classful boundary. People typically think of route aggregation as a generalized form of supernetting, especially as it pertains to BGP implementations. Supernetting is the pasting together of classful networks into supernets.

Classful and classless routing have their own unique requirements for proper deployment. RIPv1 and IGRP are classful routing protocols. RIPv2, EIGRP, OSPF, IS-IS, and BGPv4 are classless routing protocols. RIPv2, EIGRP, and BGPv4 can turn automatic summarization on and off.

RIPv2 is a robust improvement to RIPv1, providing authentication, VLSM support, passing of subnet masks in routing updates, and multicasting of routing updates.

Configuring RIPv2 requires adding the **version 2** command, and the **no auto-summary** command is normally recommended. All connected networks participating in RIP are defined with the **network** command in the form of classful networks.

You can verify RIP configurations with the **show ip protocols**, **show ip interface brief**, **show running-config**, and **show ip route** commands. You can troubleshoot RIP with the **debug ip rip** command.

Chapters 2 and 3 continue the study of classless routing with OSPF and EIGRP, respectively.

Check Your Understanding

Complete all the review questions listed here to test your understanding of the topics and concepts in this chapter. Answers are listed in Appendix A, "Answers to Check Your Understanding and Challenge Questions and Activities."

1. What does the command **ip route 186.157.5.0 255.255.255.0 10.1.1.3** specify?

    A. Both 186.157.5.0 and 10.1.1.3 use a mask of 255.255.255.0.

    B. The router should use network 186.157.5.0 to get to address 10.1.1.3.

    C. You want the router to trace a route to network 186.157.5.0 via 10.1.1.3.

    D. The router should use address 10.1.1.3 to get to devices on network 186.157.5.0.

2. When a router receives a packet with a destination address that is within an unknown subnetwork of a directly attached network, what is the default behavior if the **ip classless** command is not enabled?

    A. Drop the packet.

    B. Forward the packet to the default route.

    C. Forward the packet to the next hop for the directly attached network.

    D. Broadcast the packet through all interfaces except the one on which it was received.

3. By default, how often does RIP broadcast routing updates?

    A. Every 6 seconds

    B. Every 15 seconds

    C. Every 30 seconds

    D. Every 60 seconds

4. What is the maximum allowable hop count for RIP?

    A. 6

    B. 15

    C. 30

    D. 60

5. Which command correctly specifies RIP as the routing protocol?

    A. Router(config)#**rip**

    B. Router(config)#**router rip**

    C. Router(config-router)#**rip** {*as-number*}

    D. Router(config-router)#**router rip** {*as-number*}

6. What is the default value of the RIP hold-down timer?

    A. 30 seconds

    B. 60 seconds

    C. 90 seconds

    D. 180 seconds

7. In this line from the output of the **debug ip rip** command, what do the numbers within the parentheses signify?

```
RIP: sending v1 update to 255.255.255.255 via Ethernet1 (10.1.1.2)
```

    A. Source address

    B. Next-hop address

    C. Destination address

    D. Address of the routing table entry

8. What could cause the message "RIP: bad version 128 from 160.89.80.43" to be displayed in the output of the **debug ip rip** command?

    A. Receiving a malformed packet

    B. Sending a routing table update

    C. Receiving a routing table update

    D. Receiving a synchronization error

9. How many subnets do you gain by subnetting 172.17.32.0/20 into multiple /28 subnets?

    A. 16

    B. 32

    C. 256

    D. 1024

10. How many hosts can be addressed on a subnet that has 7 host bits?

    A. 7

    B. 62

    C. 126

    D. 252

11. How many hosts can be addressed with a prefix of /30?

    A. 1

    B. 2

    C. 4

    D. 30

12. Which of the following subnet masks would be appropriate for a Class C address used for nine LANs, each with 12 hosts?

A. 255.255.255.0

B. 255.255.255.224

C. 255.255.255.240

D. 255.255.255.252

13. What network best represents all private Class B networks?

A. 172.16.0.0/24

B. 172.16.0.0/16

C. 172.16.0.0/12

D. 172.16.0.0/8

14. Which network best represents all multicast IP addresses?

A. 224.0.0.0/24

B. 224.0.0.0/16

C. 224.0.0.0/8

D. 224.0.0.0/4

Challenge Questions and Activities

These questions and activities are purposefully designed to be similar to the more complex styles of questions you might see on the CCNA exam. Answers are listed in Appendix A.

1. Refer to Figure 1-15. Using the most efficient IP addressing scheme and VLSM, which address can you configure on one of the serial interfaces?

Figure 1-15   Using VLSM with a Serial Link

192.168.16.128/27

192.168.16.64/27   192.168.16.96/27

   A. 192.168.16.63/27

   B. 192.168.16.158/27

   C. 192.168.16.192/27

   D. 192.168.16.113/30

   E. 192.168.16.145/30

   F. 192.168.16.193/30

2. A company is using an address range of 172.18.0.0/23. Which of the following are valid host addresses if the zero subnet is usable? (Choose three.)

   A. 172.18.0.0

   B. 172.18.0.174

   C. 172.18.1.0

   D. 172.18.1.236

   E. 172.18.1.255

   F. 172.18.2.182

CHAPTER 2

Single-Area OSPF

Objectives

Upon completion of this chapter, you should be able to answer the following questions:

- How do link-state protocols maintain routing information?

- What are the features of link-state algorithms?

- What are the benefits and limitations of link-state routing?

- What are the main features of OSPF?

- How does OSPF routing compare with distance vector routing?

- How does OSPF use hierarchical routing to separate a large internetwork into separate areas?

- What are the OSPF network types?

- How does the SPF algorithm work?

- How is OSPF configured within a single area?

- How is OSPF behavior affected by modifying the OSPF router ID to a loopback address?

- How is the OSPF cost metric modified?

- How is OSPF authentication configured?

- How are OSPF timers configured?

- How is a default route propagated by OSPF?

- How are **show** commands used to verify an OSPF configuration?

- How are **debug** commands used to troubleshoot an OSPF configuration?

Key Terms

This chapter uses the following key terms. You can find the definitions in the Glossary:

continues

continued

With VLSM, CIDR, and RIPv2 under your belt, you can delve into link-state routing. This book explores the most common link-state routing protocol: Open Shortest Path First (OSPF).

OSPF is an Interior Gateway Protocol (IGP) and a classless link-state routing protocol. Because OSPF is widely deployed, knowledge of its configuration and maintenance is essential. This chapter describes OSPF's function and explains how to configure a single-area OSPF network on a Cisco router.

First, link-state routing is discussed in general. This discussion is followed by an exploration of the OSPF routing protocol and OSPF configuration.

Link-State Routing Overview

Link-state routing algorithms, also known as *shortest path first (SPF) algorithms*, are used to build a complex database of topology information. These algorithms efficiently compute the shortest path between nodes on a graph—in the case of networking, routers are the nodes and links are the edges of the graph. Whereas a distance vector algorithm has nonspecific information about distant networks and no knowledge of distant routers, a link-state routing algorithm maintains full knowledge of distant routers and how they interconnect. Understanding the operation of link-state routing protocols is critical to being able to enable, verify, and troubleshoot their operation.

Maintaining Routing Information Via Link States

To maintain routing information, link-state routing uses *link-state advertisements (LSA)*, a *topological database* (or *link-state database*), the SPF algorithm, the resulting SPF tree, and a routing table of paths and ports to each network. An LSA is a basic building block of a link-state routing protocol that provides a description of a router's local routing topology and is distributed to all other routers in the area. The topological, or link-state, database is the set of all links learned from the flooding of LSAs; each router synchronizes its topological database with all other routers in the area. Figure 2-1 shows these concepts.

OSPF and *Intermediate System-to-Intermediate System (IS-IS)* protocols are classified as link-state routing protocols. RFC 2328 describes OSPF link-state concepts and operations. Link-state routing protocols collect routing information from all other routers in the network or within a defined area of the network. After all the information is collected, each router, independent of the other routers, calculates its best paths to all destinations in the network. Because each router maintains its own view of the network, the router is less likely to propagate incorrect information that is provided by a neighboring router.

Link-state routing protocols were designed to overcome the limitations of distance vector routing protocols. Link-state routing protocols respond quickly to network changes, only send triggered updates when a network change occurs, and send periodic updates (known as link-state refreshes) at long time intervals, such as every 30 minutes. A hello mechanism determines the reachability of neighbors.

Figure 2-1   Link-State Routing Relies on Complex Mechanisms to Permit Stable, Synchronous, and High-Speed Routing

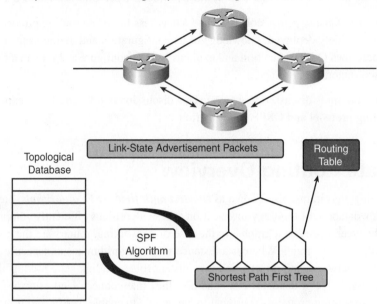

When a failure occurs in the network, such as when a neighbor becomes unreachable, link-state protocols flood LSAs by using a special multicast address throughout an area. Each link-state router takes a copy of the LSA, updates its link-state (topological) database, and forwards the LSA to all neighboring devices. LSAs cause every router within the area to recalculate routes. Because LSAs must be flooded throughout an area and all routers within that area must recalculate their routing tables, the number of link-state routers that can be in an area must be limited. Link-state routing protocols prevent the flooding of LSAs outside of any given area.

A link is similar to an interface on a router. The state of the link is a description of that interface and its relationship to its neighboring routers. A description of the interface can include, for example, the IP address of the interface, the mask, the type of network to which it is connected, the routers connected to that network, and so on. The collection of link states forms a link-state, or topological, database. The link-state database calculates the best paths through the network. Link-state routers find the best paths to destinations by applying the Dijkstra SPF algorithm against the link-state database to build the SPF tree. The best paths are then selected from the SPF tree and placed in the routing table.

Link-state protocols use a two-layer network hierarchy, as Figure 2-2 shows.

Figure 2-2   OSPF Uses a Two-Layer Hierarchy

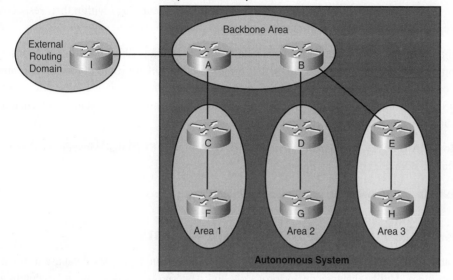

Two primary elements exist in the two-layer network hierarchy:

- **Area**—A grouping of contiguous networks. Areas are logical subdivisions of the autonomous system. Each area must connect directly to the backbone area (known as area 0).

- **Autonomous system (AS)**—Consists of a collection of networks under a common administration that share a common routing strategy. An AS, sometimes called a routing domain, can be logically subdivided into multiple areas.

Within each AS, a contiguous backbone area must be defined. All other nonbackbone areas are connected off the backbone area. The *backbone area* is the transition area because all other areas communicate through it. For OSPF, the *nonbackbone areas* can be additionally configured as a stub area, a totally stubby area, or a not-so-stubby area (NSSA) to help reduce the link-state database and routing table size; this book does not explore these options.

Routers operating within the two-layer network hierarchy have different routing entities. The terms used to refer to these entities are different for OSPF and IS-IS. Although this book does not explore IS-IS, it is worthwhile to make brief mention of the protocol here, because it is OSPF's sister link-state protocol. The following are some examples of router roles in OSPF and IS-IS networks (refers to Figure 2-2):

- Routers A and B are called backbone routers in OSPF and L2 routers in IS-IS. A backbone, or L2, router provides connectivity between different areas.

- Routers C, D, and E are called *Area Border Routers (ABR)* in OSPF and L1-L2 routers in IS-IS. ABRs, or L1-L2 routers, attach to multiple areas, maintain separate link-state databases for each area they are connected to, and route traffic destined for or arriving from other areas.

- Routers F, G, and H are called nonbackbone internal routers in OSPF, or L1 routers in IS-IS. Nonbackbone internal, or L1, routers are aware of the topology within their respective areas and maintain identical link-state databases about the areas.

- The ABR, or L1-L2 router, advertises a default route to the nonbackbone internal, or L1, router. The nonbackbone internal, or L1, router uses the default route to forward all inter-area or interdomain traffic to the ABR, or L1-L2 router. This behavior can be different for OSPF, depending on how the OSPF nonbackbone area is configured (standard/normal area, stub area, totally stubby area, or NSSA).

- Router A is an *Autonomous System Boundary Router (ASBR)* that connects to an external routing domain, or AS.

- Router I belongs to another routing domain, or AS.

Link-State Routing Protocol Algorithms

Link-state routing algorithms rely on SPF protocols to maintain a complex database of the network topology. Unlike distance vector protocols, link-state protocols develop and maintain a full knowledge of the network routers and how they interconnect. This knowledge is achieved through the exchange of LSAs with other routers in a network.

Each router that has exchanged LSAs constructs a topological database by using all received LSAs. A SPF algorithm is then used to compute reachability to networked destinations. This information is used to update the routing table; the routing table only contains the lowest-cost routes from the topological database. This process enables discovery of changes in the network topology caused by component failure or network growth.

Instead of using periodic updates, the LSA exchange is triggered by an event in the network. This can greatly speed up the convergence process because there is no need to wait for a series of timers to expire before the networked routers can begin to converge.

If the network shown in Figure 2-3 uses a link-state routing protocol, there would be no concern about connectivity between New York City and San Francisco. Depending on the actual protocol employed and the metrics selected, it is highly likely that the routing protocol will discriminate between the two paths to the same destination and try to use the best one. The cost metric determines the shortest path for link-state routing protocols. Table 2-1 summarizes the contents of the routing tables.

Figure 2-3   Cost Metric Determines Shortest Path for Link-State Routing Protocols

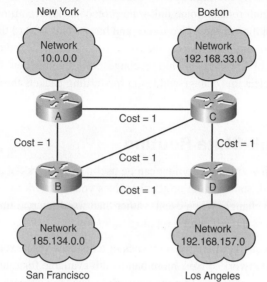

Table 2-1   Next Hops and Costs for Destination Routes

Router	Destination	Next Hop	Cost
A	185.134.0.0	B	1
A	192.168.33.0	C	1
A	192.168.157.0	B	2
A	192.168.157.0	C	2
B	10.0.0.0	A	1
B	192.168.33.0	C	1
B	192.168.157.0	D	1
C	10.0.0.0	A	1
C	185.134.0.0	B	1
C	192.168.157.0	D	1
D	10.0.0.0	B	2
D	10.0.0.0	C	2
D	185.134.0.0	B	1
D	192.168.33.0	C	1

As shown in Table 2-1, with routing entries for the New York to Los Angeles routes, a link-state protocol records both routes. Some link-state protocols can even provide a way to assess the performance capabilities of these two routes and have a bias toward the better performing one. If the better performing path, such as the route through Boston (router C), experienced operational difficulties of any kind—including congestion or component failure—the link-state routing protocol can detect this change and begin forwarding packets through San Francisco (router B).

Benefits of Link-State Routing

The link-state approach to dynamic routing can be useful in networks of any size. In a well-designed network, a link-state routing protocol enables your network to gracefully adapt to unexpected topological change. When events rather than fixed-interval timers drive updates, convergence begins more quickly after a topological change.

The overhead of the frequent, time-driven updates of a distance vector routing protocol are also avoided. This allows a network to have more bandwidth available for routing traffic rather than for network maintenance (assuming that the network is designed properly).

A side benefit of link-state routing protocols' bandwidth efficiency is that they facilitate network scalability better than either static routes or distance vector protocols. When compared with the limitations of static routes or distance vector protocols, link-state routing is clearly best in larger, more complicated networks and in networks that must be highly scalable.

There are several benefits of link-state routing protocols over the traditional distance vector algorithms, such as those used by Routing Information Protocol (RIP) and Interior Gateway Routing Protocol (IGRP):

- Link-state protocols use cost metrics to choose paths through the network. The cost metric reflects the capacity of the links on those paths.

- Routing updates are more infrequent.

- The network can be segmented into area hierarchies, which limits the scope of route changes.

- Link-state protocols send only updates of a topology change. By using triggered, flooded updates, link-state protocols can immediately report changes in the network topology to all routers in the network. This immediate reporting generally leads to fast convergence times.

- Because each router has a complete and synchronized picture of the network, it is difficult for routing loops to occur.

- Because LSAs are sequenced and aged, routers always base their routing decisions on the most recent set of information.

- With careful network design, the link-state database sizes can be minimized, which leads to smaller Dijkstra calculations and faster convergence.

Limitations of Link-State Routing

Link-state protocols do have some limitations:

- In addition to the routing table, link-state protocols require a topological database, an adjacency database, and a *forwarding table*. An *adjacency database* lists all the relationships formed between neighboring routers for the purpose of exchanging routing information. The forwarding table is a data structure consisting of a stripped down association between network prefixes and next hops. Using all these databases can require a significant amount of memory in large or complex networks.

- Dijkstra's algorithm requires CPU cycles to calculate the best paths through the network. If the network is large or complex (that is, the Dijkstra calculation is complex) or if the network is unstable (that is, the Dijkstra calculation is running on a regular basis), link-state protocols can use a significant amount of CPU time. Having said that, modern networking equipment with high-speed processors generally will have little trouble handling these calculations.

- To avoid an excessive use of memory or CPU power, a strict hierarchical network design is required to divide the network into smaller areas to reduce the size of the topology tables and the length of the Dijkstra calculation. However, this division can cause problems because areas must remain contiguous at all times. The routers in an area must always be capable of contacting and receiving LSAs from all other routers in their area. In a multi-area design, an area router must always have a path to the backbone or the router will have no connectivity to the rest of the network. Additionally, the backbone area must remain contiguous at all times to avoid some areas becoming isolated (partitioned).

- The configuration of link-state networks is usually simple, provided that the underlying network architecture has been soundly designed. If the network design is complex, the operation of the link-state protocol might have to be tuned to accommodate it. Configuring a link-state protocol in a large network can be challenging.

- Troubleshooting is usually easier in link-state networks because every router has a complete copy of the network architecture, or at least a copy of its own area of the network. But interpreting the information that is stored in the topology, neighbor databases, and the routing table requires a good understanding of link-state routing's concepts.

- Link-state protocols usually scale to larger networks than distance vector protocols do—particularly the traditional distance vector protocols, such as RIP and IGRP.

Despite all its features and flexibility, link-state routing raises the following two potential concerns:

- During the initial discovery process, link-state routing protocols can flood the network with LSAs and thereby significantly decrease the network's capability to transport data. This performance compromise is temporary, but it can be extremely noticeable. Whether this flooding process noticeably degrades network performance depends on two things: the amount of available bandwidth and the number of routers that must exchange routing information. Flooding in large networks with relatively small links, such as low-bandwidth data-link connection identifiers (DLCI) on a Frame Relay network, is more noticeable than a similar exercise on a small network with large-sized links.

■ Link-state routing is both memory- and processor-intensive. Greater demands for memory and processing require higher-end routers to accommodate these demands. Consequently, routers used with link-state routing protocols generally cost more than routers used for distance vector routing protocols.

The potential impact on performance of both drawbacks can be addressed and resolved through foresight, planning, and engineering.

Single-Area OSPF Concepts

OSPF is a routing protocol developed for IP networks by the IGP working group of the *Internet Engineering Task Force (IETF)*. OSPF was created in the mid 1980s because RIP was increasingly incapable of serving large, heterogeneous internetworks. OSPF routes packets within a single AS.

OSPF has two primary characteristics. The first is that the protocol is an open standard, which means that its specification is in the public domain. The OSPF specification is published as an RFC. RFC 2328 describes the most recent version, known as OSPF version 2. The second main characteristic is that OSPF is based on the SPF algorithm.

Comparing OSPF with Distance Vector Routing Protocols

OSPF is a link-state routing protocol, whereas RIP and IGRP are distance vector routing protocols. Routers that run distance vector algorithms send all, or a portion of, their routing tables in routing-update messages to their neighbors.

You can think of a link as an interface on a router. The state of the link describes that interface and its relationship to its neighboring routers. A description of the interface can include, for example, the interface's IP address, the subnet mask, the type of network to which it is connected, the routers connected to that network, and so on. The collection of all these link states forms a link-state database.

A router sends LSA packets to periodically advertise its link states (as opposed to routing table updates). LSAs are flooded to all routers in the area. Information about attached interfaces, metrics used, and other variables are included in OSPF LSAs. As OSPF routers accumulate link-state information, they use the SPF algorithm to calculate the shortest path to each destination.

A topological (link-state) database is essentially an overall picture of networks in relation to routers. The topological database contains the collection of LSAs received from all routers in the same area. The OSPF link-state database is pieced together from the LSAs that the OSPF routers generate. Because routers within the same area share the same information, they have identical topological databases.

OSPF can operate within a hierarchy. The largest entity within the hierarchy is the autonomous system (AS), which is a collection of networks under a common administration that share a common routing strategy. An AS can be divided into several areas, which are groups of contiguous networks and attached hosts.

OSPF Hierarchical Routing

OSPF's capability to separate a large internetwork into multiple areas is also known as hierarchical routing. Hierarchical routing enables you to separate a large internetwork (AS) into smaller internetworks (called areas).

With this technique, routing still occurs between the areas (called interarea routing), but many of the minute internal routing operations, such as recalculating the database, are kept within an area.

In Figure 2-4, if area 1 has problems with a link going up and down, routers in other areas do not need to continually run their SPF calculation because they are isolated from the area 1 problem.

Figure 2-4   OSPF Uses Areas to Provide Hierarchy

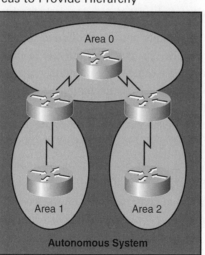

OSPF's hierarchical topology possibilities have the following important advantages:

- Reduced frequency of SPF calculations
- Smaller routing tables
- Reduced link-state update overhead

Dijkstra's Algorithm

In Dijkstra's algorithm, the best path is the lowest cost path. *Edsger Wybe Dijkstra*, a Dutch computer scientist, formulated the shortest path algorithm, known as Dijkstra's algorithm. The algorithm considers a network to be a set of nodes connected by point-to-point links, as Figure 2-5 shows.

Figure 2-5   Dijkstra's Algorithm Uses the Cost Metric

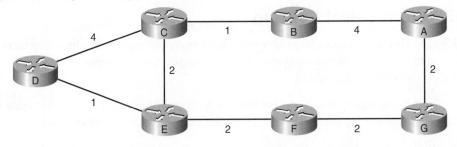

Each link has a cost. Each node has a name. Each node has a complete database of all the links and, therefore, complete information about the physical topology is known. All router link-state databases, within a given area, are identical. In Figure 2-5, node D received information that it was connected to node C with a link cost of 4 and to node E with a link cost of 1.

Dijkstra's algorithm places each router at the root of a tree and calculates the shortest path to each node based on the cumulative cost that is required to reach that destination. LSAs are flooded throughout the area using a reliable algorithm that ensures that all routers in an area have exactly the same topological database. Each router has its own view of the topology, although all the routers build a shortest path tree using the same link-state database. Each router uses the information in its topological database to calculate a shortest path tree, with itself as the root. The router then uses this tree to route network traffic.

The cost, or metric, of an interface indicates the overhead that is required to send packets across a certain interface. The *OSPF cost* of an interface is inversely proportional to that interface's bandwidth, so a higher bandwidth indicates a lower cost. More overhead, higher cost, and more time delays are involved in crossing a 56-kbps serial line than in crossing a 10-Mbps Ethernet line.

The default formula used to calculate OSPF cost is as follows:

Cost = 100,000,000 / bandwidth in bps

For example, it costs $10^8/10^7 = 10$ to cross a 10-Mbps Ethernet line, and it costs $10^8/1,544,000 = 64$ to cross a T1 line.

The shortest path algorithm calculates a loop-free topology by using the node as the starting point and examining, in turn, information it has about adjacent nodes. In Figure 2-6, node B has calculated the best path to D. The best path to D is by way of nodes C and E, which has a cost of 4. This information is converted to a route entry in B, which forwards traffic to C. Packets to D from B flow B to C to E, and then to D in this OSPF network.

Figure 2-6   Shortest Path Is Measured from Each Root Node to Build a Shortest Path Tree

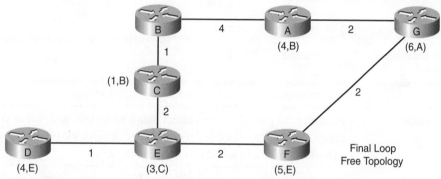

In the example shown in Figure 2-6, node B determined that, to get to node F, the shortest path has a cost of 5 (through node C). All other possible topologies either have loops or higher cost paths.

Single-Area OSPF Configuration

Configuring OSPF is simple compared to understanding the underlying OSPF concepts, such as LSA propagation and synchronization. This section explores OSPF configuration on Cisco routers, with a focus on single-area configuration.

Basic OSPF Configuration

The **router ospf** command takes a process identifier as an argument, as shown in the following syntax:

```
Router(config)#router ospf process-id
```

The *process ID* is a locally significant number between 1 and 65,535 that you select to identify the routing process. The process ID does not need to match the OSPF process ID on other OSPF routers.

The **network** command identifies which IP networks on the router are part of the OSPF network. For each network, you must also identify the OSPF area that the networks belong to, as shown in the following syntax:

```
Router(config-router)#network address wildcard-mask area area-id
```

The **network** command takes the three arguments listed in Table 2-2. This table defines the parameters of the **network** command.

Table 2-2   Parameters of **network** Command

network Command Parameters	Description
address	Can be the network, subnet, or the interface address.
wildcard-mask	Identifies the part of the IP address that is to be matched, where 0 is a match and 1 is "do not care." For example, a wildcard mask of 0.0.0.0 indicates a match of all 32 bits in the address.
area-id	Area that is to be associated with the OSPF address range. It can be specified either as a decimal value or in dotted-decimal notation.

Figure 2-7 and the accompanying Example 2-1 illustrate a basic configuration example for OSPF; configuring OSPF requires declaring which interfaces are to participate in the OSPF process. Note that the wildcard mask (or inverse mask) is normally configured in such a way to match the subnet mask in its purview. This is not required, however, and in fact, many network administrators simply use the 0.0.0.0 option to match the IP address of the interface desired to participate in the OSPF process for the referenced area. (The downside of this option is that some routers have hundreds of interfaces.) Calculating wildcard masks on non-8-bit boundaries can be error prone.

Figure 2-7   Basic OSPF Network with Each Router in Area 0

Routers that share a common segment become neighbors on that segment. In Figure 2-7, routers A and C are neighbors of router B, but not of each other.

Example 2-1   Using the network Statement in OSPF

```
Router A
<output omitted>
interface Ethernet0
 ip address 10.64.0.1 255.255.255.0
!
<output omitted>
router ospf 1
 network 10.64.0.0 0.0.0.255 area 0
<output omitted>
Router B
<output omitted>
interface Ethernet0
 ip address 10.64.0.2 255.255.255.0
!
interface Serial0
 ip address 10.2.1.2 255.255.255.252
<output omitted>
router ospf 1
network 10.2.1.0 0.0.0.3 area 0
network 10.64.0.0 0.0.0.255 area 0
<output omitted>
```

A router uses the *OSPF hello protocol* to establish neighbor relationships. Hello packets also act as keepalives to let routers know that other routers are still functional.

On *multiaccess networks* (networks supporting more than two routers), such as Ethernet networks, the hello protocol elects a designated router (DR) and a *backup designated router (BDR)*. Among other things, the *designated router* is responsible for generating LSAs for the entire multiaccess network. Designated routers allow a reduction in routing update traffic and manage *link-state synchronization*. The BDR does the same thing as the DR but overtly performs the role of DR only after the DR fails. The DR and BDR are elected based on the OSPF priority and OSPF router ID. In nonmultiaccess networks, such as a point-to-point serial link, no DR or BDR is elected.

Lab 2.3.1   Configuring the OSPF Routing Process

In this lab, you set up an IP addressing scheme for OSPF area 0 and configure and verify OSPF routing.

Loopback Interfaces

The OSPF router ID is the number by which the router is known to OSPF. To modify the OSPF router ID to a loopback address, first define a loopback interface with the following command:

```
Router(config)#interface loopback number
```

The highest IP address on an active interface at the moment of OSPF process startup, used as the router ID, can be overridden by configuring an IP address on a loopback interface. OSPF is more reliable if a loopback interface is configured because the interface is always active and cannot be in a down state like a real interface. For this reason, the loopback address needs to be used on all key routers. If the loopback address will be published with the **network** command, using a private IP address saves on registered IP address space. Note that a loopback address requires a different subnet for each router, unless the host address itself is advertised.

Using an address that is not advertised saves on real IP address space, but unlike an address that is advertised, the unadvertised address does not appear in the OSPF table and, therefore, cannot be pinged. This choice represents a trade-off between the ease of debugging the network and conserving address space.

 Lab 2.3.2   Configuring OSPF with Loopback Addresses

In this lab, you configure OSPF loopback addresses and observe the election process.

Modifying the OSPF Cost Metric

OSPF uses cost as the metric to determine the best route. A cost is associated with the output side of each router interface. Costs are also associated with externally derived routing data. Recall that the path cost is calculated using the formula 100,000,000/bandwidth, where bandwidth is expressed in bps. The system administrator can also configure cost by other methods. The lower the cost, the more likely the interface will be used to forward data traffic. Cisco IOS automatically determines cost based on the interface's bandwidth. Table 2-3 displays OSPF costs associated with various Layer 2 media.

Table 2-3   OSPF Cost Values

Link Type and Bandwidth	Cost
56-kbps serial link	1785
64-kbps serial link	1562
T1 (1.544-Mbps serial link)	64
E1 (2.048-Mbps serial link)	48
4-Mbps Token Ring	25

Table 2-3   OSPF Cost Values   *(continued)*

Link Type and Bandwidth	Cost
Standard Ethernet	10
16-Mbps Token Ring	6
FDDI	1
X.25	5208
Asynchronous	10,000
ATM	1

It is essential for proper OSPF operation that the correct interface bandwidth is set; for example:

```
Router(config)#interface serial 0/0
Router(config-if)#bandwidth 56
```

Cost can be changed to influence the outcome of the OSPF cost calculation. A common situation requiring a cost change is in a multivendor routing environment. A cost change ensures that one vendor's cost value matches another vendor's cost value. Another situation is when Gigabit Ethernet is being used. The default cost assigns the lowest cost value of 1 to a 100-Mbps link. In a 100-Mbps and Gigabit Ethernet situation, the default cost values might cause routing to take a less desirable path unless they are adjusted. The cost number can be any number between 1 and 65,535.

Use the following interface configuration command to set the link cost:

```
Router(config-if)#ip ospf cost number
```

The **ip ospf cost** command is easier to use to set the OSPF cost than the **bandwidth** command, which provides an indirect method for setting the OSPF cost.

Lab 2.3.3   Modifying OSPF Cost Metric

In this lab, you set up an OSPF area.

OSPF Authentication

By default, a router trusts that routing information is coming from a router that should be sending the information. A router also trusts that the information has not been tampered with along the route.

To guarantee this trust, routers in a specific area can be configured to authenticate each other. Cisco IOS Release 10.0 introduced *OSPF authentication*.

Each OSPF interface can present an authentication key that routers can use to send OSPF information to other routers on the segment. The authentication key, known as a password, is a shared secret between the routers. This key generates the authentication data in the OSPF packet header. The password can be up to eight characters. Use the following syntax to configure OSPF authentication:

```
Router(config-if)#ip ospf authentication-key password
```

After the password is configured, authentication must be enabled:

```
Router(config-router)#area area-number authentication
```

With simple authentication, the password is sent as plain text, which can easily be decoded if a packet sniffer captures an OSPF packet.

It is recommended that authentication information is encrypted. To send encrypted authentication information and to ensure greater security, the message-digest-key keyword is used. The md5 keyword specifies the type of message-digest hashing algorithm to use, and the *encryption-type* refers to the type of encryption, where 0 means none and 7 means proprietary. Use the interface configuration command mode syntax:

```
Router(config-if)#ip ospf message-digest-key key-id encryption-type md5 key
```

key-id is an identifier and takes the value in the range of 1 through 255. The key is an alphanumeric password up to 16 characters. Neighbor routers must use the same key identifier with the same key value.

The following is configured in router configuration mode on every router with an interface in area *area-id*:

```
Router(config-router)#area area-id authentication message-digest
```

MD5 authentication creates a message digest, which is scrambled data based on the password and the packet contents. The receiving router uses the shared password and the packet to recalculate the digest. If the digests match, the router believes that the source and contents of the packet have not been tampered with. The authentication type identifies which authentication, if any, is being used. In the case of message-digest authentication, the Authentication data field contains the key ID and the length of the message digest that is appended to the packet. The message digest is similar to a watermark that cannot be counterfeited.

Lab 2.3.4   Configuring OSPF Authentication

In this lab, you introduce OSPF authentication into the area.

OSPF Network Types and OSPF Timers

A neighbor relationship is required for OSPF routers to share routing information. A router tries to form an adjacency with at least one other router on each IP network to which it is connected.

OSPF routers determine which routers to become adjacent to based on the type of network to which they are connected. Some routers might try to become adjacent to all neighbor routers; other routers might try to become adjacent to only one or two neighbor routers. After an adjacency forms between neighbors, link-state information is exchanged.

OSPF interfaces automatically recognize three *OSPF network types*:

- Broadcast multiaccess, such as Ethernet
- Point-to-point networks
- Nonbroadcast multiaccess (NBMA), such as Frame Relay

An administrator can manually configure a fourth OSPF network type on an interface: point-to-multipoint.

In a multiaccess network, it is not known in advance how many routers will be connected. In point-to-point networks, only two routers can be connected.

In a broadcast multiaccess network segment, many routers can be connected. If every router had to establish a full adjacency with every other router and exchange link-state information with every neighbor, too much overhead would exist. If there are 5 routers, 10 adjacency relationships are needed and 10 link states are sent. If there are 10 routers, 45 adjacencies are needed. In general, for n routers, $n(n - 1)/2$ adjacencies need to be formed.

As discussed in the section, "Basic OSPF Configuration," the routers hold an election for a DR on a broadcast network. This router becomes adjacent to all other routers in the broadcast segment. All other routers on the segment send their link-state information to the DR. In turn, the DR acts as the spokesperson for the segment. The DR sends link-state information to all other routers on the segment by using the multicast address of 224.0.0.5 for all OSPF routers.

Despite the gain in efficiency that electing a DR provides, a disadvantage exists. The DR represents a single point of failure. As previously discussed, a second router is elected as a BDR to take over the duties of the DR if it should fail. To ensure that both the DR and the BDR see the link states that all routers send on the segment, the multicast address for all DRs, 224.0.0.6, is used.

On point-to-point networks, only two nodes exist and no DR or BDR is elected. Both routers become fully adjacent with each other. Table 2-4 summarizes the four network types and associated DR election.

Table 2-4   OSPF Network Types, Characteristics, and DR Election

Network Type	Characteristics	DR Election?
Broadcast multiaccess	Ethernet, Token Ring, or FDDI	Yes
NBMA	Frame Relay, X.25, SMDS	Yes
Point-to-point	PPP, HDLC	No
Point-to-multipoint	Configured by an administrator	No

OSPF uses *hello intervals* and *dead intervals* to exchange the timing of link-state information exchange. OSPF routers must use matching hello intervals and dead intervals on the same link. By default, the dead interval is four times the hello interval, which means that a router has four chances to send a hello packet before the link is declared dead.

On broadcast OSPF networks, the default hello interval is 10 seconds and the default dead interval is 40 seconds. On nonbroadcast networks, the default hello interval is 30 seconds and the default dead interval is 120 seconds. These default values result in efficient OSPF operation and seldom need to be modified.

A network engineer is allowed to choose these timer values. A justification that OSPF network performance will be improved is needed prior to changing the timers. These timers must be configured to match those of any neighboring router.

To configure the hello and dead intervals on an interface, use the following commands:

```
Router(config-if)#ip ospf hello-interval seconds
Router(config-if)#ip ospf dead-interval seconds
```

Lab 2.3.5   Configuring OSPF Timers

In this lab, you set up OSPF timers.

Propagating a Default Route

For each routing protocol, it is critical that one is able to configure the Cisco router to propagate default routes with that routing protocol. Each routing protocol behaves slightly differently in this respect.

OSPF routing ensures loop-free paths to every network in the routing domain. To reach networks outside the domain, either OSPF must know about the network or OSPF must have a default route. To have an entry for every network in the world would require enormous resources for each router.

A practical alternative is to add a default route to the OSPF router connected to the outside network. This route can be redistributed to each router in the AS through normal OSPF updates.

A router uses a configured default route to generate a gateway of last resort. The static default route configuration syntax uses the network address 0.0.0.0 and a subnet mask of 0.0.0.0:

```
Router(config)#ip route 0.0.0.0 0.0.0.0 [interface | next-hop address]
```

This is referred to as the quad-zero route. Any destination network address is matched by the ANDing algorithm applied to incoming packets on Cisco routers. The following configuration statement propagates this route to all the routers in a normal OSPF area:

```
Router(config-router)#default-information originate
```

All routers in the OSPF area learn a default route provided that the interface of the border router to the default gateway is active.

Lab 2.3.6   Propagating Default Routes in an OSPF Domain

In this lab, you configure the OSPF network so that all hosts in the OSPF area can connect to outside networks.

Verifying OSPF Configurations

You can use any one of several **show** commands to display information about an OSPF configuration. The **show ip protocols** command displays parameters about timers, filters, metrics, networks, and other information for the entire router.

The **show ip route** command displays the routes that are known to the router and how they were learned. This command is one of the best ways to determine connectivity between the local router and the rest of the internetwork.

The **show ip ospf interface** command verifies that interfaces have been configured in the intended areas. If no loopback address is specified, the active interface with the highest address is chosen as the router ID. This command also displays the timer intervals, including the hello interval, and shows the neighbor adjacencies.

The **show ip ospf neighbor** command displays OSPF neighbor information on a per-interface basis.

Troubleshooting OSPF

To display information on OSPF-related events, such as adjacencies, flooding information, designated router selection, and SPF calculation, use the **debug ip ospf events** command. Example 2-2 shows output from the **debug ip ospf events** command.

```
Example 2-2      debug ip ospf events Is a Useful Troubleshooting Command
Router1#debug ip ospf events
OSPF events debugging is on
Router1#
*Mar 1 04:04:11.926: OSPF: Rcv hello from 172.16.10.1 area 0 from Ethernet0 10.10.10.2
*Mar 1 04:04:11.930: OSPF: End of hello processing
*Mar 1 04:04:21.926: OSPF: Rcv hello from 172.16.10.1 area 0 from Ethernet 0
   10.10.10.2
*Mar 1 04:04:21.930 OSPF: End of hello processing
*Mar 1 04:04:31.926: OSPF: Rcv hello from 172.16.10.1 area 0 from Ethernet0 10.10.10.2
*Mar 1 04:04:31.930: OSPF: End of hello processing
*Mar 1 04:04:41.926: OSPF: Rcv hello from 172.16.10.1 area 0 from Ethernet 0
   10.10.10.2
*Mar 1 04:04:41.930 OSPF: End of hello processing
```

The **debug ip ospf events** output that Example 2-2 shows might appear if any of the following situations occur:

- The IP subnet masks for routers on the same network do not match.

- The OSPF hello interval for the router does not match that configured for a neighbor.

- The OSPF dead interval for the router does not match that configured for a neighbor.

If a router configured for OSPF routing is not seeing an OSPF neighbor on an attached network, perform the following tasks:

- Make sure that both routers are configured with the same IP mask, OSPF hello interval, and OSPF dead interval.

- Make sure that both neighbors are part of the same area type.

In the following line of sample output, the neighbor and this router are not both part of a stub area; that is, one is a part of a transit area and the other is a part of a stub area, as explained in RFC 1247:

```
OSPF: hello packet with mismatched E bit
```

To display information about each OSPF packet received, use the **debug ip ospf packet** privileged EXEC command. Example 2-3 shows sample output.

Example 2-3   debug ip ospf packet Provides an Intensive Means of Debugging
OSPF Behavior

```
Router1#debug ip ospf packet

OSPF: rcv. V:2 t:1 l:48 rid:200.0.0.116
      aid:0.0.0.0 chk:0 aut:2 keyid:1 seq:0x0
```

The **debug ip ospf packet** command produces one set of information for each packet received. The output varies slightly depending on which authentication is used. Table 2-5 shows a description of the output in Example 2-3.

Table 2-5   Fields in debug ip ospf packet Output

Field	Description
V:	OSPF version
t:	OSPF packet type; possible packet types are as follows:
	1—Hello
	2—Data description
	3—Link-state request
	4—Link-state update
	5—Link-state acknowledgment

Table 2-5   Fields in **debug ip ospf packet** Output   *(continued)*

Field	Description
l:	OSPF packet length in bytes
rid:	OSPF router ID
aid:	OSPF area ID
chk:	OSPF checksum
aut:	OSPF authentication type; possible authentication types are as follows:
	0—No authentication
	1—Simple password
	2—MD5
keyid:	MD5 key ID
seq:	Sequence number

As you can see from Example 2-3's output and Table 2-5, MD5 authentication is in use.

Chapter Summary

Link-state routing protocols, such as OSPF and IS-IS, are used to quickly and reliably propagate routing information within an AS. Link-state routing protocols build link-state databases, which are synchronized through link-state advertisements. The link-state protocol then applies Dijkstra's algorithm—also known as the SPF algorithm—to determine the best path(s) to each destination network to install in the routing table.

OSPF is the most commonly deployed link-state routing protocol. OSPF employs DRs and BDRs on broadcast segments to optimize propagation of link-state information. Each link uses hello and dead interval timers, depending on the OSPF network type: broadcast multiaccess, NBMA, point-to-point, or point-to-multipoint.

Configure OSPF by defining which interfaces will participate in a given OSPF process for a specific area. This is done by using **network** statements coupled with inverse masks. The inverse masks are often created to exactly match the subnet mask of the network associated with a given link; however, they can also be more broadly defined so their purview encompasses multiple interfaces; or, they can be defined simply with the 0.0.0.0 mask to exactly match an interface IP address.

Verifying OSPF configurations normally involves the commands **show ip protocol**, **show ip route**, **show ip ospf interface**, and **show ip ospf neighbor**. Troubleshooting OSPF is facilitated with the **debug ip ospf events** and **debug ip ospf packet** commands.

Chapter 3, "EIGRP and Troubleshooting Routing Protocols," continues the coverage of classless routing with Enhanced Interior Gateway Routing Protocol (EIGRP). EIGRP is a hybrid routing protocol that has some characteristics in common with both distance vector and link-state routing protocols.

Check Your Understanding

Complete all the review questions listed here to test your understanding of the topics and concepts in this chapter. Answers are listed in Appendix A, "Answers to Check Your Understanding and Challenge Questions and Activities."

1. How can link-state protocols limit the scope of route changes?

   A. By supporting classless addressing

   B. By sending the mask along with the address

   C. By only sending updates of a topology change

   D. By segmenting the network into area hierarchies

2. What is the purpose of LSAs?

   A. To construct a topological database

   B. To specify the cost to reach a destination

   C. To determine the best path to a destination

   D. To verify that a neighbor still functions

3. What are two characteristics of OSPF?

   A. Hierarchical

   B. Proprietary

   C. Open standard

   D. Similar to RIP

   E. Distance vector protocol

4. OSPF routes packets within a single _____.

   A. Area

   B. Network

   C. Segment

   D. AS

5. With OSPF, each router builds its SPF tree using the same link-state information, but each has a separate _____ of the topology.

   A. State

   B. View

   C. Version

   D. Configuration

6. Which component of the SPF algorithm is inversely proportional to bandwidth?

A. Link cost

B. Root cost

C. Link state

D. Hop count

7. Which command correctly starts an OSPF routing process using process ID 191?

A. Router(config)#**router ospf 191**

B. Router(config)#**network ospf 191**

C. Router(config-router)#**network ospf 191**

D. Router(config-router)#**router ospf process-id 191**

8. What is the purpose of the **show ip ospf interface** command?

A. To display OSPF-related interface information

B. To display general information about OSPF routing processes

C. To display OSPF neighbor information on a per-interface basis

D. To display OSPF neighbor information on a per–interface type basis

9. The output from which command includes information about the length of the OSPF packet?

A. **debug ip ospf events**

B. **debug ip ospf packet**

C. **debug ip ospf packet size**

D. **debug ip ospf mpls traffic-eng advertisements**

10. What is the default dead interval for a broadcast multiaccess link under OSPF?

A. 10

B. 30

C. 40

D. 120

Challenge Questions and Activities

These questions and activities are purposefully designed to be similar to the more complex styles of questions you might see on the CCNA exam. Answers are listed in Appendix A.

1. A router needs to be added to OSPF area 0. Which commands must be used to enable OSPF on the router? (Choose two.)

   A. RouterA(config)#**router ospf**

   B. RouterA(config)#**router ospf 1**

   C. RouterA(config-router)#**network 192.168.2.0 0.0.0.255 0**

   D. RouterA(config-router)#**network 192.168.2.0 0.0.0.255 area 0**

   E. RouterA(config-router)#**network 192.168.2.0 255.255.255.0 0**

2. See Figure 2-8. Which of the following commands configures router A for OSPF?

Figure 2-8   Variable-Length Subnet Masks with OSPF

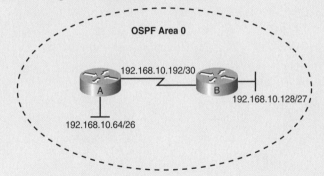

A.
```
router ospf 1
network 192.168.10.0
```

B.
```
router ospf 1
network 192.168.10.64 0.0.0.63 area 0
network 192.168.10.192 0.0.0.3 area 0
```

C.
```
router ospf 1
network 192.168.10.64 255.255.255.192
network 192.168.10.192 255.255.255.252
```

D.
```
router ospf 1
network 192.168.10.0 area 0
```

CHAPTER 3

EIGRP and Troubleshooting Routing Protocols

Objectives

Upon completion of this chapter, you should be able to answer the following questions:

- What are the features of balanced hybrid routing?

- What are the particular features of EIGRP?

- How does EIGRP compare with IGRP?

- How do you configure EIGRP?

- How do you verify the EIGRP configuration?

- What is a general process for troubleshooting routing protocols?

- How are **debug** commands used to troubleshoot a RIP configuration?

- How are **debug** commands used to troubleshoot an EIGRP configuration?

- How are **debug** commands used to troubleshoot an OSPF configuration?

Additional Topics of Interest

Some chapters contain additional coverage of previous topics or related topics that are secondary to the main goals of the chapter. You can find the additional coverage in the "Additional Topics of Interest" section near the end of the chapter. For this chapter, the following additional topic is covered:

- Troubleshooting IGRP

Key Terms

This chapter uses the following key terms. You can find the definitions in the Glossary:

Diffusing Update Algorithm (DUAL)   *page 67*

neighbor table   *page 68*

topology table   *page 68*

successor   *page 68*

feasible successor   *page 68*

Reliable Transport Protocol (RTP)   *page 69*

hello packets   *page 70*

passive state   *page 70*

acknowledgment packets   *page 70*

reply packets   *page 70*

update packets   *page 71*

query packets   *page 71*

active state   *page 71*

feasible distance   *page 75*

EIGRP is a Cisco-proprietary routing protocol that is based on IGRP. EIGRP supports CIDR and VLSM, allowing network designers to maximize address space. When compared to IGRP, a classful routing protocol, EIGRP boasts faster convergence times, improved scalability, and superior management of routing loops.

EIGRP is often described as a hybrid routing protocol that offers the best of distance vector and link-state algorithms. EIGRP is an advanced routing protocol that relies on features commonly associated with link-state protocols. Some of the best features of OSPF, such as partial updates and neighbor discovery, are similarly put to use by EIGRP; however, EIGRP is easier to configure than OSPF. EIGRP is an ideal choice for large, multiprotocol networks built primarily on Cisco routers.

This chapter discusses common EIGRP configuration tasks. The emphasis is on ways in which EIGRP establishes relationships with adjacent routers, calculates primary and backup routes, and responds to failures in known routes to a particular destination.

A network is made up of many devices, protocols, and media that allow data communication to occur. When a network component does not work correctly, it can affect the entire network. In any case, network engineers must quickly identify and troubleshoot problems when they arise. The following are some reasons network problems occur:

- Commands are entered incorrectly.

- Access lists are constructed or placed incorrectly.

- Routers, switches, or other network devices are misconfigured.

- Physical connections are bad.

A network engineer should troubleshoot in a methodical manner with the use of a general problem-solving model. It is often useful to check for physical layer problems first and then move up the layers in an organized manner. Although this chapter closes with a focus on how to troubleshoot Layer 3 protocols, it is important to troubleshoot and eliminate any problems that might exist at the lower layers.

EIGRP Concepts

Balanced hybrid routing protocols combine aspects of both distance vector and link-state protocols. The balanced hybrid routing protocol uses distance vectors with more accurate metrics to determine the best paths to destination networks. However, the balanced hybrid routing protocol differs from most distance vector protocols in that it uses topology changes instead of automatic periodic updates to trigger the routing of database updates.

The balanced hybrid routing protocol converges more rapidly than distance vector routing protocols, which is similar to link-state routing protocols. However, the balanced hybrid differs from distance vector and link-state routing protocols in that it emphasizes economy in the use of required resources, such as bandwidth, memory, and processor overhead. Enhanced Interior Gateway Routing Protocol (EIGRP) is an example of a balanced hybrid routing protocol.

EIGRP has several advantages over Routing Information Protocol (RIP) and Interior Gateway Routing Protocol (IGRP), and even some advantages over Open Shortest Path First (OSPF) and Intermediate System-to-Intermediate System (IS-IS). EIGRP's enhancements come with many complexities that take place behind the scenes. Although configuring EIGRP is relatively simple, the underlying protocol and algorithm are not so simple. This section describes EIGRP concepts, terminology, and features.

Comparing EIGRP and IGRP

EIGRP uses metric calculations similar to those that IGRP uses, and EIGRP supports the same unequal-cost path load balancing as IGRP. It is also important to note that Cisco IOS Release 12.2(13)T is the last version to support the legacy IGRP. The convergence properties and the operating efficiency of EIGRP are substantially improved compared with IGRP. EIGRP has a dramatically improved convergence time and reduced network overhead. Although the metric (bandwidth and delay, by default, and the option to use load and reliability) is the same for both IGRP and EIGRP, the weight assigned to the metric is 256 times greater for EIGRP. Automatic redistribution occurs between IGRP and EIGRP if they are using the same autonomous system number. Also of note is that EIGRP has a maximum hop count of 224 and supports route tagging during redistribution.

The convergence technology, which is based on research conducted at SRI International by Dr. J.J. Garcia-Luna-Aceves, employs *Diffusing Update Algorithm (DUAL)*. This algorithm guarantees loop-free operation at every instant throughout a route computation and allows all devices involved in a topology change to synchronize simultaneously. Routers that are not affected by topology changes are not involved in recomputations. The convergence time with DUAL rivals that of any other existing routing protocol.

EIGRP Features

In a well-designed network, EIGRP scales well and provides extremely quick convergence times with minimal network traffic. Some of the features of EIGRP are as follows:

- EIGRP has rapid convergence times for changes in the network topology. In some situations, convergence can be almost instantaneous. EIGRP uses DUAL to achieve rapid convergence. A router that runs EIGRP stores backup routes for destinations when they are available so that it can quickly adapt to alternate routes. If no appropriate route or backup route exists in the local routing table, EIGRP queries its neighbors to discover an alternate route. These queries are propagated until an alternate route is found.

- EIGRP has low usage of network resources during normal operation; only hello packets are transmitted on a stable network. Like other link-state routing protocols, EIGRP uses EIGRP hello packets to establish relationships with neighboring EIGRP routers. Each router builds a neighbor table from the hello packets that it receives from adjacent EIGRP routers. EIGRP does not send periodic routing updates like IGRP does. When a change occurs, routing table changes are only propagated, not the entire routing table. When changes are only propagated, the bandwidth required for EIGRP packets is minimized, which reduces the load that the routing protocol itself places on the network.

■ EIGRP supports automatic (classful) route summarization at major network boundaries as the default. However, unlike other classful routing protocols, such as IGRP and RIP, manual route summarization can be configured on arbitrary network boundaries to reduce the size of the routing table.

EIGRP Terminology

EIGRP relies on various tables for its computations. These include the neighbor table, the topology table, and the routing table. Table 3-1 summarizes the terms related to EIGRP.

Table 3-1   EIGRP Terminology

Term	Definition
Neighbor table (AppleTalk, Internetwork Packet Exchange [IPX], IPv4, IPv6)	Each EIGRP router maintains a neighbor table that lists adjacent routers. This table is comparable to the adjacencies database that OSPF uses, and it serves the same purpose (to ensure bidirectional communication between each of the directly connected neighbors). There is a neighbor table for each protocol that EIGRP supports.
Topology table (AppleTalk, IPX, IPv4, IPv6)	Each EIGRP router maintains a topology table for each configured routed protocol. This table includes route entries for all destinations that the router has learned.
Routing table v4, IPv6	EIGRP chooses the best (successor) routes to a destination from the topology table and places these routes in the routing table. The router maintains one routing table for each network protocol.
Successor	A route selected as the primary route to reach a destination. Successors (up to four) are the entries kept in the routing table.
Feasible successor	Considered a backup route. Backup routes are selected when the successors are identified; however, these routes are kept in a topology table. Multiple feasible successors for a destination can be retained.

Figure 3-1 displays the routing protocols supported by EIGRP.

Figure 3-1   Routing Protocols Supported by EIGRP

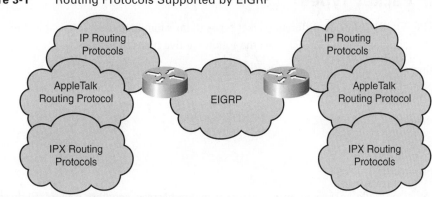

Figure 3-2 illustrates the fundamental contents of each table that EIGRP uses.

Figure 3-2   Contents of the Tables Used by EIGRP

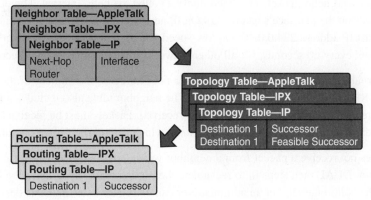

Reliable Transport Protocol (RTP) is a transport layer protocol that guarantees ordered delivery of EIGRP packets to all neighbors. On an IP network, hosts use Transmission Control Protocol (TCP) to sequence packets and ensure their timely delivery. However, EIGRP is protocol-independent, which means that it does not rely on Transmission Control Protocol/Internet Protocol (TCP/IP) to exchange routing information the way that RIP, IGRP, and OSPF do. To stay independent of IP, EIGRP uses RTP as its own proprietary transport layer protocol to guarantee delivery of routing information.

EIGRP can call on RTP to provide reliable or unreliable service as the situation warrants. With RTP, EIGRP can simultaneously multicast and unicast to different peers, which allows for maximum efficiency.

EIGRP Packet Types

Like OSPF, EIGRP relies on different packet types to maintain its tables and establish relationships with neighbor routers. EIGRP uses the following five types of packets:

- Hello
- Acknowledgment
- Update
- Query
- Reply

EIGRP relies on *hello packets* to discover, verify, and rediscover neighbor routers. Rediscovery occurs if EIGRP routers do not receive hellos from each other for a hold time interval but then reestablish communication.

Hello packets are always unreliably sent. This means that no acknowledgment is transmitted. EIGRP routers send hello packets at a fixed interval called the hello interval. The default hello interval depends on the interface's bandwidth. On IP networks, EIGRP routers send hello packets to the multicast IP address 224.0.0.10. On low-speed (T1 or slower) NBMA networks, hello packets are sent every 60 seconds; for all other networks, the hello interval is 5 seconds.

The neighbor table includes the Sequence Number field to record the number of the last received EIGRP packet that each neighbor sent. The neighbor table also includes a Hold Time field, which records the time the last packet was received. Packets must be received within the hold time interval period to maintain a *passive state*, which is a reachable and operational status.

If EIGRP does not receive a packet from a neighbor within the hold time, EIGRP considers that neighbor down. DUAL then steps in to reevaluate the routing table. By default, the hold time is three times the hello interval, but an administrator can configure both timers as desired.

OSPF requires neighbor routers to have the same hello and dead intervals to communicate. EIGRP has no such restriction. Neighbor routers learn about each of the other respective timers through the exchange of hello packets. They then use that information to forge a stable relationship regardless of unlike timers.

EIGRP routers use *acknowledgment packets* to indicate receipt of any EIGRP packet during a reliable exchange. RTP provides reliable communication between EIGRP hosts. The recipient must acknowledge a message that is received to make it reliable. Acknowledgment packets, which are hello packets without data, are used for this purpose. Unlike multicast hello packets, acknowledgment packets are unicast. Acknowledgments can be attached to other kinds of EIGRP packets, such as *reply packets*.

Update packets are used when a router discovers a new neighbor. EIGRP routers send unicast update packets to that new neighbor so that the neighbor can add to its topology table. More than one update packet can be needed to convey all the topology information to the newly discovered neighbor.

Update packets are also used when a router detects a topology change. In this case, the EIGRP router sends a multicast update packet to all neighbors, which alerts them to the change. All update packets are reliably sent.

An EIGRP router uses *query packets* whenever it needs specific information from one or all of its neighbors. A reply packet is used to respond to a query.

If an EIGRP router loses its successor and cannot find a feasible successor for a route, DUAL places the route in the *active state*. A query is then multicasted to all neighbors in an attempt to locate a successor to the destination network. Neighbors must send replies that either provide information on successors or indicate that no information is available. Queries can be multicast or unicast, while replies are always unicast. Both packet types are reliably sent.

EIGRP Configuration

Configuring EIGRP is similar to configuring RIP and IGRP. In fact, EIGRP is most similar to RIP version 2 (RIPv2) in its configuration syntax and configuration options. This section explores basic EIGRP configuration, EIGRP configuration examples, and how to verify EIGRP configurations.

Basic EIGRP Configuration

Use the **router eigrp** and **network** commands to create an EIGRP routing process:

```
Router(config)#router eigrp autonomous-system-number
Router(config-router)#network network-number
```

autonomous-system-number identifies all routers that belong within the internetwork. The number does not have to be registered, but it must match all routers within the internetwork.

The **network** command assigns a major network number to which the router is directly connected. Indicate which networks belong to the EIGRP autonomous system (AS) on the local router with the *network-number*. The EIGRP routing process associates interface addresses with the advertised network number and begins EIGRP packet processing on the specified interfaces.

Figure 3-3 displays a simple network. Example 3-1 shows the basic EIGRP configuration for the three routers in Figure 3-3.

Figure 3-3   Simple EIGRP Network

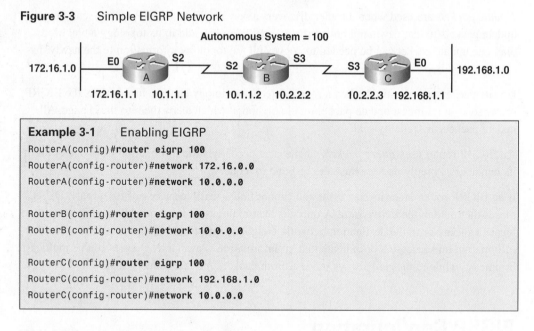

Example 3-1   Enabling EIGRP

```
RouterA(config)#router eigrp 100
RouterA(config-router)#network 172.16.0.0
RouterA(config-router)#network 10.0.0.0

RouterB(config)#router eigrp 100
RouterB(config-router)#network 10.0.0.0

RouterC(config)#router eigrp 100
RouterC(config-router)#network 192.168.1.0
RouterC(config-router)#network 10.0.0.0
```

Table 3-2 describes the router A configuration.

Table 3-2   Router A Command Descriptions

Command	Description
router eigrp 100	Enables the EIGRP routing process for AS 100
network 172.16.0.0	Associates network 172.16.0.0 with the EIGRP routing process
network 10.0.0.0	Associates network 10.0.0.0 with the EIGRP routing process

On router A, EIGRP sends updates out the interfaces in networks 10.0.0.0 and 172.16.0.0. The updates include information about networks 10.0.0.0, 172.16.0.0, and any other networks about which EIGRP learns.

When configuring serial links using EIGRP, it is important to configure the bandwidth setting on the interface. If the bandwidth for these interfaces is not changed, EIGRP assumes the default bandwidth on the link instead of the true bandwidth. If the link is slower, the router might not be able to converge, routing updates might become lost, or suboptimal path selection might result. To set the interface bandwidth, use the following syntax:

```
Router(config-if)#bandwidth kbps
```

The **bandwidth** command is only used by the routing process and must be set to match the line speed of the interface.

Cisco Systems also recommends adding the following command to all EIGRP configurations:

```
Router(config-router)#eigrp log-neighbor-changes
```

This command enables the logging of neighbor adjacency changes to monitor the stability of the routing system and to help detect problems. By default, this command is enabled.

Lab 3.2.1   Configuring EIGRP Routing

In this lab, you configure EIGRP routing.

Configuring EIGRP Summarization

Prior to Cisco IOS Release 12.2(8)T, EIGRP automatically summarized routes at the classful boundary. The classful boundary is the boundary where the network address ends, as defined by class-based addressing. This means that although router RTC in Figure 3-4 is connected to subnet 2.1.1.0, it advertises that it is connected to the entire Class A network, 2.0.0.0. In some cases, autosummarization is beneficial because it keeps routing tables as compact as possible. However, over time, it has become general consensus that it is best not to have the router automatically summarize at the classful boundary, as evidenced by Cisco Systems move to disable autosummarization as the default behavior for EIGRP.

Figure 3-4   Effect of Autosummarization Is to Summarize at the Classful Boundary

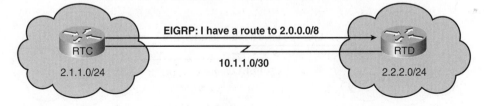

In many instances, autosummarization is not the preferred option. For example, if discontiguous subnetworks exist, autosummarization must be disabled for routing to work properly, Figure 3-5 illustrates. Autosummarization prevents routers from learning about discontinguous subnets; with summarization turned off, EIGRP routers will advertise subnets. To turn off autosummarization, use the following command:

```
Router(config-router)#no auto-summary
```

With EIGRP, a summary address can be manually configured by configuring a network prefix. With EIGRP, manual summary routes are configured on a per-interface basis, so the interface that propagates the route summary must be selected first. Then, the summary address can be defined with the **ip summary-address eigrp** command:

```
Router(config-if)#ip summary-address eigrp autonomous-system-number ip-address mask
  administrative-distance
```

Figure 3-5   Discontiguous Networks with and Without Autosummarization

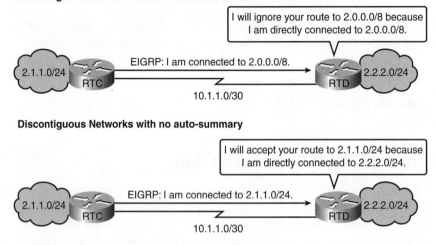

By default, EIGRP summary routes have an administrative distance of 5. Optionally, they can be configured for a value between 1 and 255.

In Figure 3-6, router RTC can be configured by using the commands shown in Example 3-2.

Figure 3-6   Granular Routing Updates with Interface Summarization

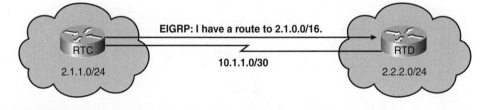

Example 3-2   Using Interface Summarization with EIGRP

```
RTC(config)#router eigrp 2446
RTC(config-router)#no auto-summary
RTC(config-router)#exit
RTC(config)#interface serial 0/0
RTC(config-if)#ip summary-address eigrp 2446 2.1.0.0 255.255.0.0
```

Router RTC adds a route to its table as follows:

```
D 2.1.0.0/16 is a summary, 00:00:22, Null0
```

Notice that the summary route is sourced from Null0 and not from an actual interface. This is because this route is used for advertisement purposes and does not represent a path that router RTC can take to reach that network. On router RTC, this route has an administrative distance of 5.

Router RTD is not aware of the summarization, but it accepts the route. The route is assigned the administrative distance of a normal EIGRP route, which, by default, is 90.

In the configuration for router RTC, autosummarization is turned off with the **no auto-summary** command. If autosummarization was not turned off, router RTD would receive two routes: the manual summary address, which is 2.1.0.0/16; and the automatic, classful summary address, which is 2.0.0.0/8. Normally, when manually summarizing, the **no auto-summary** command needs to be issued.

Verifying the EIGRP Configuration

As with OSPF, numerous **show** commands verify the EIGRP configuration. Table 3-3 summarizes these commands.

Table 3-3   EIGRP **show** Commands

Command	Description
show ip eigrp neighbors	Displays neighbors discovered by EIGRP.
show ip eigrp topology	Displays the EIGRP topology table. This command shows the topology table, the active or passive state of routes, the number of successors, and the feasible distance to the destination. *Feasible distance* is the best metric along a path to a destination network, including the metric to the neighbor advertising that path.
show ip route eigrp	Displays the current EIGRP entries in the routing table.
show ip protocols	Displays the parameters and current state of the active routing protocol process. This command shows the EIGRP AS number. It also displays filtering and redistribution numbers and neighbors and distance information.
show ip eigrp traffic	Displays the number of EIGRP packets sent and received. This command displays statistics on hello packets, updates, queries, replies, and acknowledgments.

Many network engineers use the **show ip eigrp neighbors** command when first configuring EIGRP to ensure that neighbor relationships are forming (without which no EIGRP routing can occur).

Lab 3.2.3   Verifying Basic EIGRP Configuration

In this lab, you verify EIGRP routing.

Troubleshooting Routing Protocols

Routing-protocol troubleshooting needs to begin with a logical sequence or process flow. This process flow is not a rigid outline for troubleshooting an internetwork; however, it is a foundation from which a network engineer can build a problem-solving process to suit a particular environment:

Step 1 When analyzing a network failure, make a clear problem statement:

- Define the problem in terms of a set of symptoms and potential causes.

- To properly analyze the problem, identify the general symptoms and then ascertain what kinds of problems or causes might result in these symptoms. For example, hosts might not be responding to service requests from clients, which is a symptom.

- Possible causes might include a misconfigured access host, bad interface cards, or missing router configuration commands.

Step 2 Gather the facts needed to help isolate possible causes:

- Gather the facts needed to help isolate possible causes. Ask questions of affected users, network administrators, managers, and other key people.

- Collect information from sources such as network management systems, protocol analyzer traces, output from router diagnostic commands, or software release notes.

Step 3 Consider possible problems based on the facts that have been gathered:

- Using these facts helps eliminate some of the potential problems from the list.

- Depending on the data, it might be possible to eliminate hardware as a problem, so you can then focus on software problems.

- At every opportunity, try to narrow the number of potential problems to create an efficient action plan.

Step 4 Create an action plan based on the remaining potential problems:

- Begin with the most likely problem and devise a plan in which only one variable is changed.

- Changing only one variable at a time helps to reproduce a given solution to a specific problem. Do not try to alter more than one variable at the same time. Such an action might solve the problem. However, identifying the specific change that eliminated the symptom becomes far more difficult and will not help to solve the same problem if it occurs in the future.

Step 5 Implement the action plan, performing each step carefully while testing to see whether the symptom disappears.

Step 6 Analyze the results to determine whether the problem has been resolved. If it has, the process is complete.

Step 7 If the problem has not been resolved, create an action plan based on the next most likely problem in the list. Return to Step 4, change one variable at a time, and repeat the process until the problem is solved.

Step 8 After the actual cause of the problem is identified, try to solve it:

- At this point, it is important to document the problem and the solution for future reference.

- If all attempts to this point have failed, it might now be necessary to ask for technical support from the manufacturer of the suspect equipment.

- Alternative resources include professional experts or technical engineers to help complete the troubleshooting process.

Cisco routers provide numerous integrated commands to assist you in monitoring and troubleshooting an internetwork:

- **show** commands help monitor installation behavior, normal network behavior, and isolate problem areas.

- **debug** commands assist in the isolation of protocol and configuration problems.

- TCP/IP network tools such as ping, traceroute, and Telnet help to isolate the OSI layer where the problem exists, as well as the location of the problem.

Cisco IOS **show** commands are among the most important tools for understanding the status of a router, detecting neighboring routers, monitoring the network in general, and isolating problems in the network. Chapter 1, "Introduction to Classless Routing," Chapter 2, "Single-Area OSPF," and this chapter describe the various **show** commands used with RIP, OSPF, and EIGRP. (Note that no **show** commands are specific to IGRP.)

Cisco routers provide numerous **debug** commands to assist you in troubleshooting an internetwork. EXEC **debug** commands can provide a wealth of information about interface traffic, internal error messages, protocol-specific diagnostic packets, and other useful troubleshooting data. **debug** commands isolate problems; they do not monitor normal network operation. **debug** commands look for specific types of traffic or problems. Before using a **debug** command, narrow the problems to a likely subset of causes. The **show debugging** command views which debugging features are enabled.

The remainder of this chapter explores the particular troubleshooting techniques and various **debug** commands used when troubleshooting RIP, EIGRP, and OSPF.

Troubleshooting RIP

The most common problem found in RIP that prevents RIP routes from being advertised is variable-length subnet mask (VLSM). This is because RIP version 1 (RIPv1) does not support VLSM. If the RIP routes are not being advertised, check the following:

- Layer 1 or Layer 2 connectivity issues exist.

- VLSM subnetting is configured. VLSM subnetting cannot be used with RIPv1.

- Mismatched RIPv1 and RIPv2 routing configurations exist.

- Network statements are missing or are incorrectly assigned.

- The outgoing interface is down.

- The advertised network interface is down.

Use the **debug ip rip** EXEC command to display information on RIP routing transactions. **no debug ip rip** turns off debugging for RIP. In general, the **no debug all** or **undebug all** command turns off all debugging.

Example 3-3 shows the **debug ip rip** output on router A of Figure 3-7.

Figure 3-7   Sample RIP Network for Troubleshooting

Example 3-3   Troubleshooting with **debug ip rip**

```
Router#debug ip rip
RIP protocol debugging is on
RouterA#
00:06:24: RIP: received v1 update from 10.1.1.2 on Serial2
00:06:24: 10.2.2.0 in 1 hops
00:06:24: 192.168.1.0 in 2 hops
00:06:33: RIP: sending v1 update to 255.255.255.255 via Ethernet0 (172.16.1.1)
00:06:34: network 10.0.0.0, metric 1
00:06:34: network 192.168.1.0, metric 3
00:06:34: RIP: sending v1 update to 255.255.255.255 via Serial2 (10.1.1.1)
00:06:34: network 172.16.0.0, metric 1
```

Example 3-3 shows that the router being debugged has received updates from one router at source address 10.1.1.2. That router sent information about two destinations in the routing table update. The router being debugged also sent updates (in both cases, to broadcast address 255.255.255.255 as the destination). The number in parentheses is the source address that is encapsulated into the IP header.

Other output that you might see from the **debug ip rip** command includes entries such as the following:

```
RIP: broadcasting general request on Ethernet0
RIP: broadcasting general request on Ethernet1
```

Entries like these can appear at startup or when an event occurs, such as when an interface transitions or a user manually clears the routing table.

The following output shows an entry most likely caused by a malformed packet from the transmitter:

```
RIP: bad version 128 from 160.89.80.43.
```

Troubleshooting EIGRP

Normal EIGRP operation is stable, efficient in bandwidth utilization, and relatively simple to monitor and troubleshoot.

Some possible reasons why EIGRP might not work correctly are as follows:

- Layer 1 or Layer 2 connectivity issues exist.
- AS numbers on EIGRP routers are mismatched.
- The link might be congested or down.
- The outgoing interface is down.
- The advertised network interface is down.
- Autosummarization is enabled on routers with discontiguous subnets. Use the **no auto-summary** command to disable automatic network summarization.

One of the most common reasons for a missing neighbor is a failure on the actual link. Another possible cause of missing neighbors is an expired hold-down timer. Because hellos are sent every 5 seconds on most networks, the hold time value in a **show ip eigrp neighbors** command output should normally be a value between 10 and 15.

The **debug ip eigrp** privileged EXEC command helps you analyze the packets pertaining to EIGRP routing that are sent and received on an interface, as Example 3-4 shows.

Example 3-4   Using **debug ip eigrp** to Troubleshoot

```
Router#debug ip eigrp
IP-EIGRP: Processing incoming UPDATE packet
IP-EIGRP: Ext 192.168.3.0 255.255.255.0 M 386560 - 256000 130560 SM 360960 - 256000
   104960
IP-EIGRP: Ext 192.168.0.0 255.255.255.0 M 386560 - 256000 130560 SM 360960 - 256000
   104960
IP-EIGRP: Ext 192.168.3.0 255.255.255.0 M 386560 - 256000 130560 SM 360960 - 256000
   104960
IP-EIGRP: 172.69.43.0 255.255.255.0, - do advertise out Ethernet0/1
IP-EIGRP: Ext 172.68.43.0 255.255.255.0 metric 371200 - 25600 115200
IP-EIGRP: 192.135.246.0 255.255.255.0, - do advertise out Ethernet0/1
IP-EIGRP: Ext 192.135.246.0 255.255.255.0 metric 46310656 - 45714176 596480
IP-EIGRP: 172.69.40.0 255.255.255.0, - do advertise out Ethernet0/1
IP-EIGRP: Ext 172.68.40.0 255.255.255.0 metric 2272256 - 1657856 614400
IP-EIGRP: 192.135.245.0 255.255.255.0, - do advertise out Ethernet0/1
IP-EIGRP: Ext 192.135.245.0 255.255.255.0 metric 40622080 - 40000000 622080
IP-EIGRP: 192.135.244.0 255.255.255.0, - do advertise out Ethernet0/1
```

Because the **debug ip eigrp** command generates a substantial amount of output, use it only when traffic on the network is light. Table 3-4 describes some fields in the output from the **debug ip eigrp** command shown in Example 3-4.

Table 3-4   **debug ip eigrp** Output Fields

Field	Description
IP-EIGRP:	Indicates that this is an IP EIGRP packet.
Ext	Indicates that the following address is an external destination rather than an internal destination, which would be labeled as "Int."
M	Displays the computed metric, which includes SM and the cost between this router and the neighbor. The first number is the composite metric. The next two numbers are the inverse bandwidth and the delay, respectively.
SM	Displays the metric as reported by the neighbor.

The **debug eigrp fsm** command is used for EIGRP debugging. This command displays information on DUAL feasible successor metrics and helps network engineers analyze the packets that are sent and received on an interface.

Troubleshooting OSPF

The majority of problems encountered with OSPF relate to the formation of adjacencies and the synchronization of the link-state databases.

To display information on OSPF-related events, such as adjacencies, flooding information, designated router selection, and SPF calculation, use the **debug ip ospf events** command. Example 3-5 shows output from the **debug ip ospf events** command.

Example 3-5   **debug ip ospf events** Is a Useful Troubleshooting Command

```
Router1#debug ip ospf events
OSPF events debugging is on
OSPF: hello with invalid timers on interface Ethernet0
hello interval received 10 configured 10
net mask received 255.255.255.0 configured 255.255.255.0
dead interval received 40 configured 30
```

The **debug ip ospf events** output that Example 3-5 shows might appear if any of the following situations occur:

- The IP subnet masks for routers on the same network do not match.

- The OSPF hello interval for the router does not match that configured for a neighbor.

- The OSPF dead interval for the router does not match that configured for a neighbor.

If a router configured for OSPF routing is not seeing an OSPF neighbor on an attached network, perform the following tasks:

- Make sure that both routers have been configured with the same IP mask, OSPF hello interval, and OSPF dead interval.

- Make sure that both neighbors are part of the same area type.

In the following line of sample output, the neighbor and this router are not both part of a stub area (stub areas are explored in CCNP); that is, one is a part of a transit area and the other is a part of a stub area, as explained in RFC 1247:

```
OSPF: hello packet with mismatched E bit
```

To display information about each OSPF packet received, use the **debug ip ospf packet** privileged EXEC command. Example 3-6 shows the sample output.

> **Example 3-6**   **debug ip ospf packet** Provides Detailed Output Relating to OSPF
>
> ```
> Router#debug ip ospf packet
> OSPF: rcv. v:2 t:1 l:48 rid:200.0.0.117
>       aid: 0.0.0.0 chk:6AB2 aut:0 auk:
>       rcv. v:2 t:1 l:48 rid:200.0.0.116
>       aid:0.0.0.0 chk:0 aut:2 keyid:1 seq:0x0
> ```

The **debug ip ospf packet** command produces one set of information for each packet received. The output varies slightly depending on which authentication is used. Table 3-5 gives a description of the output in Example 3-6.

Table 3-5   **debug ip ospf packet** Output Fields

Field	Description
v:	OSPF version
t:	OSPF packet type; possible packet types are as follows:
	1—Hello
	2—Data description
	3—Link-state request
	4—Link-state update
	5—Link-state acknowledgment
l:	OSPF packet length in bytes
rid:	OSPF router ID
aid:	OSPF area ID
chk:	OSPF checksum
aut:	OSPF authentication type; possible authentication types are as follows:
	0—No authentication
	1—Simple password
	2—MD5
auk:	OSPF authentication key
keyid:	MD5 key ID
seq:	Sequence number

As you can see from the output in Example 3-6, and referencing Table 3-5, MD5 authentication is in use.

Additional Topics of Interest

Some chapters of this book include additional topics of interest, which typically cover either more details about previous topics or topics that are optional or secondary to the chapter's main goals.

This chapter's "Additional Topics of Interest" section provides additional details of how to troubleshoot IGRP.

Troubleshooting IGRP

IGRP is a distance vector routing protocol that Cisco Systems developed in the 1980s. IGRP has several features that differentiate it from other distance vector routing protocols, such as RIP.

If IGRP does not appear to be working correctly, check the following:

- Layer 1 or Layer 2 connectivity issues exist.
- AS numbers on IGRP routers are mismatched.
- Network statements are missing or are incorrectly assigned.
- The outgoing interface is down.
- The advertised network interface is down.

To view IGRP debugging information, use the following commands:

```
debug ip igrp transactions [ip-address]
debug ip igrp events [ip-address]
```

Use **debug ip igrp transactions** [*ip-address*] to display IGRP transaction information.

The *ip-address* parameter is optional and indicates the IP address of an IGRP neighbor. If this option is used, the output includes only messages describing updates from that neighbor and updates that the router broadcasts toward that neighbor.

Entries such as the following occur on startup or when some event occurs, such as an interface making a transition or a user manually clearing the routing table:

```
IGRP: broadcasting request on Ethernet0
IGRP: broadcasting request on Ethernet1
```

The following type of entry can result when routing updates become corrupted between sending and receiving routers:

```
IGRP: bad checksum from 172.69.64.43
```

Use **debug ip igrp events** [*ip-address*] to display summary information on IGRP routing messages that indicate the source and destination of each update and the number of routes in each update.

To see how these commands are used to troubleshoot, first see Figure 3-8. Example 3-7 provides sample **debug ip igrp transactions** output for router A in Figure 3-8.

Figure 3-8   Sample IGRP Network for Troubleshooting

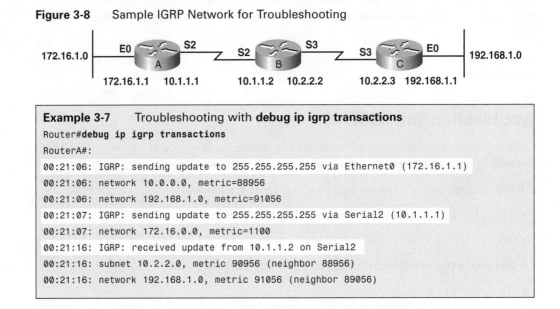

172.16.1.0   E0   S2   S2   S3   S3   E0   192.168.1.0
                    A   B   C
172.16.1.1   10.1.1.1   10.1.1.2   10.2.2.2   10.2.2.3   192.168.1.1

Example 3-7   Troubleshooting with **debug ip igrp transactions**

```
Router#debug ip igrp transactions
RouterA#:
00:21:06: IGRP: sending update to 255.255.255.255 via Ethernet0 (172.16.1.1)
00:21:06: network 10.0.0.0, metric=88956
00:21:06: network 192.168.1.0, metric=91056
00:21:07: IGRP: sending update to 255.255.255.255 via Serial2 (10.1.1.1)
00:21:07: network 172.16.0.0, metric=1100
00:21:16: IGRP: received update from 10.1.1.2 on Serial2
00:21:16: subnet 10.2.2.0, metric 90956 (neighbor 88956)
00:21:16: network 192.168.1.0, metric 91056 (neighbor 89056)
```

The output in Example 3-7 shows that the router being debugged has received an update from the router at source address 10.1.1.2, including information about two destinations (the networks being advertised). The fields are the same as in the sending output, but the metric in parentheses indicates the metric advertised by the neighbor sending the information. "Metric…inaccessible" usually means that the neighbor router has put the destination in a hold-down state.

When many networks exist in your routing table, displaying every update for every route can flood the console and make the router unusable. In this case, use the **debug ip igrp events** command to display a summary of IGRP routing information. The output of this command indicates the source and destination of each update and the number of routes in each update. Messages are not generated for each route. Example 3-8 illustrates typical output of **debug ip igrp events**. This output comes from router A in Figure 3-8.

In Figure 3-8, router A exchanges update IGRP messages with its neighbors. The router that is being debugged has sent two updates (in both cases, to broadcast address 255.255.255.255 as the destination address). The type of route information is categorized as subnet (interior), network (system), or exterior (exterior). The number of each type of route and the total number of routes are also indicated.

Example 3-8   Troubleshooting with **debug ip igrp events**

```
Router#debug ip igrp events
IGRP event debugging is on
RouterA#
00:23:44: IGRP: sending update to 255.255.255.255 via Ethernet0 (172.16.1.1)
00:23:44: IGRP: Update contains 0 interior, 2 system, and 0 exterior routes.
00:23:44: IGRP: Total routes in update: 2
00:23:44: IGRP: sending update to 255.255.255.255 via Serial2 (10.1.1.1)
00:23:45: IGRP: Update contains 0 interior, 1 system, and 0 exterior routes.
00:23:45: IGRP: Total routes in update: 1
00:23:48: IGRP: received update from 10.1.1.2 on Serial2
00:23:48: IGRP: Update contains 1 interior, 1 system, and 0 exterior routes.
00:23:48: IGRP: Total routes in update: 2
```

To delve into more detail about using the **debug ip igrp transactions** command, here is a troubleshooting scenario (see Figure 3-9).

Figure 3-9   IGRP Network Fails

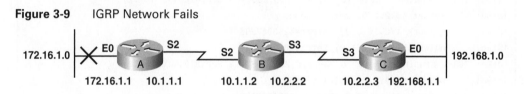

In Figure 3-9, the Ethernet network attached to router A fails. Router A sends a triggered update to router B that indicates that network 172.16.0.0 is inaccessible (with a metric of 4294967295), as Example 3-9 illustrates. Router B sends back a poison reverse update.

Example 3-9   Troubleshooting an IGRP Network (Router A)

```
RouterA#
00:31:15: %LINEPROTO-5-UPDOWN: Line protocol on Interface Ethernet0, changed state to
  down
00:31:15: IGRP: edition is now 3
00:31:15: IGRP: sending update to 255.255.255.255 via Serial2 (10.1.1.1)
00:31:15: network 172.16.0.0, metric=4294967295
00:31:16: IGRP: Update contains 0 interior, 1 system, and 0 exterior routes.
00:31:16: IGRP: Total routes in update: 1
00:31:16: IGRP: broadcasting request on Serial2
00:31:16: IGRP: received update from 10.1.1.2 on Serial2
00:31:16: subnet 10.2.2.0, metric 90956 (neighbor 88956)
00:31:16: network 172.16.0.0, metric 4294967295 (inaccessible)
00:31:16: network 192.168.1.0, metric 91056 (neighbor 89506)
00:31:16: IGRP: Update contains 1 interior, 2 system, and 0 exterior routes.
00:31:16: IGRP: Total routes in update: 3
```

In Example 3-10, router B receives the triggered update from router A, sends a poison reverse to router A, and sends a triggered update to router C, thereby notifying both routers that network 176.16.0.0 is "possibly down."

Example 3-10　Troubleshooting an IGRP Network (Router B)

```
RouterB#debug ip igrp transactions
IGRP protocol debugging is on
RouterB#
1d19h: IGRP: sending update to 255.255.255.255 via Serial2 (10.1.1.2)
1d19h:     subnet 10.2.2.0, metric=88956
1d19h:     network 192.168.1.0, metric=89056
1d19h: IGRP: sending update to 255.255.255.255 via Serial3 (10.2.2.2)
1d19h:     subnet 10.1.1.0, metric=88956
1d19h:     network 172.16.0.0, metric=89056
1d19h: IGRP: received update from 10.1.1.1 on Serial2
1d19h:     network 172.16.0.0, metric 4294967295 (inaccessible)
1d19h: IGRP: edition is now 10
1d19h: IGRP: sending update to 255.255.255.255 via Serial2 (10.1.1.2)
1d19h:     subnet 10.2.2.0, metric=88956
1d19h:     network 172.16.0.0, metric=4293967295
1d19h:     network 192.168.1.0, metric=89056
1d19h: IGRP: sending update to 255.255.255.255 via Serial3 (10.2.2.2)
1d19h:     subnet 10.1.1.0, metric=88956
1d19h:     network 172.16.0.0, metric=4294967295
```

Example 3-11　Troubleshooting an IGRP Network 2 (Router B)

```
RouterB#show ip route
Codes: C - connected, S - static, I - IGRP, R - RIP, M - mobile, B - BGP
       D - EIGRP, EX, - EIGRP external, O - OSPF, IA - OSPF inter area
       N1 - OSPF NSSA external type 1, N2 - OSPF NSSA external type 2
       E1 - OSPF external type 1, E2 - OSPF external type 2, E - EGP
       I - IS-IS, L1 - IS-IS level-1, L2 - IS-IS level-2, * - candidate default
       U - per-user static route, o - ODR
       T - traffic engineered route

Gateway of last resort is not set

I 172.16.0.0/16 is possibly down, routing via 10.1.1.1, Serial2
  10.0.0.0/24 is subnetted, 2 subnets
C    10.1.1.0 is directly connected, Serial2
C    10.2.2.0 is directly connected, Serial3
I 192.168.1.0/24 [100/89506] via 10.2.2.3, 00:00:14, Serial3
```

In addition to sending updates, router B places the route to network 172.16.0.0 in the hold-down state for 280 seconds. While in the hold-down state, the route to network 172.16.0.0 is marked as "possibly down" in the routing table, as Example 3-11 shows. Router B still tries to send traffic to network 172.16.0.0 until the hold-down timer expires.

In Example 3-12, a network engineer unsuccessfully attempts to ping 172.16.1.1.

Example 3-12   Troubleshooting an IGRP Network 3 (Router B)

```
RouterB#ping 172.16.1.1

Type escape sequence to abort.
Sending 5, 100-byte ICMP Echos to 172.16.1.1, timeout is 2 seconds:
.....
Success rate is 0 percent (0/5)
RouterB#
```

If the Ethernet link on router A comes back up, router A sends another triggered update to router B stating that network 172.16.0.0 is now accessible (with metric 89056), as Example 3-13 shows. Router B receives the triggered update.

Example 3-13   Troubleshooting an IGRP Network 4 (Router B)

```
RouterB#debug ip igrp transactions
RouterB#
1d20h: IGRP: received update from 10.1.1.1 on Serial2
1d20h:     network 172.16.0.0, metric 89056 (neighbor 1100)
RouterB#
```

Although router B receives the update, router B keeps the route in the hold-down state. Router B does not remove the route from the hold-down state and update its routing table until the hold-down timer expires.

In Example 3-14, the hold-down timer has not yet expired, so the route is still "possibly down."

Example 3-14   Troubleshooting an IGRP Network 5 (Router B)

```
RouterB#show ip route
Codes: C - connected, S - static, I - IGRP, R - RIP, M - mobile, B - BGP
       D - EIGRP, EX, - EIGRP external, O - OSPF, IA - OSPF inter area
       N1 - OSPF NSSA external type 1, N2 - OSPF NSSA external type 2
       E1 - OSPF external type 1, E2 - OSPF external type 2, E - EGP
       I - IS-IS, L1 - IS-IS level-1, L2 - IS-IS level-2, * - candidate default
       U - per-user static route, o - ODR
       T - traffic engineered route

Gateway of last resort is not set

I 172.16.0.0/16 is possibly down, routing via 10.1.1.1, Serial2
   10.0.0.0/24 is subnetted, 2 subnets
C    10.1.1.0 is directly connected, Serial2
C    10.2.2.0 is directly connected, Serial3
I 192.168.1.0/24 [100/89506] via 10.2.2.3, 00:00:14, Serial3
```

However, the administrator at router B can now successfully ping network 172.16.0.0, as Example 3-15 shows.

Example 3-15   Troubleshooting an IGRP Network 6 (Router B)

```
RouterB#ping 172.16.1.1

Type escape sequence to abort.
Sending 5, 100-byte ICMP Echos to 172.16.1.1, timeout is 2 seconds:
!!!!!
Success rate is 100 percent (5/5)
```

Chapter Summary

EIGRP is an IGP that scales well and provides quick convergence times with minimal network traffic. EIGRP is an enhanced version of IGRP, which was developed by Cisco, but EIGRP has improved convergence properties and operating efficiency over IGRP. New versions of the IOS no longer support IGRP.

Although IGRP and EIGRP are compatible with each other, there are some differences. EIGRP offers multiprotocol support, but IGRP does not. The EIGRP metric is the same as the IGRP metric except for a multiplier of 256 (which makes the EIGRP metrics larger).

EIGRP routers keep route and topology information readily available in RAM. Like OSPF, EIGRP saves this information in three tables. The neighbor table lists adjacent routers, the topology table is made up of all the EIGRP routes in the AS, and the routing table holds the best routes to a destination. DUAL, which is the EIGRP distance vector algorithm, takes the information supplied in the neighbor and the topology tables and calculates the lowest cost routes to each destination. The preferred primary route is called the successor route, and the backup route is called the feasible successor.

EIGRP is a balanced hybrid routing protocol (also referred to as an advanced distance vector routing protocol) and acts as a link-state protocol when updating neighbors and maintaining routing information. Advantages include rapid convergence, efficient use of bandwidth, support for VLSM and CIDR, support for multiple network layers, and independence from routed protocols.

DUAL results in the fast convergence of EIGRP. Each router has constructed a topology table that contains information about how to route to specific destinations. Each topology table identifies the routing protocol, or EIGRP; the lowest cost of the route, which is called feasible distance; and the cost of the route as advertised by the neighboring router, called reported distance.

EIGRP configuration commands vary depending on which protocol is used. Some examples of these protocols are IP, IPX, and AppleTalk. The **network** command configures only connected networks. EIGRP automatically summarizes routes at the classful boundary only prior to Cisco IOS Release 12.2(8)T. If discontiguous subnetworks exist, autosummarization must be disabled for routing to work properly. Manual summarization is done at the interface level with the **ip summary-address eigrp** command. The **show ip eigrp** command can verify an EIGRP configuration. The **debug ip eigrp** command can display information on EIGRP packets and troubleshoot EIGRP.

Troubleshooting at Layer 3 can be approached in a systematic fashion by using an eight-step troubleshooting methodology. Network engineers rely on **show** and **debug** commands to troubleshoot routing protocols. RIP, IGRP, EIGRP, and OSPF have their own set of **debug** commands that are tailored for culling important information that is used to troubleshoot issues with the respective routing protocol.

Check Your Understanding

Complete all the review questions listed here to test your understanding of the topics and concepts in this chapter. Answers are listed in Appendix A, "Answers to Check Your Understanding and Challenge Questions and Activities."

1. In this output line from the **debug ip rip** command, what do the numbers within the parentheses signify?

   ```
   RIP: sending v1 update to 255.255.255.255 via Ethernet1 (10.1.1.2)
   ```

   A. Source address

   B. Next-hop address

   C. Destination address

   D. Address of the routing table entry

2. What could cause the message "RIP: bad version 128 from 160.89.80.43" to display in the output of the **debug ip rip** command?

   A. Receiving a malformed packet

   B. Sending a routing table update

   C. Receiving a routing table update

3. Which command displays metric information that is contained in an IGRP update?

   A. **debug ip igrp events**

   B. **debug ip igrp transactions**

   C. **debug ip igrp events summary**

   D. **debug ip igrp transactions summary**

4. How is the bandwidth requirement for EIGRP packets minimized?

   A. By propagating only data packets

   B. By propagating only hello packets

   C. By propagating only routing table changes and hello packets

   D. By propagating the entire routing table to only those routers affected by a topology change

5. Which command correctly specifies that network 10.0.0.0 is directly connected to a router that runs EIGRP?

   A. Router(config)#**network 10.0.0.0**

   B. Router(config)#**router eigrp 10.0.0.0**

   C. Router(config-router)#**network 10.0.0.0**

   D. Router(config-router)#**router eigrp 10.0.0.0**

6. Which command displays the amount of time since the router heard from an EIGRP neighbor?

   A. **show ip eigrp traffic**

   B. **show ip eigrp topology**

   C. **show ip eigrp interfaces**

   D. **show ip eigrp neighbors**

7. The output from which command includes information about the length of the OSPF packet?

   A. **debug ip ospf events**

   B. **debug ip ospf packet**

   C. **debug ip ospf packet size**

   D. **debug ip ospf mpls traffic-eng advertisements**

8. What command(s) advertises the summary route 172.16.0.0/12 in EIGRP AS 1 out of interface Serial 0/0?

   A. Router(config)#**ip summary-address 172.16.0.0 255.240.0.0 eigrp 1 serial0/0**

   B. Router(config)#**interface serial0/0**
      Router(config-if)#**ip summary-address eigrp 1 172.16.0.0 255.240.0.0**

   C. Router(config)#**ip summary-address 172.16.0.0 255.255.0.0 eigrp 1 serial0/0**

   D. Router(config)#**interface serial0/0**
      Router(config-if)#**ip summary-address 172.16.0.0 255.240.0.0 eigrp 1 serial0/0**

9. What are the five EIGRP packet types?

   A. Reply, query, hello, update, acknowledgment

   B. Reply, query, hello, acknowledgment, LSU

   C. Query, hello, acknowledgment, LSA, LSU

   D. Reply, query, hello, RTP, acknowledgment

10. Which command displays the active or passive state of routes?

   A. **show ip eigrp traffic**

   B. **show ip eigrp topology**

   C. **show ip eigrp interfaces**

   D. **show ip eigrp neighbors**

Challenge Questions and Activities

These questions and activities are purposefully designed to be similar to the more complex styles of questions you might see on the CCNA exam. Answers are listed in Appendix A.

1. In Figure 3-10, two routers are configured to use EIGRP. Packets are not being forwarded between the two routers. What could be the problem?

Figure 3-10 EIGRP and VLSM

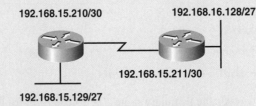

A. EIGRP does not support VLSM.

B. The routers were not configured to monitor neighbor adjacency changes.

C. The default bandwidth was used on the routers.

D. An incorrect IP address was configured on a router interface.

2. In Figure 3-11, routers A and B have EIGRP configured and automatic summarization has been disabled on both routers. Which one of the following router commands summarizes the attached routes and to which interface is the command applied? (Choose two.)

Figure 3-11 Interface Summarization with EIGRP

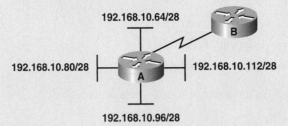

A. **ip summary-address eigrp 1 192.168.10.64 255.255.255.192**

B. **ip area-range eigrp 1 192.168.10.80 255.255.255.224**

C. **summary-address 192.168.10.80 0.0.0.31**

D. **ip summary-address eigrp 1 192.168.10.64 0.0.0.63**

E. Serial interface on Router A

F. Serial interface on Router B

3. When EIGRP is configured on a router, which table of DUAL information calculates the best route to each designated router?

A. Router table

B. Topology table

C. DUAL table

D. CAM table

E. ARP table

CHAPTER 4

Switching Concepts

Objectives

Upon completion of this chapter, you should be able to answer the following questions:

- What are the functions of Layer 2 switches?

- What are the primary LAN switch frame transmission modes?

- How does a LAN switch associate a MAC address with a port?

- How do switches forward and filter frames?

Additional Topics of Interest

Some chapters contain additional coverage of previous topics or related topics that are secondary to the main goals of the chapter. You can find the additional coverage in the "Additional Topics of Interest" section near the end of the chapter. For this chapter, the following additional topics are covered:

Introduction to Ethernet/802.3 LANs

Key Terms

This chapter uses the following key terms. You can find the definitions in the Glossary:

cyclic redundancy check (CRC)   *page 98*

frame check sequence (FCS)   *page 98*

flooding   *page 100*

filtering   *page 101*

age time   *page 101*

application-specific integrated circuit (ASIC)   *page 101*

Content Addressable Memory (CAM)   *page 102*

port-based memory buffering   *page 103*

shared memory buffering   *page 103*

store and forward   *page 104*

cut-through   *page 104*

fragment-free   *page 104*

LAN design has evolved. Fifteen years ago, network designers used hubs and bridges to build networks. Now, switches and routers are the key components in LAN design, and the capabilities and performance of these devices continue to improve.

With the use of repeaters in Ethernet networks, performance suffered as too many devices shared the same segment. Network engineers then added bridges to create multiple collision domains. As networks grew in size and complexity, the bridge evolved into the modern switch, allowing microsegmentation of the network. Modern networks are now built with switches and routers, often with both functionalities in one device.

Many modern switches are capable of performing varied and complex tasks in the network. This chapter provides an introduction to network segmentation and describes the basics of switch operation.

Switches and bridges perform much of the heavy work in LANs where they make nearly instantaneous decisions when frames are received. This chapter describes in detail how switches learn the physical addresses of nodes, and how switches transmit and filter frames. This chapter also describes the principles of LAN segmentation and collision domains.

Switches are Layer 2 devices that increase available bandwidth and reduce network congestion. A switch can segment a LAN into microsegments, which are segments with only a single host. Microsegmentation creates multiple collision-free domains from one large domain. As a Layer 2 device, the LAN switch increases the number of collision domains, but all hosts connected to the switch are still part of the same broadcast domain.

Introduction to LAN Switching

The exploration of LAN switching begins with a discussion of LAN segmentation by way of bridges, routers, and switches. This section then looks at types of switching and associated latency. The remainder of this book is devoted to LAN switching.

LAN Segmentation

A network can be divided into smaller units called segments. Figure 4-1 shows a sample segmented Ethernet network. The entire network contains 15 computers. Of these 15 computers, six are servers and nine are workstations. Each segment uses the carrier sense multiple access collision detect (CSMA/CD) access method and maintains traffic between users on the segment. Each segment is its own collision domain.

Figure 4-1   Bridges, Switches, and Routers Provide LAN Segmentation

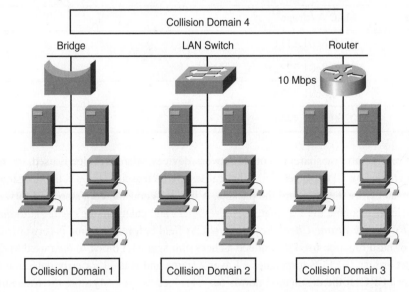

Segmentation allows network congestion to be significantly reduced within each segment. When data transmits within a segment, the devices within that segment share the total available bandwidth. Data that is passed between segments is transmitted over the network backbone through a bridge, router, or switch.

Bridges are Layer 2 devices that forward data frames based on the Media Access Control (MAC) address. Bridges read the source MAC address of the data packets to discover the devices that are on each segment. The source MAC addresses are then used to populate the MAC address table. This allows bridges to block packets that do not need to be forwarded from the local segment. Frames entering a bridge with a destination MAC address that does not appear in the MAC address table are forwarded out all ports except the ingress port. Figure 4-2 shows several devices (and their MAC addresses) connected to a bridge. Table 4-1 shows the mapping between the interfaces and the MAC addresses that the bridge stores.

Figure 4-2   MAC Addresses Are Used for Communication Within an Ethernet Collision Domain

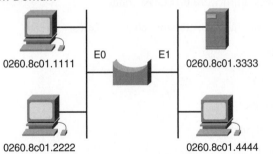

Table 4-1   Interface-to-MAC-Address Mapping

Interface	MAC Address
E0	0260.8c01.1111
E0	0260.8c01.2222
E1	0260.8c01.3333
E1	0260.8c01.4444

Although bridges are transparent to other network devices, when a bridge is used, the network latency increases by 10 to 30 percent. What causes the increased latency is the decisions bridges make before they forward the packets. A bridge is considered a store and forward device. Bridges examine the Destination Address field and calculate the *cyclic redundancy check (CRC)* in the *Frame Check Sequence (FCS)* field before the frame is forwarded. A CRC is a type of hash function used to produce a checksum against a block of data used to detect and correct errors. The FCS terminates a Layer 2 frame and is used for error detection and correction via a CRC. If the destination port is busy, bridges temporarily store the frame until that port becomes available.

Segmentation with bridging has the following characteristics:

- Segmentation provides fewer users per segment.
- Bridges store, and then forward frames based on Layer 2 addresses.
- Layer 3 protocol independence.
- Increased latency on the network.

Routers provide network segmentation and add a latency factor of 20 to 30 percent over a switched network. The latency increases because routers operate at the network layer and use the IP address to determine the best path to the destination node. Although platform dependent, routers also tend to require more software processing than switches.

Bridges and switches provide segmentation within a single network or subnetwork. Routers provide connectivity between networks and subnetworks. Routers do not forward broadcasts, but switches and bridges do forward broadcast frames.

Segmentation with routing has the following characteristics:

- More manageable
- Greater functionality
- Multiple active paths
- Smaller broadcast domains
- Operates at Layer 3

Switches decrease bandwidth shortages and network bottlenecks, such as those between several workstations and a remote file server. Switches segment LANs into microsegments, which decrease the size of collision domains. However, all hosts connected to a (Layer 2) switch are still in the same broadcast domain.

Segmentation with switches has the following characteristics:

- Eliminates the impact of collisions through microsegmentation

- Low latency and high frame-forwarding rates at each port

- Works with existing 802.3 (CSMA/CD) compliant network interface cards (NIC) and cabling

In a completely switched Ethernet LAN, the source and destination nodes function as if they are the only nodes on the network. When these two nodes establish a link (or virtual circuit), they have access to the maximum available bandwidth. These links provide significantly more throughput than Ethernet LANs connected by bridges or hubs. This virtual network circuit is established within the switch and exists only when the nodes need to communicate.

Basic Operations of a Switch

Switches use microsegmentation to reduce collision domains and network traffic. This reduction results in more efficient use of bandwidth and increased throughput. LAN switches have replaced shared hubs, and they are designed to work with already-in-place cable infrastructures.

Switches perform the following two basic operations:

- **Switch data frames**—Process of receiving a frame on a switch interface, selecting the correct forwarding switch port(s), and forwarding the frame.

- **Maintain switch operations**—Switches build and maintain forwarding tables. Switches also construct and maintain a loop-free topology across the LAN.

Figures 4-3 through 4-6 show the basic operations of a switch. In Figure 4-3, data is sent from A to B.

Figure 4-3   Frame Generated by A Is Destined for B

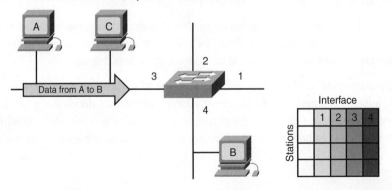

The switch's MAC address table has no entry for the MAC address of A, so it inserts a new entry into the table and forwards the frame out ports 1, 2, and 4, as shown in Figure 4-4.

Note

A switch or bridge maintains a MAC address table to track the locations of devices that are connected to it. The size of the MAC address table varies depending on the switch or bridge. For example, the Catalyst 2950 Series can hold up to 8192 entries.

When a switch or bridge is first initialized, the MAC address table is empty. With an empty MAC address table, the switch or bridge must forward each frame to all connected ports other than the one on which the frame arrived. Forwarding a frame to all connected ports except the incoming port is called *flooding* the frame. Flooding is the least efficient way to transmit data across a switch or bridge because it wastes bandwidth.

Switches and bridges implement memory so that they can independently receive and transmit frames on each port.

Figure 4-4   MAC Address of A Is Added to the MAC Address Table and the Frame Is Flooded

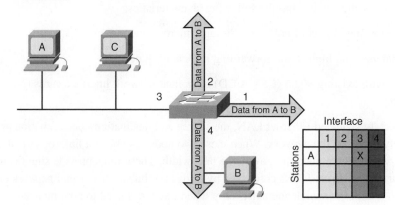

Subsequently, in Figure 4-5, B responds to the transmission with data from B to A, and the switch installs an entry for B in the MAC address table.

Figure 4-5   Unicast Ethernet Frame Transmission Toward Ingress Port

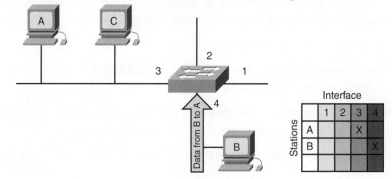

Finally, in Figure 4-6, the switch forwards the frame out port 3 back to A.

To recap, a switch forwards packets based on the MAC address table; the MAC address table maps MAC addresses to port numbers. Switches operate at Layer 2, installing entries in the MAC address table based on the source MAC address of ingress frames.

When a destination MAC address does not appear in the MAC address table, or when the destination MAC address is a multicast or broadcast address, the switch floods the frame (which means it forwards the frame out of all the ports except for the switch port through which the frame entered). Broadcast and multicast addresses never appear as the source address of a frame.

Figure 4-6   Unicast Frame Transmission from Egress Port

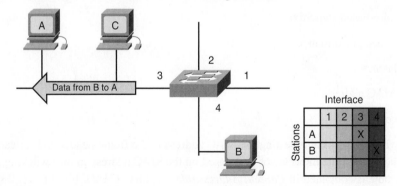

When the destination MAC address appears in the MAC address table, the switch only forwards the frame out the associated port. Frame *filtering* is the process of sending unicast Ethernet frames out of a single port once based on MAC address table entries, thus preserving bandwidth on the links connected to other switch ports.

Ethernet Switch Latency

Switch latency is the period of time when a frame enters a switch to the time it takes the frame to exit the switch. Latency is directly related to the configured switching process and volume of traffic.

Latency is measured in fractions of a second. Network devices operate at incredibly high speeds, so every additional millisecond (ms) of latency adversely affects network performance.

Layer 2 and Layer 3 Switching

There are two primary methods of switching data frames: Layer 2 switching and Layer 3 switching. Routers and Layer 3 switches use Layer 3 switching to switch packets. Layer 2 switches and bridges use Layer 2 switching to forward frames.

The difference between Layer 2 and Layer 3 switching is the type of information inside the frame that determines the correct output interface. Layer 2 switching is based on MAC address information; Layer 3 switching is based on network layer addresses (IP addresses). The features and functionality of Layer 3 switches and routers have numerous similarities. The only major difference between the packet-switching operation of a router and a Layer 3 switch is the physical implementation. In general-purpose routers, packet switching takes place in software, using microprocessor-based engines, whereas a Layer 3 switch performs packet forwarding using *application-specific integrated circuit (ASIC)* hardware. ASICs are integrated circuits designed to perform a specific function.

Note

When a MAC address table entry is created, it stays in the table until the *age time*. If a source station does not transmit another frame to the switch before the age time expires, the associated entry is not refreshed and is removed from the MAC address table. Because the MAC address table has a limited size, the age time helps to limit flooding by remembering the most active stations in the network. The age time also accommodates station moves. Aging allows the switch or bridge to forget an entry about a station that has been removed. If a station is moved from one port to another port, the switch or bridge immediately learns the new location of the station as soon as that station begins to transmit frames to the switch or bridge on the new port.

Here are some characteristics of Layer 2 switching:

- Hardware-based switching
- Wire-speed performance
- Low latency
- Uses MAC addresses
- Low cost

Layer 2 switching looks at a destination MAC address in the frame header and forwards the frame to the appropriate interface or port based on the MAC address in the switching table. The switching table is contained in *Content Addressable Memory (CAM)*. If the Layer 2 switch does not know where to send the frame, it broadcasts the frame out all ports to the network. When a reply is returned, the switch records the new address in the CAM.

Layer 3 switching is a function of the network layer. The Layer 3 header information is examined and the packet is forwarded based on the IP address.

Here are some characteristics of Layer 3 switching:

- Hardware-based packet forwarding
- High-performance packet switching
- High-speed scalability
- Low latency
- Lower per-routed-port cost
- Flow-based accounting
- Robust security
- Full QoS support

Traffic flow in a switched or flat network is inherently different from the traffic flow in a routed or hierarchical network. Hierarchical networks offer more flexible traffic flow than flat networks.

Symmetric and Asymmetric Switching

LAN switching can be classified as symmetric or asymmetric based on how bandwidth is allocated to the switch ports. A symmetric switch provides switched connections between ports with the same bandwidth. Multiple simultaneous conversations increase throughput.

Asymmetric switching provides connections between ports of unlike bandwidth, such as a combination of 100-Mbps and 1000-Mbps ports. Asymmetric switching enables more bandwidth to be dedicated to the server switch port to prevent a bottleneck. This allows smoother traffic flows where multiple clients communicate with a server at the same time. Memory buffering is required on an asymmetric switch. The use of buffers keeps the frames in proper sequence between different data rate ports.

An Ethernet switch might use a buffering technique to store and forward frames. Buffering can also be used when the destination port is busy. The area of memory where the switch stores the data is called the memory buffer. This memory buffer can use two methods to forward frames: port-based memory buffering and shared memory buffering.

In *port-based memory buffering*, frames are stored in queues that are linked to specific incoming ports. A frame is only transmitted to the outgoing port after all the frames ahead of it in the queue are successfully transmitted. It is possible for a single frame to delay the transmission of all the frames in memory because of a busy destination port. This delay occurs even if the other frames could be transmitted to open destination ports.

Shared memory buffering deposits all frames into a common memory buffer that all ports on the switch share. The amount of buffer memory required by a port is dynamically allocated. The frames in the buffer are linked dynamically to the destination port. This allows the packet to be received on one port and then transmitted to another port without moving it to a different queue.

The switch keeps a map of frame-to-port links showing where a packet needs to be transmitted. After the frame has been successfully transmitted, the map link is cleared. The memory buffer is shared. The number of frames stored in the buffer is restricted by the size of the entire memory buffer, not a single port buffer. This permits larger frames to transmit with fewer dropped frames. This is important to asymmetric switching, where frames are being exchanged between different rate ports.

Frame Transmission Modes

Ethernet switches and bridges increase the available bandwidth by reducing the number of devices that contend for the segment bandwidth. Ethernet switches and bridges also make intelligent frame-forwarding decisions by examining the source and destination MAC address of incoming frames.

Ethernet switches and bridges operate at Layer 2 of the Open System Interconnection (OSI) reference model. Because of their high-speed internal architecture and large number of ports, Ethernet switches offer much higher throughput than a traditional bridge.

Here is a review of the functions that switches and bridges perform:

- An Ethernet switch or bridge learns the MAC addresses of the devices that are attached to each of its ports. The switches and bridges do this by listening in on the incoming traffic to examine the source MAC addresses of the incoming frames on the switch and bridge ports. The MAC address-to-port mappings are stored in a MAC database. This MAC database is often called the MAC address table or the CAM table.

■ When an Ethernet switch or bridge receives a frame, the switch or bridge consults the MAC database to determine which port can reach the station identified as the destination in the frame. If the destination MAC address is found in the MAC database, the frame only transmits on that port identified as the destination in the frame. If the destination MAC address is not found in the MAC database, the frame transmits on all outgoing ports except the incoming port.

Three primary operating modes handle frame switching:

■ *Store and forward*—In store and forward mode, the switch or bridge receives the complete frame, and then forwards it. The destination and source addresses are read, the cyclic redundancy check (CRC) is performed, the relevant filters are applied, and the frame is forwarded. If the CRC is bad, the frame is discarded. Latency through the switch or bridge varies with frame length.

■ *Cut-through*—In cut-through mode, the switch or bridge checks the destination address as soon as the header is received and immediately begins forwarding the frame. The latency significantly decreases compared to store and forward mode. The delay in cut-through switching remains constant regardless of frame size because this switching mode starts to forward the frame as soon as the switch or bridge reads the destination addresses. In some switches and bridges, only the destination addresses are read. Some switches and bridges continue to read the CRC and keep a count of errors. Although the switch or bridge will not stop an errored frame, if the error rate is too high, the switch or bridge can be set— either manually or automatically—to use store and forward mode instead. This is often known as adaptive cut-through, which combines the low-latency advantage of cut-through and the error protection offered by store and forward.

■ *Fragment-free* (modified cut-through)—In fragment-free mode, the switch or bridge reads the first 64 bytes (minimum Ethernet frame size) before forwarding the frame. Usually, collisions happen within the first 64 bytes of a frame. When a collision occurs, a fragment (a frame less than 64 bytes) is created. By reading 64 bytes, the switch or bridge can filter out collision (fragment) frames. Fragment-free mode has higher latency than cut-through mode. Fragment-free mode can detect fragment frames and discard them instead of forwarding them, in contrast to cut-through, which forwards fragment frames if the destination address exists.

Figure 4-7 summarizes the three frame transmission modes.

Figure 4-7   Frame Transmission Modes Include Cut-Through, Store and Forward, and
Fragment-Free

Cut-Through
- Switch checks destination
  address and immediately
  begins forwarding frame.

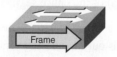

Store and Forward
- Complete frame is
  received and checked
  before forwarding.

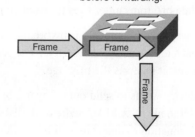

Fragment-Free
- Switch checks the first
  64 bytes, then immediately
  begins forwarding frame.

Switch Operation

LAN switches are considered multiport bridges with no collision domain because of microsegmentation. Data is exchanged at high speeds by switching the frame to its destination. By reading the destination MAC address Layer 2 information, switches can achieve high-speed data transfers. This process leads to low latency levels and a high rate of speed for frame forwarding.

Ethernet switching increases a network's available bandwidth by creating dedicated network segments (or point-to-point connections) and connecting them in a virtual network within the switch. This virtual network circuit exists only when two nodes need to communicate. This network is called a virtual circuit because it exists only when needed and is established within the switch.

Although the LAN switch reduces the size of collision domains, all hosts connected to the switch are still in the same broadcast domain. Therefore, a broadcast from one node can still be seen by all the other nodes connected through the LAN switch.

Switches are data link layer devices that enable multiple physical LAN segments to interconnect into a single larger network. Switches forward and flood traffic based on MAC addresses. Because switching is performed in hardware instead of in software, it is significantly faster than traditional bridging. Each switch port gives the full bandwidth of the medium to each host.

Broadcast Domains

Communication in a network occurs in three ways. The most common way is by unicast transmissions. In a unicast transmission, one transmitter tries to reach one receiver.

Another way to communicate is known as a multicast transmission. Multicast transmission occurs when one transmitter tries to reach only a subset (group) of the entire segment.

The final way to communicate is by broadcasting. Broadcasting occurs when one transmitter tries to reach all the network receivers. The server station sends out one message and everyone on that segment receives the message.

When a device wants to send out a Layer 2 broadcast, the destination MAC address in the frame is set to all 1s. A MAC address of all 1s is FF:FF:FF:FF:FF:FF in hexadecimal. By setting the destination to this value, all the devices accept and process the broadcasted frame.

The broadcast domain at Layer 2 is referred to as the MAC broadcast domain. This domain consists of all devices on the LAN that receive frame broadcasts by a host to all other machines on the LAN.

A switch is a Layer 2 device. When a switch receives a broadcast, it forwards it to each port on the switch except the incoming port. Each attached device must process the broadcast frame. This leads to reduced network efficiency because available bandwidth is used for broadcasting purposes.

When two switches are connected, as in Figure 4-8, the broadcast domain increases. In this example, a broadcast frame is forwarded to all connected ports on Switch 1. Switch 1 is connected to Switch 2. The frame is propagated to all devices connected to Switch 2.

Figure 4-8   Broadcast Domains Encompass Collision Domains

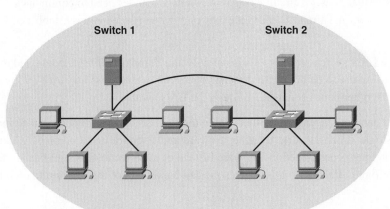

The overall result is a reduction in available bandwidth. This happens because all devices in the broadcast domain must receive and process the broadcast frame.

Routers are Layer 3 devices. Routers do not propagate broadcasts. Routers segment both collision and broadcast domains.

Communication Between Switches and Workstations

When a workstation connects to a LAN, it transmits data independently of the other devices connected to the LAN media. The workstation simply transmits data frames from a NIC to the network medium.

If desired, the workstation can be attached directly to another workstation by using a crossover cable. Crossover cables connect the following devices:

- Workstation to workstation
- Switch to switch
- Switch to hub
- Hub to hub
- Router to router
- Router to PC

Straight-through cables connect the following devices:

- Switch to router
- Switch to workstation or server
- Hub to workstation or server

Many modern switches now automatically adjust the port pinout to support the particular cable attached, whether it is a crossover or straight-through cable.

Switches, which are Layer 2 devices, use intelligence to learn the MAC addresses of the devices that are attached to its ports. This data is entered into a switching table. After the table is complete, the switch can read the destination MAC address of an incoming data frame on a port and immediately forward it. Until a device transmits, the switch does not know its MAC address.

Switches provide significant scalability on a network. Switches are normally connected to each other by way of trunk links. Chapter 9, "VLAN Trunking Protocol," discusses trunks in detail.

Additional Topics of Interest

Some chapters of this book include additional topics of interest, which typically cover either more details about previous topics or topics that are optional or secondary to the chapter's main goals.

This chapter's "Additional Topics of Interest" section provides additional details of Ethernet/802.3 LANs, which is also explored in CCNA 1. We review the content here because the theory underlies the operation of LAN switching.

Introduction to Ethernet/802.3 LANs

This section describes the roots of modern Ethernet LANs, emphasizing the evolution of Ethernet/802.3, which is the most commonly deployed LAN architecture. A look at the historical context of LAN development and various network devices that can be used at different layers of the OSI model will help you better understand the reasons why network devices have evolved as they have.

Ethernet/802.3 LAN Development

The earliest LAN technologies used either Thick Ethernet or Thin Ethernet infrastructures. The media have not been used for almost a decade, but it helps to understand the limitations of these infrastructures. For Thick Ethernet, some limitations were as follows:

- Limited to 500 meters before signal degrades.
- Limitation on number and placement of hosts.
- Adding users requires network interruptions.
- Expensive, thick, and hard to pull.
- 10 Mbps.

For Thin Ethernet, some limitations were as follows:

- Limited to 185 meters before signal degrades.
- Difficult to pull.
- Adding users requires network interruptions.
- 10 Mbps.

The addition of hubs and UTP cabling into the network offered an improvement on Thick and Thin Ethernet technology. A hub is a Layer 1 device; it is sometimes referred to as an Ethernet concentrator or a multiport repeater. Hubs allow more users to have better access to the network. Hubs regenerate data signals, which allow networks to extend to greater distances. Hubs do not make any decisions when data signals are received. They simply regenerate and amplify the data signals to all connected devices, except for the device that originally sent the signal. Hubs are not used in modern networks and are no longer widely available.

By design, Ethernet is a shared technology where all users on a given LAN segment compete for the same available bandwidth. This situation is analogous to several cars that simultaneously try to access a one-lane road. Because the road has only one lane, only one car can access it at a time. As hubs were added to the network, more users competed for the same bandwidth.

Collisions are a natural occurrence in traditional Ethernet networks. If two or more devices try to transmit simultaneously, a collision occurs. This situation is analogous to two cars that try to merge into a single lane and cause a collision. Traffic is backed up until the collision clears. Excessive collisions in a network result in slow network response times. This indicates that the network is too congested or has too many users who need to access the network at the same time.

Layer 2 devices are more intelligent than Layer 1 devices. Layer 2 devices make forwarding decisions based on MAC addresses contained within the headers of transmitted data frames.

A bridge, which is a Layer 2 device, divides (or segments) a network. Bridges collect and selectively pass data frames between two network segments, as Figure 4-9 illustrates.

Figure 4-9   Bridges Create Smaller Collision Domains

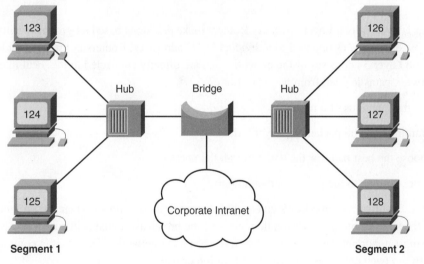

To do this, bridges learn the MAC address of devices on each connected segment. With this information, the bridge builds a MAC address table and forwards or blocks traffic based on that table. This results in smaller collision domains and greater network efficiency. Bridges do not restrict broadcast traffic. However, they do provide greater traffic control within a network. Bridges have the following advantages over hubs:

- Bridges are more intelligent than hubs.

- Bridges eavesdrop on conversations to learn and maintain MAC address tables.

- Bridges collect and pass frames between two network segments.

- Bridges control traffic to the network.

Modern networks no longer use bridges. Switches have replaced them.

A switch is (traditionally) a Layer 2 device and is sometimes referred to as a multiport bridge. Switches make forwarding decisions based on MAC addresses contained within data frames. Switches learn the MAC addresses of devices connected to each port, and this information is entered into a switching table.

Switches create a virtual circuit between two connected devices that want to communicate. When the virtual circuit is created, a dedicated communication path is established between the two devices. The implementation of a switch on the network provides microsegmentation. This creates a collision-free environment between the source and destination, which allows maximum utilization of the available bandwidth. Switches can facilitate multiple, simultaneous virtual circuit connections. This is analogous to a highway that is divided into multiple lanes with each car having its own dedicated lane.

The disadvantage of Layer 2 devices is that they forward broadcast frames to all connected devices on the network. Excessive broadcasts in a network result in slow network response times.

A router is essentially a Layer 3 device. Routers make decisions based on groups of network addresses, or classes, as opposed to individual MAC addresses. Routers use routing tables to record the Layer 3 addresses of the networks that are directly connected to the local interfaces and network paths learned from neighbor routers.

Here are the functions of a router:

- Examine inbound packets of Layer 3 data.

- Choose the best path for the data through the network.

- Route the data to the proper outbound port.

Routers do not forward broadcasts unless they are configured to do so. Therefore, routers reduce the size of both the collision domains and the broadcast domains in a network. Routers are the most important devices to regulate traffic on large networks. They enable communication between two computers regardless of location or operating system.

LANs typically employ a combination of Layer 1, Layer 2, and Layer 3 devices. To reiterate the correspondence between device type and OSI layer, see the following list:

- Repeaters and hubs are Layer 1 devices.

- Bridges and switches are Layer 2 devices.

- Routers are Layer 3 devices.

Keep in mind, however, that newer switches typically employ Layer 3 and higher functionality. Implementation of these devices depends on factors that are specific to the particular needs of the organization.

Factors That Impact Network Performance

In addition to a large number of network users, several other factors, which are illustrated in Figure 4-10, have combined to test the limits of traditional LANs:

- The multitasking environment present in current desktop operating systems, such as Windows, UNIX/Linux, and Mac OS X, allows for simultaneous network transactions. This increased capability has lead to an increased demand for network resources.

- The use of network-intensive applications, such as the World Wide Web, has increased. Client/server applications allow administrators to centralize information and make it easier to maintain and protect information.

- Client/server applications do not require workstations to maintain information or provide hard disk space to store it. Given the cost benefit of client/server applications, such applications are likely to become even more widely used in the future.

Figure 4-10   Identifying Network Bandwidth Requirements

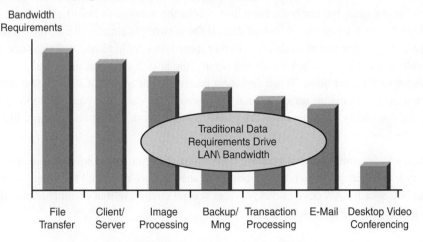

Elements of Ethernet/802.3 Networks

Ethernet is a broadcast transmission technology. Network devices, such as computers, printers, and file servers, communicate with one another over a shared network medium. The performance of a shared medium Ethernet/802.3 LAN can be negatively affected by several factors:

- Data frame delivery of Ethernet/802.3 LANs is of a broadcast nature.

- CSMA/CD method allows only one station to transmit at a time.

- Multimedia applications with higher bandwidth demand, such as video, coupled with the broadcast nature of Ethernet, can create network congestion.

- Normal latency occurs as frames travel across the network medium and through network devices.

Ethernet uses CSMA/CD and can support fast transmission rates. Fast Ethernet (or 100BASE-T) provides transmission speeds up to 100 Mbps. Gigabit Ethernet provides transmission speeds up to 1000 Mbps and 10 Gigabit Ethernet (10GigE) provides transmission speeds up to 10,000 Mbps. Ethernet's goal is to provide a best-effort delivery service and allow all devices on the shared medium to transmit on an equal basis. Collisions are a natural occurrence on Ethernet networks and can become a major problem. Here are some indicative signs of excessive collisions:

- Slow network response

- Slow file transfer

- Increased user complaints

Duplex and Speed

Originally, Ethernet was a half-duplex technology. Half-duplex allows hosts to either transmit or receive at one time, but not both. Each host checks the network to see whether data is being transmitted before it transmits additional data. If the network is already in use, the transmission is delayed. Despite transmission deferral, two or more hosts could transmit at the same time. This results in a collision. When a collision occurs, the host that detects the collision first sends a jam signal to the other hosts. When each host receives a jam signal, it stops data transmission, and then waits for a random period of time to retransmit the data. The backoff algorithm generates this random delay. As more hosts are added to the network, collisions are more likely to occur.

Ethernet LANs become saturated because users run network intensive software, such as client/server applications, which causes hosts to transmit more often and for longer time periods. The NIC which LAN devices use provides several circuits so that communication among devices can occur, as Figure 4-11 shows.

Figure 4-11   NICs Employ Several Circuits to Enable Communication

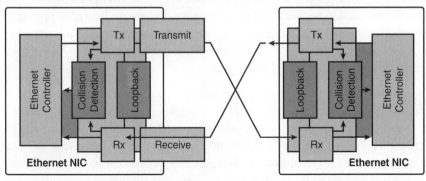

Half-duplex transmission mode implements CSMA/CD. The traditional shared LAN operates in half-duplex mode and is susceptible to transmission collisions across the wire. To summarize, half-duplex is characterized by the following:

- CSMA/CD

- Connectivity with hubs (see Figure 4-12)

- Unidirectional data flow

- Higher potential for collisions

Figure 4-12   Hubs Support Half-Duplex Environments

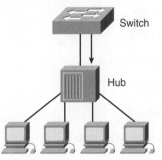

Full-duplex Ethernet significantly improves network performance without the expense of installing new media. Full-duplex transmission between stations is achieved by using point-to-point Ethernet, Fast Ethernet, Gigabit Ethernet, and 10GigE connections. This arrangement is collision free. Frames sent by the two connected end nodes cannot collide because the end nodes use two separate circuits in the Category 3, 5, 5e, or 6 cable. Each full-duplex connection uses only one port.

Full-duplex port connections are point-to-point links between switches or end nodes, but not between shared hubs. Nodes that are directly attached to a dedicated switch port with NICs that support full duplex need to be connected to switch ports that are configured to operate in full-duplex mode. The Ethernet, Fast Ethernet, Gigabit Ethernet, and 10GigE NICs sold today offer full-duplex capability. In full-duplex mode, the collision detect circuit is disabled. Gigabit Ethernet and 10GigE NICs are solely full duplex.

Full duplex allows the transmission of a packet and the reception of a different packet at the same time. This simultaneous transmission and reception requires the use of two pairs of wires in the cable and a switched connection between each node. This connection is a point-to-point connection and is collision free. Because both nodes can transmit and receive at the same time, there are no negotiations for bandwidth. Full-duplex Ethernet can use a cable infrastructure that is already in place, as long as the medium meets the minimum Ethernet standards.

To transmit and receive simultaneously, a dedicated switch port is required for each node. Full-duplex Ethernet connections can be 10 Mbps, 100 Mbps, 1000 Mbps, or 10,000 Mbps point-to-point connections. The NICs on all connected devices must have full-duplex capabilities.

The full-duplex Ethernet switch takes advantage of the two pairs of wires in the cable and creates a direct connection between the transmit (Tx) at one end of the circuit and the receive (Rx) at the other end. With the two stations connected in this manner, a collision-free environment is created as the transmission and receipt of data occurs on separate noncompetitive circuits.

Summarizing full-duplex links, as Figure 4-13 shows, are characterized by the following:

- Point-to-point only

- Doubles bandwidth between nodes

- Attached to dedicated switch port

- Requires full-duplex support on both ends

- Collision free

- Collision-detect circuit disabled

- Two 10, 100, 1000, or 10,000 Mbps data paths

Nodes attached to hubs that share their connection to a switch port must operate in half-duplex mode because the end stations must be able to detect collisions. Standard (shared) Ethernet configuration efficiency is typically rated at 50 to 60 percent of the bandwidth. Full-duplex Ethernet offers 100 percent efficiency in both directions. With Standard Ethernet, this produces a potential 20-Mbps throughput, which results from 10 Mbps Tx and 10 Mbps Rx. Today, the vast majority of Ethernet infrastructures consist of full-duplex links.

Figure 4-13   Full-Duplex Links Are Used Throughout Modern Ethernet LANs

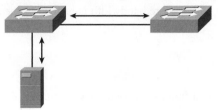

Network Congestion

Advances in technology produce faster and more intelligent desktop computers and workstations. The combination of more powerful workstations and network-intensive applications has created a need for greater network capacity (bandwidth). All these factors place a strain on networks. Figure 4-14 shows the connection between various applications and bandwidth requirements.

Figure 4-14   Applications Vary in Bandwidth Requirements

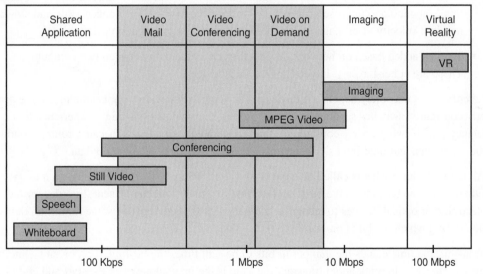

The following types of media have increased in transmission over networks:

- Large graphics files

- Full-motion video

- Multimedia applications

Also, the number of users on a network has increased. As more people use networks to share larger files, access file servers, and connect to the Internet, network congestion occurs. This results in slower response times, longer file transfers, and less productive network users. To relieve network congestion, either more bandwidth is needed or the available bandwidth must be used more efficiently.

Network Latency

Latency (or delay) is the time a frame or a packet takes to travel from the source station to the final destination. It is important to quantify the total latency of the path between the source and the destination for LANs and WANs. In the specific case of an Ethernet LAN, it is important to understand latency and its effect on network timing as it is used to determine if CSMA/CD will work properly.

Latency has at least three sources:

- Time it takes the source NIC to place voltage pulses on the wire, and the time it takes the destination NIC to interpret these pulses. This is sometimes called NIC delay (typically, around 1 microsecond for a 10BASE-T NIC).

- Actual propagation delay while the signal takes time to travel through the cable. Typically, this is about 0.556 microseconds per 100 m for Category 5 UTP. Longer cable and slower nominal velocity of propagation (NVP) results in more propagation delay.

- Latency added based on network devices that are in the path between two computers. These are either Layer 1, Layer 2, or Layer 3 devices.

Latency does not solely depend on distance and number of devices. For example, if three properly configured switches separate two workstations, the workstations might experience less latency than if two properly configured routers separated them. This is because routers conduct more complex and time-intensive functions. A router must analyze Layer 3 data.

All networks have what is called bit-time or slot time. Many LAN technologies, such as Ethernet, define bit-time as the basic unit of time in which 1 bit can be sent. In order for the electronic or optical devices to recognize a binary 1 or 0, there must be some minimum duration during which the bit is on or off.

Transmission time equals the number of bits to be sent times the bit-time for a given technology. Another way to think about transmission time is the interval between the start and end of a frame transmission or between the start of a frame transmission and a collision. Small frames take a shorter amount of time. Large frames take a longer amount of time.

A bit on an 10-Mbps Ethernet network has a 100-ns transmission window or bit-time. One ns is one billionth of a second (or .000000001 seconds). A byte equals 8 bits. Therefore, 1 byte takes a minimum of 800 ns to transmit. A 64-byte frame, which is the smallest 10BASE-T Ethernet frame that allows CSMA/CD to function properly, has a transmission time of 51,200 ns (51.2 microseconds, denoted 51.2 μs). (μ is the Greek letter mu, pronounced "myew.") One microsecond is one millionth of a second (or .000001 seconds). A 512-byte frame has a transmission time of approximately 410 µs (obtained by multiplying 51.2 by 8). Transmission of a 1000-byte frame from the source requires 800 µs. A 1518-byte Ethernet frame requires 1214 µs; 1518 is the maximum frame size for Ethernet.

The time at which the frame actually arrives at the destination station depends on the additional latency introduced by the network. This latency can be caused by various delays, including the following:

- NIC delays

- Propagation delays

- Layer 1, Layer 2, or Layer 3 device delays

The distance that a LAN can cover is limited because of attenuation. Attenuation means that a signal weakens as it travels through the network. The resistance in the cable or medium through which the signal travels causes the loss of signal strength. An Ethernet repeater is a physical layer device on the network that boosts or regenerates the signal on an Ethernet LAN. Figure 4-15 shows an Ethernet hub.

When a repeater is used to extend the distance of a LAN, as shown in Figure 4-16, a single network can cover a greater distance and more users can share that same network. However, the use of repeaters and hubs adds to problems associated with broadcasts and collisions. It also has a negative effect on the overall performance of the shared media LAN.

Figure 4-15   (End-of-Life) Cisco Hub Used as a Multiport Repeater

Figure 4-16   Repeaters Increase the Frequency of Collisions

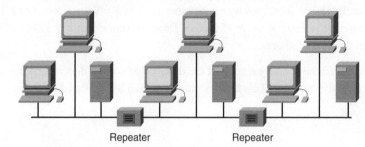

Repeater   Repeater

Chapter Summary

Segmentation divides a network into smaller units to reduce network congestion and enhance security. The CSMA/CD access method on each segment maintains traffic between users. Segmentation with a Layer 2 bridge is transparent to other network devices, but latency is increased significantly. The more work done by a network device, the more latency the device introduces into the network. Routers provide segmentation of networks but can add a latency factor of 20 to 30 percent over a switched network. This latency increases because a router operates at the network layer and uses the IP address to determine the best path to the destination node. A switch can segment a LAN into microsegments, which decreases the size of collision domains. However, all hosts connected to the switch are still in the same broadcast domain.

Switching decreases congestion in Ethernet LANs. Switching is the process of receiving an incoming frame on one interface and delivering that frame out another interface. Some routers now use Layer 3 switching to route a packet. Switches use Layer 2 switching to forward frames. A symmetric switch provides switched connections between ports with the same bandwidth. An asymmetric LAN switch provides switched connections between ports of unlike bandwidth, such as a combination of 100-Mbps and 1000-Mbps ports.

A memory buffer is an area of memory where a switch stores data. It can use two methods to forward frames, including port-based memory buffering and shared memory buffering.

Three frame transmission modes are used to forward frames. Store and forward receives the entire frame before forwarding. Cut-through mode forwards the frame as it is received, which decreases latency. Fragment-free mode reads the first 64 bytes (minimum Ethernet frame size) before forwarding the frame.

Check Your Understanding

Complete all the review questions listed here to test your understanding of the topics and concepts in this chapter. Answers are listed in Appendix A, "Answers to Check Your Understanding and Challenge Questions and Activities."

1. Which two functions can bridges and OSI Layer 2 switches provide? (Choose two.)

    A. Packet routing

    B. Jitter avoidance

    C. Address learning

    D. Frame filtering

    E. Loop avoidance using a routing protocol

2. Ethernet switching or bridging _____ the available bandwidth of a network by creating _____ network segments.

    A. Increases, shared

    B. Decreases, shared

    C. Increases, dedicated

    D. Decreases, dedicated

3. Which frame transmission mode reads the destination address of a frame only before forwarding it?

    A. Cut-through

    B. Fragment-free

    C. Store and forward

    D. All transmission modes

4. Which feature do switches and bridges implement so that they can independently receive and transmit frames on each port?

    A. Loop avoidance

    B. Buffer memory

    C. Store and forward mode

    D. Two-way forwarding

5. What information in a frame does a switch or bridge use to make frame-forwarding decisions?

A. Source port

B. Source address

C. Destination port

D. Destination address

6. When a frame arrives with a known destination address, where does the switch or bridge forward it?

A. Source port

B. Broadcast port

C. Destination port

D. All ports except the source port

7. Which three frame types are flooded to all ports except the source port on a switch? (Choose three.)

A. Unicast frames

B. Multicast frames

C. Broadcast frames

D. Frames with a known destination address

E. Frames with an unknown destination address

8. Which devices can segment an Ethernet collision domain? (Choose three.)

A. Hub

B. Router

C. Switch

D. Bridge

E. Repeater

F. Workstation

9. Which of the following describe asymmetric switching? (Choose three.)

A. Requires memory buffering

B. Creates a bottleneck on a network

C. Helps prevent bottlenecks on a network

D. Provides switched connections between ports of unlike bandwidth

E. Provides switched connections between ports of like bandwidth

10. Which layer of the OSI model does a LAN switch use to make a forwarding decision?

   A. Layer 1

   B. Layer 2

   C. Layer 3

   D. Layer 4

Challenge Questions and Activities

These questions and activities are purposefully designed to be similar to the more complex styles of questions you might see on the CCNA exam. Answers are listed in Appendix A.

  1. See Figure 4-17. How many broadcast domains will there be in the entire network if Hub1 is replaced with a Layer 2 switch?

Figure 4-17   Broadcast Domains

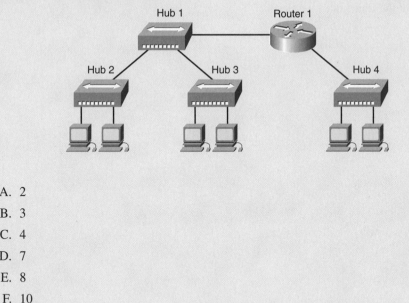

   A. 2

   B. 3

   C. 4

   D. 7

   E. 8

   F. 10

  2. See Figure 4-18. An Ethernet switch has developed the MAC address table shown at the top of the figure. What action will the switch take when it receives the frame shown at the bottom of the figure?

Figure 4-18   MAC Address Table and MAC Header

Station	Interface1	Interface2	Interface3	Interface4
00-00-3D-1F-11-01			X	
00-00-3D-1F-11-02				X
00-00-3D-1F-11-03	X			

Destination	Source	Data	CRC
00-00-3D-1F-11-03	00-00-3D-1F-11-01		

A. Forward the frame out all interfaces.

B. Forward the frame out all interfaces except Interface3.

C. Discard the frame.

D. Forward the frame out Interface1.

E. Forward the frame out Interface2.

F. Forward the frame out Interface3.

CHAPTER 5

LAN Design and Switches

Objectives

Upon completion of this chapter, you should be able to answer the following questions:

- What are the requirements of network design?

- What affects network availability?

- Into which three OSI layers is network design broken?

- What are the characteristics of the access, distribution, and core layers of the hierarchical design model?

Key Terms

This chapter uses the following key terms. You can find the definitions in the Glossary:

access layer   page 124

distribution layer   page 124

core layer   page 124

virtual LAN (VLAN)   page 125

Domain Name System (DNS)   page 125

collision domain   page 125

microsegmentation   page 127

availability   page 128

cut sheets   page 130

unshielded twisted-pair (UTP)   page 132

shielded twisted-pair (STP)   page 132

horizontal cross-connect (HCC)   page 132

vertical cross-connect (VCC)   page 133

asymmetric switching   page 135

symmetric switching   page 135

Designing a network is a challenging process that requires extensive planning. A network requires many features to be reliable, manageable, and scalable. To design reliable, manageable, and scalable networks, network designers must realize that each of the major components of a network has distinct design requirements.

Each of the access, distribution, and core LAN design layers discussed in this chapter requires switches that are best suited for the task at hand. The features, functions, and technical specifications for each switch vary based on the LAN design layer (access, distribution, core) for which the switch is intended. For the best network performance, you need to understand the role of each layer and then choose the switch that best suits the layer requirements.

LAN Design

Network design has become more difficult despite improvements in equipment performance and media capabilities. The use of multiple media types and LANs that interconnect with other networks add to the complexity of the network environment. Good network designs improve performance and reduce the difficulties associated with network growth and evolution.

A LAN spans a single room, a building, or a set of buildings that are close together. A group of buildings that are close to each other and belong to a single organization is referred to as a campus. You must identify the following aspects of the network before designing a large LAN:

- An *access layer* that connects end users to the LAN

- A *distribution layer* that provides policy-based connectivity between end-user LANs

- A *core layer* that provides the fastest connection between the distribution points

LAN Design Goals

The first step in LAN design is to establish and document the goals of the design. These goals are unique to each organization or situation. The following describes the requirements of most network designs:

- **Functionality**—Design the network to work as it needs to. It must allow users to meet their job requirements and provide user-to-user and user-to-application connectivity with reasonable speed and reliability.

- **Scalability**—Design the network to be expandable. The initial design should grow without major changes to the overall design.

- **Adaptability**—Design the network with a vision toward future technologies. It should not include elements that would limit implementation of new technologies as they become available.

- **Manageability**—Design the network to facilitate network monitoring and management to ensure continuous stability of operation.

LAN Design Considerations

Many organizations have upgraded their current LANs or plan to implement new LANs. This expansion in LAN design is because of the development of high-speed technologies, such as Gigabit Ethernet and 10-Gigabit Ethernet. This expansion is also because of complex LAN architectures that use LAN switching and virtual LANs (VLAN). A *VLAN* is a group of devices on one or more LANs that can communicate as if they were attached to the same wire, when in fact they are located on a number of different LAN segments.

To maximize available LAN bandwidth and performance, address the following LAN design considerations:

- The function and placement of servers
- Collision domain issues
- Segmentation issues
- Broadcast domain issues

Servers allow network users to communicate and to share files, printers, and application services. Servers typically do not function as workstations. Servers run specialized operating systems, such as NetWare, Windows NT, UNIX, and Linux. Each server is usually dedicated to one function, such as e-mail or file sharing.

Servers can be categorized as either enterprise servers or workgroup servers. An enterprise server supports all the users on the network as it offers services, such as e-mail or Domain Name System (DNS). *DNS* is the Internet-wide system by which a hierarchical set of DNS servers collectively hold all the name-to-IP address mappings, with DNS servers referring users to the correct DNS server in order to successfully resolve a DNS name. E-mail or DNS is a service that everyone in an organization needs because it is a centralized function. A workgroup server supports a specific set of users and offers services such as word processing and file sharing.

As seen in Figure 5-1, you should place enterprise servers in the main distribution facility (MDF). Whenever possible, the traffic to enterprise servers should travel only to the MDF and not be transmitted across other networks. However, some networks use a routed core or might even have a server farm for the enterprise servers. In these cases, network traffic travels across other networks and usually cannot be avoided. Ideally, you should place workgroup servers in the intermediate distribution facilities (IDF) closest to the users who access the applications on these servers. This allows traffic to travel the network infrastructure to an IDF and does not affect other users on that network segment. Layer 2 LAN switches located in the MDF and IDFs should have 1000 Mbps or more allocated to these servers.

Ethernet nodes use carrier sense multiple access collision detect (CSMA/CD). Each node must contend with all other nodes to access the shared medium, or *collision domain*, as illustrated in Figure 5-2.

Figure 5-1   Servers Are Typically Placed at a Point of Convergence in the Network, Such as Within an IDF or MDF

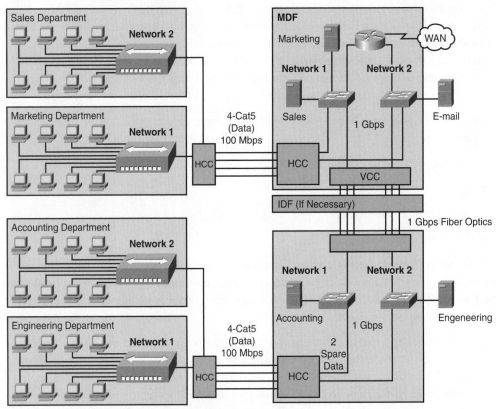

Figure 5-2   Collisions Increase Multiplicatively with the Number of Hosts

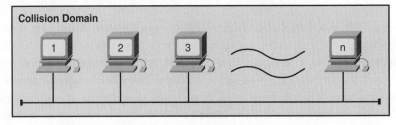

If two nodes transmit at the same time, a collision occurs. Collisions destroy the transmitted frame and send a jam signal to all nodes on the segment. The nodes wait a random period of time, and then resend the data. Excessive collisions can reduce the bandwidth of a network segment to 35 or 40 percent of the available bandwidth. Note that modern networks normally have one device per switch port (or two in the case of an IP phone cascaded with an end station), which means that collisions are not as likely.

Microsegmentation is when a single collision domain is split into smaller collision domains, as seen in Figure 5-3. Smaller collision domains reduce the number of collisions on a LAN segment and allow for greater utilization of bandwidth. You can use Layer 2 devices to segment a LAN. Routers, on the other hand, provide Layer 3 segmentation.

Figure 5-3   Microsegmentation Increases the Number of Collision Domains

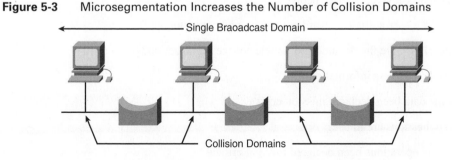

A broadcast occurs when the destination MAC address is set to FF-FF-FF-FF-FF-FF. A broadcast domain refers to the set of devices that receive a broadcast data frame that originates from any device within that set. All hosts that receive a broadcast data frame must process it. This process consumes the resources and available bandwidth of the host. Layer 2 devices such as bridges and switches reduce the size of a collision domain but do not reduce the size of the broadcast domain. Routers reduce the size of the collision domain and the size of the broadcast domain at Layer 3.

LAN Design Methodology

For a LAN to be effective and serve the needs of its users, you should design and implement it based on a planned series of systematic steps:

Step 1 Gather the requirements and expectations.

Step 2 Analyze the requirements and data.

Step 3 Design the Layer 1, 2, and 3 LAN structure, or topology.

Step 4 Document the logical and physical network implementation.

The process to gather information helps to clarify and identify any current network problems. This information includes the history of the organization and current status, its projected growth, operation policies and management procedures, office systems and procedures, and the viewpoints of the people who will use the LAN.

For the first step in the design methodology, ask the following questions to gather information:

- Who will use the network?
- What is the corporate structure?
- What is the skill level of these people?
- What are the user attitudes toward computers and computer applications?
- How developed are the documented policies of the organization?
- What is the business information flow?
- Has some data been declared mission critical?
- What applications are in use?
- Have some operations been declared mission critical?
- What protocols are allowed on the network?
- What are the performance characteristics of the current network?
- Are only certain desktop hosts supported?
- Who is responsible for LAN addresses, naming, topology design, and configuration?
- What is the current topology?
- What are the human, hardware, and software resources of the organization?
- How are these resources currently linked and shared?
- What financial resources does the organization have available?

Documentation of the requirements allows for an informed estimate of costs and timelines for projected LAN design implementation. You need to understand the performance issues of the network.

Availability measures the usefulness of the network. The following are a few of the many factors that affect availability:

- Throughput
- Response time
- Access to resources

Every customer has a different definition of availability. For example, customers might need to transport voice and video over the network. These services could require more bandwidth than is available on the network or backbone. To increase availability, you can add more resources, but that increases the cost of the network. Network designs should provide the greatest availability for the least cost.

The second step in the network design is to analyze the requirements of the network and its users. The needs of network users constantly change. As more voice and video-based network applications become available, the necessity to increase network bandwidth grows, too.

A LAN that cannot provide prompt and accurate information to its users is useless. You must take steps to ensure that the information requirements of the organization and its workers are met.

The third step is to decide on an overall LAN topology that will satisfy the user requirements. Two common LAN topologies are displayed in Figure 5-4.

Figure 5-4   The Star Topology Is a Special Case of the Extended Star Topology

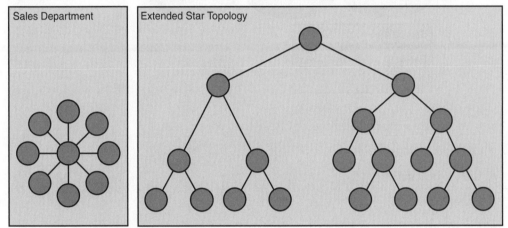

This book concentrates on the star topology and extended star topology. The star topology and extended star topology use Ethernet 802.3 CSMA/CD technology. The extended star topology is the predominant configuration in industry.

Not to be confused with the core-distribution-access model, you can break down LAN topology design into the following three unique categories of the OSI reference model:

- Network layer (Layer 3)

- Data link layer (Layer 2)

- Physical layer (Layer 1)

By looking through the filter of the respective OSI layer, a network engineer can properly incorporate products and technologies within the campus or enterprise network.

The fourth and final step in LAN design methodology is to document the physical and logical topology of the network. The physical topology of the network refers to the way in which various LAN components are connected. The logical design of the network refers to the flow of data in a network and to the name and address schemes used in the implementation of the LAN design solution, as illustrated in Figure 5-5.

Figure 5-5   Logical Design Includes Name and Address Schemes

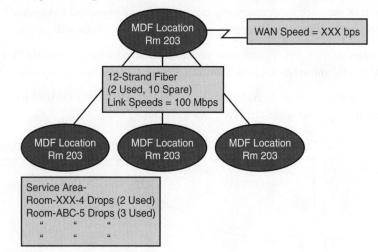

The following are important elements of LAN design documentation:

- OSI layer topology map

- LAN logical map

- LAN physical map

- *Cut sheets*, as shown in Table 5-1

- VLAN logical map, as shown in Figure 5-6

- Layer 3 logical map, as shown in Figure 5-7

- Address maps, as shown in Figure 5-8

Table 5-1   Cut Sheet for IDF Location—Rm XXX

Connection	Cable ID	Cross Connection Paired#/Port#	Type of Cable	Status
IDF1 to Rm 203	203-1	HCC1/Port 13	Category 6 UTP	Used
IDF1 to Rm 203	203-2	HCC1/Port 14	Category 6 UTP	Not used
IDF1 to Rm 203	203-3	HCC2/Port 3	Category 6 UTP	Not used
IDF1 to MDF	IDF1-1	VCC1/Port 1	Single-mode fiber	Used
IDF1 to MDF	IDF1-2	VCC1/Port 2	Single-mode fiber	Used

Figure 5-6   VLAN Logical Design

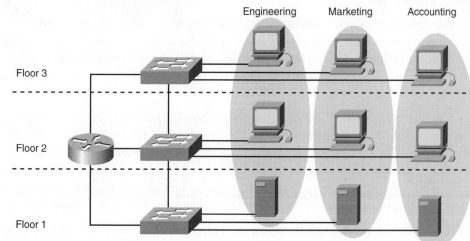

Figure 5-7   IP Networks Are Displayed in a Layer 3 Logical Map

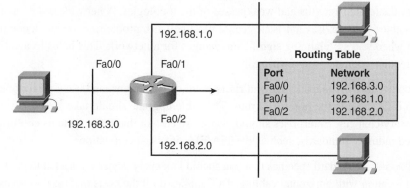

Figure 5-8   Address Maps Provide a Detailed View of IP Addresses for Key Devices and Interfaces

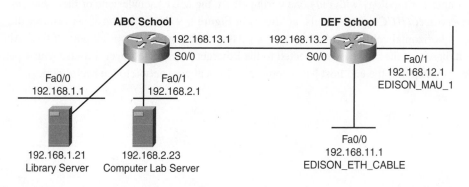

Layer 1 Design

One of the most important components to consider in network design is the cables. Today, most LAN cabling is based on Fast Ethernet or Gigabit Ethernet technology. Both Fast Ethernet and Gigabit Ethernet can utilize full-duplex functionality, where independent transmit and receive circuits permit concurrent, collision-free, two-way communication. A logical bus topology that employs CSMA/CD can also be used with Standard Ethernet.

Design issues at Layer 1 include the type of cabling to be used, such as copper or fiber optic, and the overall structure of the cabling. Certain restrictions apply; for example, the 100BASE-TX standard specifies a baseband technology employing Category 5e *unshielded twisted-pair (UTP)* cable with a length limitation of 100 m. UTP is a cable type consisting of twisted pairs of copper wires, where the cable itself has little shielding. Similarly, 100BASE-FX specifies a baseband technology employing multimode fiber (two strands) with a length limitation of 2 km.

The TIA/EIA-568-A standard details the layout and wiring connection schemes. Layer 1 media types include Category 5, 5e, or 6 UTP, or *shielded twisted-pair (STP)*, and single-mode and multimode fiber-optic cable. STP is a type of cable consisting of twisted pairs of copper wires with shielding around each pair of wires, as well as another shield around all of the wires in the cable.

Carefully evaluate the strengths and weaknesses of the topologies. A network is only as effective as the cables you use. Layer 1 issues cause most network problems. Conduct a complete cable audit when you are planning significant changes for a network. This helps to identify areas that require upgrades and rewiring.

Use fiber-optic cable in the backbone and risers in all cable designs, and use Category 5e or Category 6 UTP cable in the horizontal runs. The cable upgrade should take priority over any other necessary changes. Enterprises should also make certain that these systems conform to well-defined industry standards, such as the TIA/EIA-568-A specifications.

The TIA/EIA-568-A standard specifies that you should link every device connected to the network to a central location with horizontal cabling. This applies if all the hosts that need to access the network are within the 100-m distance limitation for Category 5e and Category 6 UTP Ethernet.

In a simple star topology with only one wiring closet, the MDF includes one or more *horizontal cross-connect (HCC)* patch panels, as shown in Figure 5-9. HCC patch cables connect the Layer 1 horizontal cabling with the Layer 2 LAN switch ports. The uplink port of the LAN switch, based on the model, is connected to the Ethernet port of the Layer 3 router with a patch cable. At this point, the end host has a complete physical connection to the router port.

Figure 5-9   HCC Connects Layer 1 Cabling to Layer 2 Switch Ports

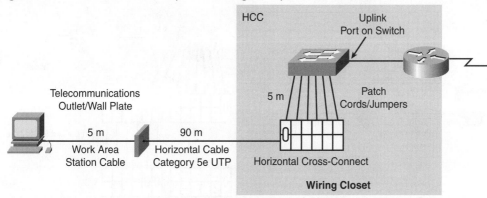

When hosts in larger networks exceed the 100 m limitation for Category 5e UTP, more than one wiring closet is required. Multiple wiring closets mean multiple catchment areas. The secondary wiring closets are referred to as IDFs, as illustrated in Figure 5-10.

Figure 5-10   IDFs Interconnect via the MDF

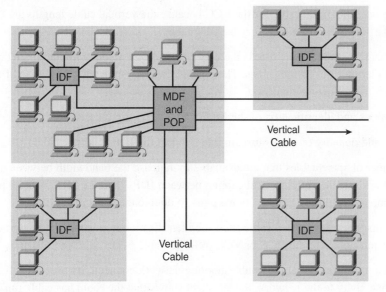

TIA/EIA-568-A standards specify to connect IDFs to the MDF by vertical cabling, also called backbone cabling. A **_vertical cross-connect (VCC)_**, as shown in Figure 5-11, interconnects the various IDFs to the central MDF.

Figure 5-11   VCC Interconnects IDFs to MDF

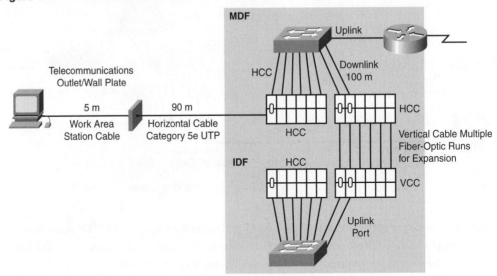

You normally use fiber-optic cable for the VCC because the vertical cable lengths are typically longer than the 100-m limit for Category 5e UTP cable.

The logical diagram, as in Figure 5-5, is the network topology model without all the details of the exact installation paths of the cables. The logical diagram is the basic road map of the LAN, which includes the following elements:

- The locations and identification of the MDF and IDF wiring closets.

- The type and quantity of cables used to interconnect the IDFs with the MDF.

- The number of spare cables that are available to increase the bandwidth between the wiring closets. For example, if the vertical cabling between IDF 1 and the MDF is at 80 percent utilization, you could use two additional pairs to double the capacity.

- Detailed documentation of all cable runs, the identification numbers, and the port on which the run is terminated at the HCC or VCC (refer to Table 5-1).

The logical diagram is essential for troubleshooting network connectivity problems. If Room 203 loses connectivity to the network, the cut sheet shows that the room has cable run 203-1, which is terminated on HCC1 port 13. You can use cable testers to determine Layer 1 failure. If Layer 1 has failed, you can use one of the other two runs to re-establish connectivity and troubleshoot run 203-1.

Layer 2 Design

The purpose of Layer 2 devices in the network, such as bridges and switches, is to switch frames based on destination MAC address information, provide error detection, and reduce congestion in the network. Devices at Layer 2 determine the size of the collision domains.

Collisions and collision domain size are two factors that negatively affect the performance of a network. Microsegmentation of the network reduces the size of collision domains and reduces collisions, as illustrated in Figure 5-12. Microsegmentation is implemented through the use of switches. The goal is to boost performance for a workgroup or a backbone. You can use switches with hubs to provide the appropriate level of performance for different users and servers.

Figure 5-12   LAN Switches Provide Microsegmentation

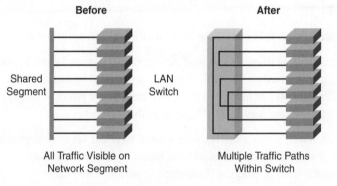

Another important characteristic of a LAN switch is the way it allocates bandwidth on a per-port basis. This supplies more bandwidth to vertical cabling, uplinks, and servers. This type of switching is referred to as asymmetric switching. *Asymmetric switching* provides switched connections between ports of unlike bandwidth, such as a combination of 100-Mbps and 1-Gbps ports. *Symmetric switching* provides switched connections between ports of similar bandwidth.

The desired capacity of a vertical cable run is greater than that of a horizontal cable run. The installation of a LAN switch at the MDF and IDF allows the vertical cable run to manage the data traffic from the MDF to the IDF (refer to Figure 5-11). The horizontal runs between the IDF and the workstations use Category 5e or Category 6 UTP. A horizontal cable drop should not be longer than 100 m. In a normal environment, 100 Mbps is adequate for the horizontal drop. Asymmetric LAN switches allow 100-Mbps and 1-Gbps ports on a single switch.

The next task in the LAN design process is to determine the number of 100-Mbps or 1-Gbps ports needed in the MDF and every IDF. This is accomplished by reviewing the user requirements for the number of horizontal cable drops per room and the number of total drops in any catchment area. This includes the number of vertical cable runs. For example, suppose that user requirements dictate that four horizontal cable runs are installed in each room. The IDF services a catchment area of 18 rooms. Therefore, four drops in each of the 18 rooms equals $4 \times 18 =$ 72 LAN switch ports.

The number of hosts that are physically connected to any single port on the switch determines the size of a collision domain. This also affects the bandwidth that is available to any host. In an ideal situation, only one host is connected on a LAN switch port. The collision domain would consist only of the source host and destination host via a virtual circuit. The size of the collision domain would be two for the life of the virtual circuit. Because of the small size of this collision domain, collisions should be nonexistent when just two hosts communicate with each other.

You can eliminate collision domains by using one host, or one host and one IP phone, per switch port. Provide bandwidth requirements for the hosts in accordance to the specifications you gathered in the requirements phase of the network design process.

Layer 3 Design

A router is a Layer 3 device. It is one of the most intelligent devices in the network topology.

You can use Layer 3 devices to create unique LAN segments. Layer 3 devices allow communication between segments based on Layer 3 addresses, such as IP addresses. Implementation of Layer 3 devices allows for segmentation of the LAN into unique physical and logical networks. Routers also allow for connectivity to WANs, such as the Internet.

Layer 3 routing determines traffic flow between unique physical network segments based on Layer 3 addresses. A router forwards data packets based on destination addresses. A router does not forward broadcasts, such as Address Resolution Protocol (ARP) requests. Therefore, the router interface is considered the entry and exit point of a broadcast domain. It stops broadcasts to other LAN segments.

Routers provide scalability because they serve as firewalls for broadcasts. They can divide networks into subnetworks, or subnets, based on Layer 3 addresses, as pictured in Figure 5-7.

In deciding whether to use routers or switches in LAN design, you should determine the problem that you need to solve. If the problem is related to protocol rather than issues of contention, routers are the appropriate solution. Routers solve problems with excessive broadcasts, protocols that do not scale well, security issues, and network layer addresses. Routers are generally more expensive and more difficult to configure than switches. However, the line between Layer 3 switches are and routers is blurring over time; the price point and availability are such that a pervasive Layer 3 switched infrastructure will be the norm within the decade. Layer 3 switches perform wire-speed routing, as well as QoS and security functions.

Figure 5-1 shows an example of an implementation that has multiple networks. All data traffic from Network 1 that is destined for Network 2 has to go through the router. This implementation has two broadcast domains, and the two networks have unique Layer 3 network address schemes. You can create multiple physical networks if you patch the horizontal cabling and vertical cabling into the appropriate Layer 2 switch. This implementation also provides robust security because all traffic in and out of the LAN must pass through the router.

After you deploy an IP address scheme for a client, you should clearly document it. Set a standard convention for addresses of important hosts on the network, as in Table 5-2.

Table 5-2   Logical Addressing Mapped to the Physical Network

Logical Address	Physical Network Devices
x.x.x.1–x.x.x.10	Router, LAN, and WAN ports
x.x.x.11–x.x.x.20	LAN switches
x.x.x.21–x.x.x.30	Enterprise servers
x.x.x.31–x.x.x.80	Workgroup servers
x.x.x.81–x.x.x.254	Hosts

Keep this address scheme consistent throughout the entire network. Address maps, as shown in Figures 5-8 and 5-13, provide a snapshot of the network.

Figure 5-13   Logical Network Addressing Map

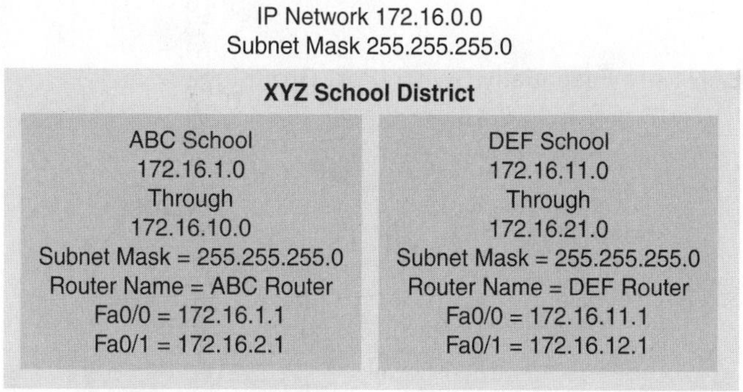

IP Network 172.16.0.0
Subnet Mask 255.255.255.0

XYZ School District

ABC School	DEF School
172.16.1.0	172.16.11.0
Through	Through
172.16.10.0	172.16.21.0
Subnet Mask = 255.255.255.0	Subnet Mask = 255.255.255.0
Router Name = ABC Router	Router Name = DEF Router
Fa0/0 = 172.16.1.1	Fa0/0 = 172.16.11.1
Fa0/1 = 172.16.2.1	Fa0/1 = 172.16.12.1

Physical maps of the network, as illustrated in Figure 5-14, make it easier to troubleshoot the network.

VLAN implementation combines Layer 2 switching and Layer 3 routing technologies to limit both collision domains and broadcast domains. In a traditional VLAN implementation (refer to Figure 5-6), VLANs provide security with the creation of VLAN groups that communicate with other VLANs only through a router.

A physical port association implements VLAN assignment, as in Figure 5-15. Ports P1, P4, and P6 have been assigned to VLAN 1. VLAN 2 has ports P2, P3, and P5. Communication between VLAN 1 and VLAN 2 can occur only through the router. This limits the size of the broadcast domains and uses the router to determine whether VLAN 1 can talk to VLAN 2.

Figure 5-14   Physical Network Maps Ease Troubleshooting

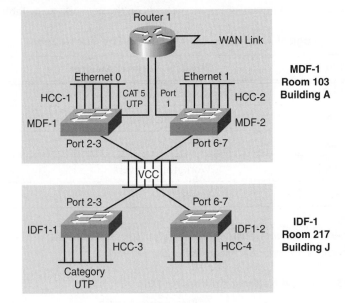

Figure 5-15   VLANs Are Essentially Switch Port Groupings

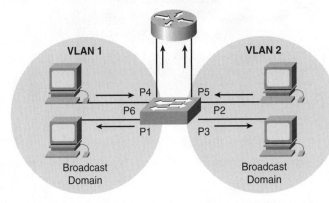

LAN Switches

LAN switches have evolved considerably since the early days of Layer 2 switches, which did not support VLANs. Second-generation switches supported VLANs, but they relied on routers for inter-VLAN communication. Third-generation switches, such as the Cisco Catalyst 3750, began to have the route processors built into the switches. Now, with the exception of access layer switches, switches are becoming less distinguishable from routers; most switches now support routing, and many routers now support the internal addition of modular switches.

Switched LANs and the Hierarchical Design Model

The construction of a LAN that satisfies the needs of both medium and large-sized organizations is more likely to be successful if you use a hierarchical design model. In a hierarchical design model, it is easier to make changes to the network as the organization grows. This chapter discusses the three layers of the hierarchical design model:

- **Access layer**—Gives users in workgroups access to the network.

- **Distribution layer**—Provides policy-based connectivity.

- **Core layer**—Provides optimal transport between sites. The core layer is often referred to as the backbone.

This hierarchical model applies to any network design. It is important to realize that these three layers can exist in clear and distinct physical entities. However, this is not a requirement. These layers are defined to aid in successful network design and to represent functionality that must exist in a network.

Access Layer Overview

The access layer is the entry point to the network for user workstations and servers. In a campus LAN, the device used at the access layer is typically a Layer 2 switch. Figure 5-16 illustrates the access layer.

Figure 5-16   The Access Layer Is an Entry Point to the Network, Particularly for End Users

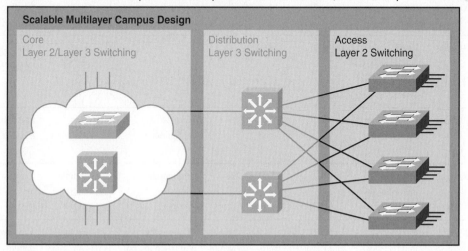

Access layer functions also include MAC layer filtering and microsegmentation. MAC layer filtering allows switches to direct frames only to the switch port that is connected to the destination device. The switch creates small Layer 2 segments called microsegments. The collision domain can be as small as one or two devices. Layer 2 switches are used in the access layer.

Access Layer Switches

Access layer switches generally operate at Layer 2 of the OSI model and provide services such as VLAN membership. Ultramodern switched networks now use pervasive Layer 3 switching (including the access layer). The main purpose of an access layer switch is to allow end users into the network. An access layer switch should provide this functionality with low cost and high port density.

The following Cisco switches are legacy switches, with the exception of the Catalyst 2950, and are commonly used at the access layer:

- Catalyst 1900 series
- Catalyst 2820 series
- Catalyst 2950 series
- Catalyst 4000 series
- Catalyst 5000 series

Table 5-3 describes the functionality for each of these switches.

Table 5-3   Features of Access Layer Switches

Catalyst	Type	Supported OSI Layers	Ethernet Ports	Fast Ethernet Ports	Gigabit Ethernet Ports	Enterprise Size
1900 series	Fixed configuration	Layer 2	12 or 24	2	0	Small to medium
2820 series	Fixed configuration with modular expansion slots	Layer 2	24	2	0	Small to medium
2950 series	Fixed configuration	Layer 2	0	12 or 24 configurable	0 or 2	Small to medium speed
4000 series	Modular—multiple slots per chassis	Layer 2 and Layer 3	Configurable ports—up to 240	Configurable ports—up to 240	Configurable ports—up to 240	Varies with options chosen
5000 series	Modular—multiple slots per chassis	Layer 2 and Layer 3	Configurable ports—up to 528	Configurable ports—up to 266	Configurable ports—up to 38	Varies with options chosen

The Catalyst 1900 or 2820 series switches were effective access layer devices for small campus networks. The Catalyst 2950 series switch effectively provides access for servers and users that require higher bandwidth. This is achieved with Fast Ethernet and Gigabit Ethernet switch ports. The Catalyst 4000 and 5000 series switches include Gigabit Ethernet ports. They were effective access devices for numerous users in large campus networks. The Catalyst 4500 has replaced the Catalyst 4000 and Catalyst 5000 in this role. Figure 5-17 displays a Catalyst 4503 switch.

Now, having seen the legacy products provided by Cisco so far in this section, note that, as of this writing, the Catalyst switch product lines being sold are the 500, 2960, 3560, 3750, 4500, 4900, and 6500. The 500, 2960, 3560, and 3750 are frequently used in the access layer; however, it is important to note that there are no hard-and-fast restrictions as to what switch to use at what layer in the core-distribution-access layer model. See www.cisco.com/en/US/products/hw/switches for the latest information.

Figure 5-17   The Catalyst 4500 Series Is Often Used at the Access Layer in an Enterprise Network

Distribution Layer Overview

The distribution layer of the network, pictured in Figure 5-18, is between the access and core layers. It helps to define and separate the core. The purpose of this layer is to provide a boundary definition where packet manipulation can take place. The distribution layer segments networks into broadcast domains. You can apply policies, and access control lists can be used at the distribution layer to filter packets. The distribution layer does not allow problems originating at the access or distribution layer from affecting the core layer. Switches in this layer operate at Layer 2 and Layer 3. The following are some of the distribution layer functions in a switched network:

- Aggregation of the wiring closet connections

- Broadcast/multicast domain definition

- VLAN routing

- Any media transitions that need to occur

- Security

Figure 5-18   The Distribution Layer Is Typically Where Policy Is Incorporated

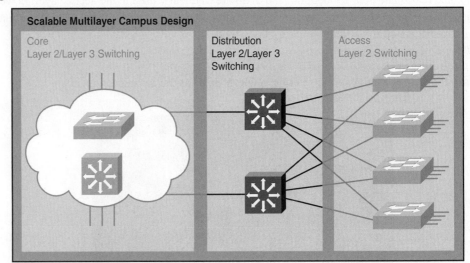

Distribution Layer Switches

Distribution layer switches are the aggregation points for multiple access layer switches. The switch must be able to accommodate the total amount of traffic from the access layer devices.

The distribution layer switch must have high performance. The distribution layer switch is a point at which a broadcast domain is delineated. The distribution layer combines VLAN traffic and is a focal point for policy decisions about traffic flow. For these reasons, distribution layer switches operate at both Layer 2 and Layer 3 of the OSI model. Switches in this layer are referred to as multilayer switches. These multilayer switches combine the functions of a router and a switch in one device. They are designed to switch traffic to gain higher performance than a standard router. If they do not have an associated router module, an external router is used for the Layer 3 function.

The distribution layer often used the following legacy Cisco switches:

- Catalyst 2926G

- Catalyst 5000 series

- Catalyst 6000 series

Currently, Catalyst 4500, 4900, and 6500 switches are deployed at the distribution layer. A Catalyst 6513 is displayed in Figure 5-19.

Figure 5-19   The Catalyst 6513 Is About as Good as It Gets for a Distribution Layer Switch, Circa 2006

Core Layer Overview

The core layer is a high-speed switching backbone, illustrated in Figure 5-20. If the core switch does not have an associated router module, an external router is used for the Layer 3 function. This layer of the network design should not perform packet manipulation. Packet manipulation, such as access list filtering, would slow down the switching of packets. A core infrastructure with redundant alternate paths gives stability to the network in the event of a single device failure.

Figure 5-20   Core Layer Is Devoted to High-Speed Switching of Numerous Packets

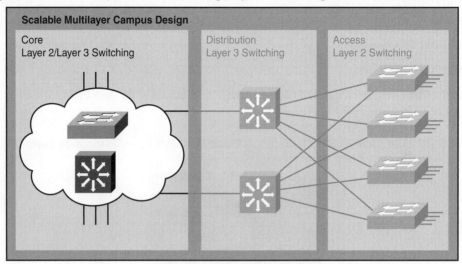

You can design the core to use Layer 2 or Layer 3 switching. The current trend is to perform wire-speed Layer 3 switching at the core.

Core Layer Switches

The core layer is the backbone of the campus switched network. The switches in this layer can use various Layer 2 technologies. Provided that the distance between the core layer switches is not too great, the switches can use Ethernet technology. Other Layer 2 technologies, such as ATM cell switching, can also be used. In a network design, the core layer can be a routed, or Layer 3, core. Core layer switches are designed to provide efficient Layer 3 functionality when needed. Consider such factors as need, cost, and performance before making a choice.

The core layer often used the following legacy Cisco switches:

- Catalyst 8500 series
- IGX 8400 series
- Lightstream 1010

Currently, the core layer of enterprise networks uses Catalyst 6500 switches, Cisco 12000 Series Routers, and (occasionally) Cisco CRS-1 (Carrier Routing System) devices.

Chapter Summary

LAN design depends on the requirements of individual organizations but typically focuses on functionality, scalability, manageability, and adaptability. For a LAN to be effective, you should design and implement it based on a planned series of systematic steps. The steps call for you to gather and analyze data and requirements; implement Layers 1, 2, and 3; and document everything. The following are important elements of LAN design documentation:

- OSI layer topology map

- LAN logical map

- LAN physical map

- Cut sheets

- VLAN logical map

- Layer 3 logical map

- Address maps

Layer 1 design issues include the type of cables to be used and the overall structure of the cabling. This also includes the TIA/EIA-568-A standard for layout and connection of wiring schemes. Layer 1 media types include those that support 100-Mbps and 1-Gbps transmission, such as Category 5, Category 5e, and Category 6 UTP or STP cable, and single- and multimode fiber-optic cable.

The logical diagram of the LAN includes the locations and identification of the MDF and IDF wiring closets, the type and quantity of cables used to interconnect the IDFs with the MDF, and the number of spare cables available to increase the bandwidth between the wiring closets.

Layer 2 devices provide flow control, error detection, and error correction, and they reduce congestion in the network. Microsegmentation of the network reduces the size of collision domains and reduces collisions.

Routers are Layer 3 devices that you can use to create unique LAN segments. They allow communication between segments based on Layer 3 addresses, such as IP addresses. Implementation of Layer 3 devices allows for segmentation of the LAN into unique physical and logical networks. Routers also allow for connectivity to WANs such as the Internet.

VLAN implementation combines Layer 2 switching and Layer 3 routing technologies to limit both collision domains and broadcast domains. VLANs were traditionally used to create logical groupings according to function; now they are used more as a means of grouping IP subnets than anything else. Routers or route processors are used to enable communication between VLANs.

The hierarchical design model includes three layers. The access layer gives users in workgroups access to the network. The distribution layer provides policy-based connectivity. The core layer provides optimal transport between sites. The core layer is often referred to as the backbone.

Access layer switches operate at Layer 2 of the OSI model and offer services such as VLAN membership. The main purpose of an access layer switch is to allow end users into the network. An access layer switch should supply this functionality with low cost and high port density.

The distribution layer switch is a point at which a broadcast domain is delineated. The distribution layer combines VLAN traffic and is a focal point for policy decisions about traffic flow. For these reasons, distribution layer switches operate at both Layer 2 and Layer 3 of the OSI model. Switches in this layer are referred to as multilayer switches.

The core layer is a high-speed switching backbone. This layer of the network design should not perform packet manipulation. Packet manipulation, such as access list filtering, would slow down the switching of packets. A core infrastructure with redundant alternate paths gives stability to the network in the event of a single device failure.

Check Your Understanding

Complete all the review questions listed here to test your understanding of the topics and concepts in this chapter. Answers are listed in Appendix A, "Answers to Check Your Understanding and Challenge Questions and Activities."

1. A core layer switch can operate at which OSI layers? (Choose two.)

    A. Data link

    B. Network

    C. Access

    D. Session

    E. Transport

2. Refer to Figure 5-21. A server that is running DNS for the entire network also has an application that only the media services group uses. How will this server be classified, and where should it be located in the network?

Figure 5-21   MDF and IDF

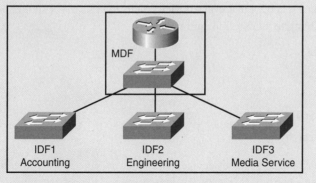

    A. Enterprise, IDF3

    B. Workgroup, IDF2

    C. Enterprise, IDF2

    D. Workgroup, MDF

    E. Enterprise, MDF

3. What is required for workstations on one VLAN to communicate with servers on another VLAN?

   A. The workstations and servers must be on the same collision domain.

   B. VLAN security must be disabled.

   C. The switch ports must be assigned membership to both VLANs.

   D. A router must be configured to connect the VLANs.

4. Which LAN design requirement addresses the need to accommodate growth of the network without requiring major changes to the design?

   A. Adaptability

   B. Availability

   C. Functionality

   D. Reliability

   E. Scalability

   F. Manageability

5. Which standard specifies that every device connected to a LAN should be linked by horizontal cabling to a central location?

   A. CSMA/CD

   B. IEEE 802.3

   C. ISO 9000

   D. TIA/EIA-568-A

   E. OSI physical layer

6. What are the responsibilities of devices located at the core layer of the hierarchical design model? (Choose two.)

   A. Access list filtering

   B. Packet manipulation

   C. High-speed backbone switching

   D. Interconnection of distribution layer devices

   E. Inter-VLAN routing

7. In order, which layers of the hierarchical design model provide network policies, optimal transport between sites, and user connectivity?

  A. Core, distribution, access

  B. Distribution, access, core

  C. Access, core, distribution

  D. Distribution, core, access

8. At which layer of the hierarchical model of network design do workstations and servers enter the network?

  A. Entry

  B. Access

  C. Distribution

  D. Core

  E. Connection

9. Which of the following services are provided by enterprise servers? (Choose two.)

  A. Domain Name System

  B. User applications

  C. File sharing

  D. E-mail

  E. Print sharing

10. Which network devices reduce the size of collision domains and provide error detection?

  A. Bridges

  B. Hubs

  C. NICs

  D. Repeaters

  E. Switches

CHAPTER 6

Catalyst Switch Configuration

Objectives

Upon completion of this chapter, you should be able to answer the following questions:

- How do you start up a Catalyst switch?

- How do you identify the conditions reflected by the LEDs on Catalyst switches?

- How do you view the initial boot output from a Catalyst switch?

- How do you log in to a Catalyst switch?

- How do you identify the types of online help functions associated with the CLIs?

- How do you configure a Catalyst switch from the command line?

- How do you verify the initial switch operation?

- What are the default settings for a Cisco Catalyst switch?

- How do you configure an access layer Catalyst switch with an IP address and a default gateway?

- What are the two duplex modes used with Catalyst switches?

- How do you configure the duplex options in Catalyst switches?

- How do you set permanent and static addresses in the MAC address table?

- How do you configure port security?

- How do you add, move, and change MAC addresses on access layer Catalyst switches?

- How do you manage Catalyst switch configuration files?

Key Terms

This chapter uses the following key terms. You can find the definitions in the Glossary:

A switch is a Layer 2 network device that acts as the concentration point for the connection of workstations, servers, routers, hubs, and other switches.

Switches are multiport bridges that utilize a star topology on Ethernet LANs. A switch provides many dedicated, point-to-point virtual circuits between connected network devices. Collisions are not likely to occur.

Because of the dominant role of switches in modern networks, the ability to understand and configure switches is essential for network support.

New switches have a preset configuration with factory defaults. This configuration rarely meets the needs of network engineers. You can configure and manage switches from a *command-line interface (CLI)*. You can also configure and manage network devices through a web-based interface on a browser.

Network engineers must be familiar with all tasks associated with the management of networks with switches. Some of these tasks include maintenance of the switch and the Cisco IOS. Other tasks include management of the interfaces and tables for optimal, reliable, and secure operation. Basic switch configuration, Cisco IOS upgrades, and password recovery are essential skills for a network engineer.

Starting the Switch

Switches are dedicated, specialized devices that contain a CPU, RAM, and an operating system. Switches usually have several ports that hosts can connect to and specialized ports for the purpose of management. You can manage switches and view and change the configuration through the console port.

Physical Startup of the Catalyst Switch

Many Cisco Catalyst switches have no power switch to turn them on and off. They simply connect or disconnect from a power source.

The initial startup of a Catalyst switch requires completion of the following steps:

How To

Step 1 Before starting the switch, verify the following:

- All network cable connections are secure.

- Your terminal is connected to the console port.

- Your console terminal application, such as HyperTerminal, is selected.

Step 2 Attach the power cable plug to the switch power supply socket.

The switch starts. There is no on/off switch on some Catalyst switches, including the Catalyst 2950.

Step 3 Observe the boot sequence as follows:

- Look at the LEDs on the switch chassis.

- Observe the Cisco IOS Software output text on the console.

Switch Port Types

Several switches from the Cisco Catalyst 2950 series are shown in Figure 6-1. Models include 12-port, 24-port, and 48-port. The top two switches in Figure 6-1 are fixed configuration switches that offer Fast Ethernet on all ports. The next three switches are asymmetrical switches with two fixed fiber or copper Gigabit Ethernet ports. The bottom four switches are asymmetrical models with modular *Gigabit Interface Converter (GBIC)* slots, which can accommodate a variety of copper and fiber media options.

Figure 6-1   Catalyst 2950 Series Switches Are Used at the Access Layer

Many newer Cisco devices, such as the Cisco 3800 series routers and the Catalyst 3750 switches, now include *small-form-factor pluggable (SFP)* slots for SFP modules, instead of the GBIC slots. The SFP slots are much smaller, requiring much less real estate on the Cisco devices. Figure 6-2 illustrates the SFP slots for Catalyst 3750 switches.

Figure 6-2   Four Slots on the Right of These Catalyst 3750 Switches Are SFP Slots

Switch LED Indicators

The front panel of a switch has several lights to help monitor system activity and performance. These lights are called LEDs. Figure 6-3 illustrates the LEDs on the front of a Catalyst 2950 switch.

Figure 6-3   Catalyst 2950 Switches Have Four Types of LEDs

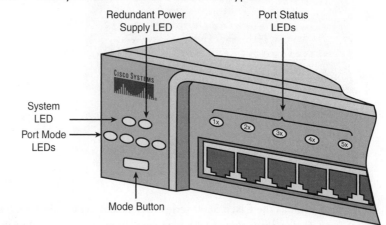

The following LEDs are seen on the front of a Catalyst 2950 switch:

- System LED
- Redundant Power Supply (RPS) LED
- Port Mode LEDs
- Port Status LEDs

The System LED shows whether the system is receiving power and functioning correctly. The RPS LED indicates whether the redundant power supply is in use. Table 6-1 explains these LEDs.

Table 6-1   System LED and RPS LED

Switch LED	Description
System LED	Off: System is not powered up.
	Green: System is powered and operational.
	Amber: System malfunction occurred; one or more POST errors occurred.
Redundant power supply	Off: Redundant power supply is off or is not installed.
	Green: Redundant power supply is operational.
	Flashing green: Redundant power supply is connected but unavailable because it is providing power to another device.
	Amber: Redundant power supply is installed but not operational.
	Flashing amber: Internal power supply failed, and redundant power supply is providing power to the switch.

After the power cable is connected, the switch initiates a series of tests called the *power-on self test (POST)*. POST runs automatically to verify that the switch functions correctly. The System LED indicates the success or failure of POST. If the System LED is off but the switch is plugged in, POST is running. If the System LED is green, POST was successful. If the System LED is amber, POST failed. POST failure is considered a fatal error. You should not expect reliable operation of the switch if POST fails.

The Port Status LEDs also change during POST. The Port Status LEDs turn amber for approximately 30 seconds as the switch discovers the network topology and searches for loops. If the Port Status LEDs turn green, the switch has established a link between the port and a target, such as a computer. If the Port Status LEDs turn off, the switch has determined that nothing is plugged into the port.

The Port Mode LEDs indicate the state of the Mode button. The modes determine how the Port Status LEDs are interpreted. To select or change the port mode, press the Mode button repeatedly until the Mode LEDs indicate the desired mode.

The Port Status LEDs indicate various port states. The Port Status LED display modes depend on the value of the Mode LEDs. Table 6-2 describes the Port Status LED display modes.

Table 6-2   Catalyst 2950 Port Status LED Display Modes

Port LED Display Mode	Description
Port status (STAT LED on)	Off: No link is present. Green: The link is present but has no activity. Flashing green: The link is present with traffic activity. Alternating green and amber: The link has a fault. Error frames can affect connectivity. Excessive collisions and cyclic redundancy check (CRC), alignment, and jabber errors are monitored for a link-fault indication. Amber: The port is not forwarding because the port was disabled by management, suspended because of an address violation, or suspended by Spanning Tree Protocol (STP) because of network loops.
Bandwidth utilization (UTL LED on)	Green: The current bandwidth utilization is displayed over the amber LED background on a logarithmic scale. Amber: Backplane utilization is maximal because the switch was powered on. Green and amber: This depends on the model, as follows: If all LEDs on Catalyst 2950-12, 2950-24, 2950C-24, and 2950T-24 switches are green, the switch is using 50% or more of the total bandwidth. If the far-right LED is off, the switch is using more than 25% but less than 50% of the total bandwidth, and so on. If only the far-left LED is green, the switch is using less than 0.0488% of the total bandwidth. If all LEDs on Catalyst 2950G-12-EI switches are green, the switch is using 50% or more of the total bandwidth. If the LED for Gigabit Interface Converter (GBIC) module slot 2 is off, the switch is using more than 25% but less than 50% of the total bandwidth. If LEDs for both GBIC module slots are off, the switch is using less than 25% of the total bandwidth, and so on. If all LEDs on Catalyst 2950G-24-EI and 2950G-24-EI-DC switches are green, the switch is using 50% or more of the total bandwidth.

Table 6-2   Catalyst 2950 Port Status LED Display Modes   *(continued)*

Port LED Display Mode	Description
Bandwidth utilization (UTL LED on)	Green: The current bandwidth utilization is displayed over the If the LED for GBIC module slot 2 is off, the switch is using more than 25% but less than 50% of the total bandwidth. If LEDs for both GBIC module slots are off, the switch is using less than 25% of the total bandwidth, and so on. If all LEDs on Catalyst 2950G-48-EI switches are green, the switch is using 50% or more of the total bandwidth. If the LED for the upper GBIC module slot is off, the switch is using more than 25% but less than 50% of the total bandwidth. If LEDs for both GBIC module slots are off, the switch is using less than 25% of the total bandwidth, and so on.
Full duplex mode (FDUP LED on)	Green: Ports are configured in full-duplex mode. Off: Ports are configured in half-duplex mode.

Viewing Initial Bootup Output from the Switch

To configure or check the status of a switch, connect a computer to the switch to establish a communication session. Use a rollover cable to connect the console port on the back of the switch to a COM port on the back of the computer, as illustrated in Figure 6-4.

Figure 6-4   Console Connection to the Switch Is the Most Common Configuration Method

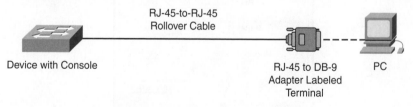
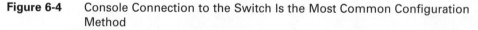

Start HyperTerminal on the computer. A dialog box is displayed, as shown in Figure 6-5. The correct serial port must be configured in HyperTerminal.

Figure 6-5   Choose Serial Port

You must name the connection when you initially configure the HyperTerminal communication with the switch. Select the COM port to which the switch is connected from the pull-down menu, and click the **OK** button. A second dialog box is displayed. Set up the parameters as shown in Figure 6-6, and click the **OK** button. Clicking the **Restore Defaults** button normally results in a functional combination of port settings.

Figure 6-6   COM1 Properties Dialog Box

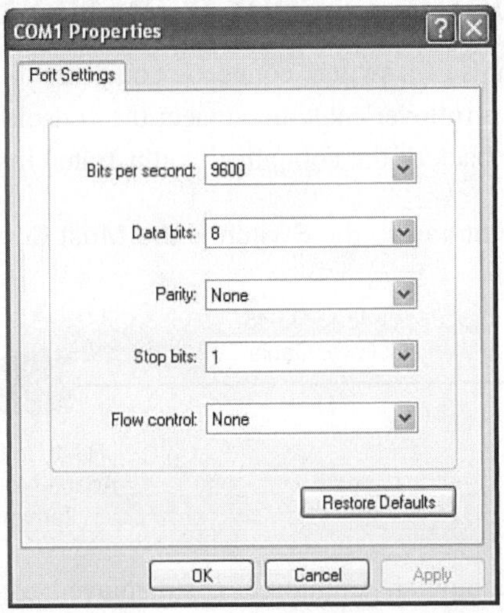

Plug the switch into a wall outlet (we assume the previous steps were carried out prior to plugging in the switch). The initial bootup output from the switch should be displayed on the HyperTerminal screen, as in Example 6-1. This output shows information about the switch, details about POST status, and data about the switch hardware. Hardware platform and Flash image information is displayed during bootup.

Example 6-1   Hardware Platform and Flash Information Displayed During Bootup

```
C2950 Boot Loader (C2950-HBOOT-M) Version 12.1(11r)EA1, RELEASE
SOFTWARE (fcl)
Complied Mon 22-Jul-02 18:57 by antonino
WS-C2950G-12-EI starting...
Base ethernet MAC Address: 00:05:DC:C9:79:00
Xmodem file system is available.
Initializing Flash...
flashfs[0]: 162 files, 3 directories
<output omitted>
...done initializing flash.
Boot Sector Filesystem (bs:) installed, fsid: 3
Parameter Block Filesystem (pb:) installed, fsid: 4
Loading "flash:/c2950-i6q412-mz.121-20.EA1.bin"...#######
<output omitted>
Model revision number: 02
Model number: WS-C2950G-12-EI
System serial number: FAB0517QOOB
System serial number: FAB0517QOOB

--- System Configuration Dialog ---

Would you like to enter the initial configuration dialog?
[yes/no]:n
Cisco Internetwork Operating System Software
IOS (tm) C2950 Software(C2950-I6Q4L2-M)Version 12.1(19)EA1,
RELEASE SOFTWARE (fcl)
Copyright  1986-2003 by cisco Systems, Inc.
Compiled Tue 09-Dec-03 00:12 by yenanh

Press RETURN to get started!

Switch>
```

After POST completes successfully on a Catalyst 2950 switch, you see a prompt to enter the initial configuration for the switch. You can use an automatic setup program, called the System Configuration dialog, to assign switch IP information, host and cluster names, and passwords and to create a default configuration for continued operation. You can configure the switch manually or with the assistance of the System Configuration dialog. If using the CLI to customize the configuration, choose "**n**" at the prompt to skip the System Configuration Dialog. See Example 6-1.

Using the System Configuration Dialog

If you choose to use the System Configuration dialog to obtain a basic switch configuration, complete the initial configuration by answering each question as it appears, as shown in Example 6-2.

Example 6-2   Using the System Configuration Dialog

```
        --- System Configuration Dialog ---
Would you like to enter the initial configuration dialog? [yes/no]: y
At any point you may enter a question mark '?' for help.
Use ctrl-c to abort configuration dialog at any prompt.
Default settings are in square brackets '[]'.
Basic management setup configures only enough connectivity
for management of the system, extended setup will ask you
to configure each interface on the system
Would you like to enter basic management setup? [yes/no]: no
First, would you like to see the current interface summary? [yes]: no
Configuring global parameters:
  Enter host name [Switch]: cat
  The enable secret is a password used to protect access to
  privileged EXEC and configuration modes. This password,
  after entered, becomes encrypted in the configuration.
  Enter enable secret: cisco
  The enable password is used when you do not specify an
  enable secret password, with some older software versions,
  and some boot images.
  Enter enable password: enable_password
  The virtual terminal password is used to protect
  access to the router over a network interface.
  Enter virtual terminal password: vty_password
  Configure SNMP Network Management? [no]: no
Configuring interface parameters:
Do you want to configure Vlan1  interface? [yes]: yes
  Configure IP on this interface? [yes]: yes
    IP address for this interface: 10.1.1.140
    Subnet mask for this interface [255.0.0.0] : 255.255.255.0
    Class A network is 10.0.0.0, 24 subnet bits; mask is /24
Do you want to configure GigabitEthernet0/1  interface? [yes]: n
<output omitted>
Do you want to configure GigabitEthernet0/12  interface? [yes]: n
Would you like to enable as a cluster command switch? [yes/no]: n
```

After you enter the required settings, the setup program displays the configuration to be confirmed, as displayed in Example 6-3.

Example 6-3   Option to Use Config Generated by Setup

```
hostname cat
enable secret 5 $1$oV63$8z7cBuveTibpCn1Rf5uI01
enable password enable_password
line vty 0 15
password vty_password
no snmp-server
!
!
interface Vlan1
ip address 10.1.1.140 255.255.255.0
!
interface GigabitEthernet0/1
<output omitted>
interface GigabitEthernet0/12
!
end
[0] Go to the IOS command prompt without saving this config.
[1] Return back to the setup without saving this config.
[2] Save this configuration to nvram and exit.
Enter your selection [2]:2
Building configuration...
[OK]
Use the enabled mode 'configure' command to modify this configuration.
Enter 2 to complete the initial configuration.
```

Logging On with the Switch CLI and Using the Help Facility

When you configure Catalyst switches from the CLI that runs on the console or a remote terminal, the Cisco IOS Software provides a CLI called the EXEC. The EXEC interprets the commands that you enter and carries out the corresponding operations. This topic describes how to log in to a Catalyst switch to begin the initial configuration.

For security purposes, the EXEC has the following two levels of access to commands:

- **User mode**—Typical tasks include those that check the status of the switch. User mode is indicated by the > prompt.

- **Privileged mode**—Typical tasks include those that change the configuration of the switch. Privileged mode is indicated by the # prompt.

To change from user EXEC mode to privileged EXEC mode, enter the **enable** command. The switch then prompts for the enable password if one is configured. Enter the correct enable password. By default, the enable password is not configured. For security reasons, the network device does not echo the password that you enter. However, if you are configuring a network device over a modem link or using Telnet, the password is sent in clear text. Telnet does not offer a method to secure packets.

The privileged EXEC mode command set includes all commands from user EXEC mode, some with more options available. It also has a number of additional commands, including the **configure** command. The **configure** command allows you to access other command modes. Because you use these modes to configure the switch, you should password-protect access to privileged EXEC mode to prevent unauthorized use.

The Catalyst switch uses Cisco IOS Software with several command-line input help facilities, including context-sensitive help:

- **Context-sensitive help**—Provides a list of commands and the arguments associated with a specific command

- **Console error messages**—Identifies problems with any switch commands that you enter incorrectly so that you can alter or correct them

- **Command history buffer**—Allows recall of long or complex commands or entries for re-entry, review, or correction

At any time during an EXEC session, you can enter a question mark (?) to get help. The following two types of context-sensitive help are available:

- **Word help**—Enter the **?** command to get word help for a list of commands that begin with a particular character sequence. Enter the character sequence followed immediately by the question mark. Do not include a space before the question mark. The switch then displays a list of commands that start with the characters that you entered.

- **Command syntax help**—Enter the **?** command to get command syntax help to see how to complete a command. Enter a question mark in place of a keyword or argument. Include a space before the question mark. The network device then displays a list of available command options, with <cr> standing for a carriage return.

The CLI help facilities on the Catalyst switches are similar to the help facilities on the routers.

Configuring the Switch

To configure global switch parameters such as the switch hostname or the switch IP address used for switch management purposes, you use the global configuration mode. To configure a particular port (interface), you use the interface configuration mode. This section details basic configuration tasks for Catalyst 2950 switches (similarly, for Catalyst 2960 switches).

Catalyst Switch Default Configuration

A Cisco Catalyst switch comes with factory default settings that you can display with **show** commands. For many parameters, the default configuration will suit your needs. However, you might want to change some of the default values to meet your specific network needs. The default values vary according to the features of the switch. The Catalyst 2950 switch has the following default configurations in place:

- IP address: 0.0.0.0

- CDP: Enabled

- 100BASE-T port: Autonegotiate duplex mode

- Spanning tree: Enabled

- Console password: None

When you power up a switch for the first time, it has default data in the running configuration file. The default hostname is "Switch." No passwords are set on the console or *virtual terminal (VTY)* lines, as illustrated in Example 6-4. A VTY line is a CLI created on a networking device for a Telnet or Secure Shell session. The **show running-config** command displays the current active (running) configuration file of the switch. This command requires privileged EXEC mode access. The IP address, subnet mask, and default gateway settings are displayed here.

Example 6-4   Default Output for show running-config Command

```
Switch#show running-config
Building configuration...

Current configuration : 1626 bytes
!
version 12.1
no service pad
service timestamps debug uptime
service timestamps log uptime
service password-encryption
!
hostname Switch
!
```

continues

Example 6-4   Default Output for **show running-config** Command   *(continued)*

```
<output omitted>
!
interface Vlan1
 no ip directed-broadcast
 no ip route-cache
!
ip http server
!
!
line con 0
 transport input none
 stopbits 1
line vty 5 15
!
end
```

You can give a switch an IP address for management purposes. You configure this on the virtual interface, VLAN 1. By default, the switch has no IP address, as seen in Example 6-4.

Set the switch ports or interfaces to auto mode, as shown in Example 6-5. The **show interface f0/2** command displays statistics and status information for interface f0/2. Both the switch trunks and the switch line ports are considered interfaces. The resulting output varies, depending on the network for which you have configured an interface.

Example 6-5   Default f0/2 Settings, Followed by Some Nondefault f0/1 Settings

```
Switch#show interface f0/2
FastEthernet0/2 is down, line protocol is down
  Hardware is Fast Ethernet, address is 0009.e8a1.5882 (bia 0009.e8a1.5882)
  MTU 1500 bytes, BW 10000 Kbit, DLY 1000 usec,
      reliability 255/255, txload 1/255, rxload 1/255
  Encapsulation ARPA, loopback not set
  Keepalive set (10 sec)
  Auto-duplex, Auto-speed
  input flow-control is off, output flow-control is off
  ARP type: ARPA, ARP Timeout 04:00:00
  Last input never, output 35w3d, output hang never
  Last clearing of "show interface" counters never
  Input queue: 0/75/0/0 (size/max/drops/flushes); Total output drops: 0
  Queueing strategy: fifo
  Output queue :0/40 (size/max)
  5 minute input rate 0 bits/sec, 0 packets/sec
```

Example 6-5 Default f0/2 Settings, Followed by Some Nondefault f0/1 Settings *(continued)*

```
  5 minute output rate 0 bits/sec, 0 packets/sec
     1 packets input, 64 bytes, 0 no buffer
     Received 0 broadcasts, 0 runts, 0 giants, 0 throttles
     0 input errors, 0 CRC, 0 frame, 0 overrun, 0 ignored
     0 watchdog, 0 multicast, 0 pause input
     0 input packets with dribble condition detected
     1 packets output, 64 bytes, 0 underruns
     0 output errors, 0 collisions, 2 interface resets
     0 babbles, 0 late collision, 0 deferred
     0 lost carrier, 0 no carrier, 0 PAUSE output
     0 output buffer failures, 0 output buffers swapped out
Switch#show interface f0/1
FastEthernet0/1 is up, line protocol is up
  Hardware is Fast Ethernet, address is 0009.e8a1.5881 (bia 0009.e8a1.5881)
  MTU 1500 bytes, BW 100000 Kbit, DLY 1000 usec,
     reliability 255/255, txload 1/255, rxload 1/255
  Encapsulation ARPA, loopback not set
  Keepalive set (10 sec)
  Full-duplex, 100Mb/s
  input flow-control is off, output flow-control is off
  ARP type: ARPA, ARP Timeout 04:00:00
  Last input never, output 00:00:01, output hang never
  Last clearing of "show interface" counters never
  Input queue: 0/75/0/0 (size/max/drops/flushes); Total output drops: 0
  Queueing strategy: fifo
  Output queue :0/40 (size/max)
  5 minute input rate 4000 bits/sec, 6 packets/sec
  5 minute output rate 6000 bits/sec, 6 packets/sec
     8520416 packets input, 1513361550 bytes, 0 no buffer
     Received 236675 broadcasts, 43761 runts, 0 giants, 0 throttles
     65590 input errors, 10816 CRC, 10988 frame, 0 overrun, 0 ignored
     0 watchdog, 9635 multicast, 0 pause input
     0 input packets with dribble condition detected
     28105321 packets output, 2931629249 bytes, 0 underruns
     0 output errors, 0 collisions, 2 interface resets
     0 babbles, 0 late collision, 0 deferred
     0 lost carrier, 0 no carrier, 0 PAUSE output
     0 output buffer failures, 0 output buffers swapped out
```

Table 6-3 shows some commonly referenced fields in the show interface f0/1 output of
Example 6-5.

Table 6-3   Fields in the **show interface f0/1** Output of Example 6-5

Output	Description
FastEthernet0/1 is up address is 0009.e8a1.5881	Indicates that the interface hardware is functioning correctly, and the line protocol status is operational and active. Shows the MAC address that identifies the interface hardware.
Full-duplex, 100 Mbps	Shows the type mode of connection. Other possibilities include half duplex, 10 megabits per second (Mbps).
CRC	Shows that there were "10816 CRC" errors. Incrementing CRC errors can indicate duplex mismatch or a malfunctioning Ethernet adapter in an attached device.

VLAN membership is displayed using the **show vlan** command. Example 6-6 illustrates that in the default configuration, all switch ports are in VLAN 1.

Example 6-6   Default Port VLAN Membership

```
Switch#show vlan

VLAN Name                             Status    Ports
---- -------------------------------- --------- -------------------------------
1    default                          active    Fa0/1, Fa0/2, Fa0/3, Fa0/4
                                                Fa0/5, Fa0/6, Fa0/7, Fa0/8
                                                Fa0/9, Fa0/10, Fa0/11, Fa0/12
                                                Gi0/1, Gi0/2
1002 fddi-default                     active
1003 token-ring-default               active
1004 fddinet-default                  active
1005 trnet-default                    active

VLAN Type  SAID     MTU   Parent RingNo BridgeNo Stp  BrdgMode Trans1 Trans2
---- ----- -------- ----- ------ ------ -------- ---- -------- ------ ------
1    enet  100001   1500  -      -      -        -    -        0      0
1002 fddi  101002   1500  -      -      -        -    -        0      0
1003 tr    101003   1500  -      -      -        -    -        0      0
1004 fdnet 101004   1500  -      -      -        ieee -        0      0
1005 trnet 101005   1500  -      -      -        ibm  -        0      0
```

VLAN 1 is the default management VLAN.

By default, the flash directory has a file that contains the IOS image, a file called env_vars, and a subdirectory called html. After you configure the switch, the flash directory contains a file called config.text and a VLAN database. As shown in Example 6-7, the flash directory does not contain a config.text file or a VLAN database file called vlan.dat.

Example 6-7   Output of show flash

```
Switch#show flash
Directory of flash:/

    2  -rwx         273    Jan 01 2006 00:01:16  env_vars
    4  -rwx         108    Mar 01 2005 00:01:25  info
    5  -rwx     2490607    Mar 01 2005 00:02:41  c2950-i6q4l2-mz.121-9.EA1.bin
    6  drwx         640    Mar 01 2005 00:03:34  html
   19  -rwx         108    Mar 01 2005 00:03:34  info.ver

7741440 bytes total (3574784 bytes free)
Switch#dir flash:
Directory of flash:/

    2  -rwx         273    Jan 01 2006 00:01:16  env_vars
    4  -rwx         108    Mar 01 2005 00:01:25  info
    5  -rwx     2490607    Mar 01 2005 00:02:41  c2950-i6q4l2-mz.121-9.EA1.bin
    6  drwx         640    Mar 01 2005 00:03:34  html
   19  -rwx         108    Mar 01 2005 00:03:34  info.ver

7741440 bytes total (3574784 bytes free)
```

You can verify the IOS version and the configuration register settings with the **show version** command in Example 6-8. This command displays the configuration of the system hardware, software version, names and sources of configuration files, and boot images.

Example 6-8   Output of show version

```
Switch#show version
Cisco Internetwork Operating System Software
IOS (tm) C2950 Software (C2950-I6Q4L2-M), Version 12.1(9)EA1, RELEASE SOFTWARE
  (fc1)
Copyright  1986-2002 by cisco Systems, Inc.
Compiled Wed 24-Apr-02 06:57 by antonino
Image text-base: 0x80010000, data-base: 0x804E8000

ROM: Bootstrap program is CALHOUN boot loader

Switch uptime is 35 weeks, 3 days, 6 hours, 24 minutes
System returned to ROM by power-on
System image file is "flash:c2950-i6q4l2-mz.121-9.EA1.bin"
```

continues

Example 6-8   Output of **show version**   *(continued)*

```
cisco WS-C2950G-12-EI (RC32300) processor (revision C0) with 20815K bytes of memory.
Processor board ID FHK0631Y067
Last reset from system-reset
Running Enhanced Image
12 FastEthernet/IEEE 802.3 interface(s)
2 Gigabit Ethernet/IEEE 802.3 interface(s)

32K bytes of flash-simulated non-volatile configuration memory.
Base ethernet MAC Address: 00:09:E8:A1:58:80
Motherboard assembly number: 73-7410-04
Power supply part number: 34-0965-01
Motherboard serial number: FOC06230KCF
Power supply serial number: PHI06230BDD
Model revision number: C0
Motherboard revision number: B0
Model number: WS-C2950G-12-EI
System serial number: FHK0631Y067
Configuration register is 0xF
```

Table 6-4 describes some output fields from the **show version** command.

Table 6-4   Fields in the **show version** Output

Output	Description
IOS version	Information identifying the software by name and version number. Always specify the complete version number when reporting a possible software problem. In the example, the switch is running IOS version 12.1(9)EA1.
Switch uptime	Current days and time since the system was last booted. In the example, the switch uptime is 35 weeks, 3 days, 6 hours, and 24 minutes.
Switch platform	The hardware platform information including revision and RAM.

In this default state, the switch has one broadcast domain, and you can use the CLI to manage and configure the switch through the console port. The STP is also enabled. It allows the bridge to construct a loop-free topology across an extended LAN.

For small networks, the default configuration might be sufficient. You obtain the benefits of better performance with microsegmentation immediately.

Lab 6.2.1   Verifying Default Switch Configuration

In this lab, you investigate the default configuration of a 2900 series switch.

Basic Catalyst Switch Configuration

It is useful to be able to reconfigure a Catalyst switch from scratch. For a nonmodular IOS-based Catalyst switch, such as the 2960, 3550, 3560, and 3750, the procedure for returning the device to its default configuration is illustrated in Example 6-9.

Example 6-9   Returning the Switch to Its Default Configuration

```
Switch#switch delete vlan.dat5
Delete filename [vlan.dat]?
Delete flash:vlan.dat? [confirm]
Switch#erase startup-config
<output omitted>
Switch#reload
```

To reiterate, the procedure to return the switch to its default configuration is as follows:

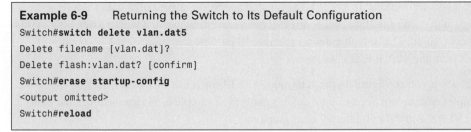

Step 1 To remove the current VLAN information, delete the VLAN database file called **vlan.dat** from the flash directory.

Step 2 Erase the backup configuration file called **startup-config**.

Step 3 Restart the switch with the **reload** command.

One of the first tasks in configuring a switch is to name it. Naming the switch allows you to better manage the network by being able to uniquely identify each switch within the network. The name of the switch is considered the hostname; it is the name displayed at the system prompt. The switch name is assigned in global configuration mode. In Example 6-10, the switch name is set to AccessSwitch.

You should give a switch a hostname, and you should set passwords on the console and VTY lines, as illustrated in Example 6-10.

Example 6-10   Configuring the Hostname and Line Passwords

```
Switch(config)#hostname AccessSwitch
AccessSwitch(config)#line console 0
AccessSwitch(config-line)#password cisco
AccessSwitch(config-line)#login
AccessSwitch(config-line)#line vty 0 15
AccessSwitch(config-line)#password cisco
AccessSwitch(config-line)#login
```

Assign an IP address to a switch so that you can access the switch remotely using Telnet or other TCP/IP applications. Normally, VLAN 1 is assigned an IP address for remote management access, as in Example 6-10. It is necessary to use the **no shutdown** command to make the *Switch Virtual Interface (SVI)*, interface VLAN 1, operational. An SVI is a logical representation of a VLAN as one interface to a routing or bridging function of a switch. It is essentially an evolution of the concept of bridge virtual interface (BVI) commonly used on Cisco routers in the 1990s. Configuring the management VLAN for IP permits Telnet access to the switch and is required if you will be using *Simple Network Management Protocol (SNMP)* to manage the switch.

Assign a default gateway to a Layer 2 switch using the **ip default-gateway** command. That way, when you are working from the CLI, you can access other networks. Enter the IP address of the next-hop router interface that is directly connected to the switch where a default gateway is being configured. The default gateway receives IP packets with unresolved destination IP addresses from the switch EXEC processes.

Note that when you configure a switch to route with IP (on a Layer 3 switch such as the 3560, for example), you do not need to set a default gateway. Example 6-11 demonstrates the management VLAN and default-gateway configuration.

Example 6-11   Configuring the Switch for Management

```
AccessSwitch(config)#interface VLAN1
AccessSwitch(config-if)#ip address 192.168.1.2 255.255.255.0
AccessSwitch(config-if)#no shutdown
AccessSwitch(config-if)#exit
AccessSwitch(config)#ip default-gateway 192.168.1.1
AccessSwitch(config)#exit
AccessSwitch#show interfaces vlan 1
Vlan1 is up, line protocol is up
  Hardware is CPU Interface, address is 0008.a445.9b40 (bia 0008.a445.9b40)
  Internet address is 192.168.1.2/24
```

After you have configured the default gateway, the switch has connectivity to the remote networks with which the switch needs to communicate.

By default, VLAN 1 is the management VLAN. You use the management VLAN to manage all the network devices on a network. In a switch-based network, all network devices should be in the management VLAN. All ports belong to VLAN 1 by default. A best practice is to remove all the access ports from VLAN 1 and place them in another VLAN. This allows for management of network devices while keeping traffic from the network hosts off the management VLAN. Alternatively, you can change the management VLAN to something other than VLAN 1. Many network engineers advocate switching the management VLAN away from VLAN 1.

Use the **no ip address** interface configuration command to remove an IP address for interface VLAN 1 or to disable IP processing. This enables you to configure a different VLAN as the management VLAN.

The Fast Ethernet switch ports default to auto-speed and auto-duplex. This allows the interfaces to negotiate these settings. Network engineers can manually configure the interface speed and duplex values if necessary. The next section looks carefully at speed and duplex considerations.

 Some network devices can provide a web-based interface for configuration and management purposes. After you have configured a switch with an IP address and gateway, you can access it this way. A web browser can access this service using the IP address and port 80, which is the default port for HTTP. Example 6-12 illustrates the configuration. You can turn the HTTP service on or off, and you can choose the port address for the service.

```
Example 6-12     Configuring HTTP Support
AccessSwitch#configure terminal
AccessSwitch(config)#ip http ?
  access-class          Restrict access by access-class
  authentication        Set http authentication method
  path                  Set base path for HTML
  port                  HTTP port
  server                Enable HTTP server
AccessSwitch(config)#ip http server
AccessSwitch(config)#ip http port ?
  <0-65535<             HTTP port
AccessSwitch(config)#ip http port 80
```

The *Cisco Virtual Switch Manager (CVSM)* is a web-based graphical user interface (GUI) used to configure and monitor Catalyst 2900XL/3500XL, 2940, 2950, 3550, 3560, 3750, and 3750 metro series switches. The CVSM requires you to configure an IP address for the switch and to communicate IP connectivity with a web browser, such as Microsoft Internet Explorer. When the GUI is initialized by opening a browser with the switch's URL, an applet is downloaded to the browser from the switch. Note that CatalystExpress 500 switches and Catalyst 2940, 2950, 2955, 2960, 2970, 3550, 3560, 3750, 4500, and 4900 series switches now support Cisco Network Assistant (CNA). As of this writing, CNA Version 4.0 is available as a free download from Cisco.com and is the most recent GUI designed for Catalyst switches. CNA 4.0 is a centralized management application that simplifies the administration task of Catalyst switches, with a user-friendly GUI to easily configure, troubleshoot, and enable and monitor the network.

You must download from Cisco.com special Catalyst IOS images that include an additional HTML package so that CVSM and CNA will work with your switches. *Cluster Management Suite (CMS)* is another GUI-based management interface supported by certain Catalyst switch series. The web-based GUIs that you use to configure Catalyst switches change fairly often, so check periodically to see what the latest version and associated product name is for the relevant software.

 Lab 6.2.2 Basic Switch Configuration

In this lab, you configure a switch with a name and an IP address.

Duplex and Speed Configuration

Half-duplex transmission mode implements Ethernet carrier sense multiple access collision detect (CSMA/CD). The traditional shared LAN operates in half-duplex mode and is susceptible to transmission collisions across the wire.

Full-duplex Ethernet significantly improves network performance without the expense of installing new media. You can achieve full-duplex transmission between stations by using point-to-point Ethernet, Fast Ethernet, and Gigabit Ethernet connections. This arrangement is collision free. Frames sent by the two connected end nodes cannot collide because the end nodes use two separate circuits in the Category 5 or Category 3 cable. Each full-duplex connection uses only one port.

Full-duplex port connections are point-to-point links between switches or end nodes but not between shared hubs. Most Ethernet, Fast Ethernet, and Gigabit Ethernet NICs sold today offer full-duplex capability. In full-duplex mode, the collision detect circuit is disabled.

Nodes that are attached to hubs that share their connection to a switch port must operate in half-duplex mode because the end stations must be able to detect collisions.

Standard shared Ethernet configuration efficiency is typically rated at 50 to 60 percent of the 10-Mbps bandwidth. Full-duplex Ethernet offers 100 percent efficiency in both directions (10-Mbps transmit and 10-Mbps receive).

The following list summarizes the operation of half-duplex versus full-duplex:

- Half-duplex relies on CSMA/CD.

- Half-duplex supports only unidirectional data flow.

- Half-duplex has a higher potential for collisions.

- Half-duplex involves the use of hubs.

- Full-duplex is point-to-point only (one-to-one correspondence between connected devices and switch ports).

- Full-duplex requires full-duplex support on both ends.

- Full-duplex is collision free.

- Full-duplex has the collision-detect circuit disabled.

Use the **duplex** {**auto** | **full** | **half**} interface configuration command to specify the duplex mode of operation for switch ports. The following describes the duplex parameters on the Catalyst 2950 series:

- **auto** sets autonegotiation of duplex mode.
- **full** sets full-duplex mode.
- **half** sets half-duplex mode.

For Fast Ethernet and 10/100/1000 ports, the default is **auto**. For 100BASE-FX ports, the default is **full**. The 10/100/1000 ports operate in either half- or full-duplex mode when you set them to 10 or 100 Mbps, but when you set them to 1000 Mbps, they operate only in full-duplex mode. 100BASE-FX ports operate only at 100 Mbps, full-duplex mode.

To determine the default duplex mode settings for the GBIC-module ports, refer to the documentation that came with your GBIC module.

To verify duplex settings, use the **show interfaces** command, as you saw in Example 6-5. Recall that this command displays statistics and status reports for all or specified interfaces.

Autonegotiation can, at times, produce unpredictable results. A problem sometimes occurs when an attached device does not support autonegotiation and is operating in full duplex. By default, the Catalyst switch sets the corresponding (auto-configuring) switch port to half-duplex mode in this case. This configuration—half duplex on one end and full duplex on the other—causes late collision errors at the half-duplex end. To avoid this situation, manually set the duplex parameters of the switch to match the attached device.

If the switch port is in full-duplex mode and the attached device is in half-duplex mode, check for frame check sequence (FCS) errors on the switch full-duplex port. What is critical is that the setting on the switch is compatible with the setting on the NIC.

You can use the **show interfaces** command to check for FCS late collision errors.

Managing the MAC Address Table

Switches use the MAC address tables to forward traffic between ports. These MAC tables include dynamic, permanent, and static addresses.

Dynamic addresses are source MAC addresses that the switch learns and then drops when they are not refreshed and aged out. The switch provides dynamic addressing by learning the source MAC address of each frame that it receives on each port. Then, it adds the source MAC address and its associated port number to the MAC address table. As the switch adds or removes stations from the network, it updates the MAC address table, adding new entries and aging out those that are currently not in use.

An administrator can specifically assign permanent addresses to certain ports. Unlike dynamic addresses, permanent addresses are not aged out.

The maximum size of the MAC address table varies with different switches. For example, the Catalyst 2950 series switch can store up to 8192 MAC addresses. When the MAC address table is full, traffic for all new unknown addresses is flooded.

The **show mac-address-table** command is illustrated in Example 6-13. You enter this command in the privileged EXEC mode to examine the addresses that a switch has learned.

Example 6-13   Viewing the MAC Address Table

```
AccessSwitch#show mac-address-table
         Mac Address Table
-------------------------------------------

Vlan    Mac Address      Type       Ports
----    -----------      ----       -----
   1    0005.9a3c.7800   STATIC     Fa0/9
   1    0006.5b2f.c095   DYNAMIC    Fa0/1
   1    0009.e800.2401   DYNAMIC    Fa0/12
   1    0014.2275.601e   DYNAMIC    Gi0/2
   1    0040.9632.c466   STATIC     Fa0/9
   1    0040.9646.80ae   STATIC     Fa0/9
Total Mac Addresses for this criterion: 6
```

The **clear mac-address-table dynamic** command purges dynamically learned entries, as illustrated in Example 6-14. (Compare to Example 6-13.)

Example 6-14   Clearing Dynamic Entries in the MAC Address Table

```
AccessSwitch#clear mac-address-table dynamic
AccessSwitch#show mac-address-table
         Mac Address Table
-------------------------------------------

Vlan    Mac Address      Type       Ports
----    -----------      ----       -----
   1    0005.9a3c.7800   STATIC     Fa0/9
   1    0006.5b2f.c095   DYNAMIC    Fa0/1
   1    0009.e800.2401   DYNAMIC    Fa0/12
   1    0040.9632.c466   STATIC     Fa0/9
   1    0040.9646.80ae   STATIC     Fa0/9
Total Mac Addresses for this criterion: 5
```

You can permanently assign a MAC address to an interface. The following are possible reasons for assigning a permanent MAC address to an interface:

- The switch will not automatically age out the MAC address.

- You must attach a specific server or user workstation to the port, and you know the MAC address.

- You want enhanced security.

You can use the following global configuration mode command to configure a static MAC address for a switch:

```
mac address-table static mac-addr vlan vlan-id interface interface-id
```

Note that IOS Release 12.1(11)EA1 replaced the mac-address-table static command with the mac address-table static command. Example 6-15 illustrates the use of the mac **address-table static** command.

Example 6-15   Statically Configuring a Port-to-MAC Mapping

```
AccessSwitch(config)#mac address-table static 0004.5600.67ab vlan 1 interface
                     fastethernet0/2
AccessSwitch(config)#end
AccessSwitch#show mac-address-table
          Mac Address Table
-------------------------------------------

Vlan    Mac Address       Type        Ports
----    -----------       ----        -----
  1     0004.5600.67ab    STATIC      Fa0/2
  1     0005.9a3c.7800    STATIC      Fa0/9
  1     0006.5b2f.c095    DYNAMIC     Fa0/1
  1     0009.e800.2401    DYNAMIC     Fa0/12
  1     0014.2275.601e    DYNAMIC     Gi0/2
  1     0040.9632.c466    STATIC      Fa0/9
  1     0040.9646.80ae    STATIC      Fa0/9
Total Mac Addresses for this criterion: 7
```

Lab 6.2.3   Managing the MAC Address Table

In this lab, you create a basic switch configuration and manage the MAC table.

Lab 6.2.4   Configuring Static MAC Addresses

In this lab, you create a static address entry in the switch MAC table.

Configuring Port Security

You can use the port security feature to restrict input to an interface by limiting and identifying MAC addresses of the stations that are allowed to access the port. When you assign secure MAC addresses to a secure port, the port does not forward packets with source addresses that are outside the group of defined addresses.

On the Catalyst 2950 series, use the **switchport port-security** interface command without keywords to enable port security on an interface. Use the **switchport port-security** interface command with keywords, as illustrated in Example 6-16, to configure a secure MAC address, a maximum number of secure MAC addresses, or the violation mode. Use the **no** form of this command to disable port security or set the parameters to their default state.

Example 6-16   Port Security Options

```
Switch(config-if)#switchport port-security ?
  aging          Port-security aging commands
  mac-address    Secure mac address
  maximum        Max secure addrs
  violation      Security Violation Mode
  <cr>
```

The full syntax for the **switchport port-security** interface mode command is as follows:

```
switchport port-security [mac-address mac-address] |
[mac-address sticky [mac-address]] | [maximum value] |
[violation {protect | restrict | shutdown}]
```

Note that a port must be in access mode to enable port security, and port security is disabled by default. The following describes the methods by which you can add secure addresses to the address table after you set the maximum number of secure MAC addresses allowed on a port:

- Manually configure all the addresses.

- Allow the port to dynamically configure all the addresses.

- Configure a number of MAC addresses and allow the rest of the addresses to be dynamically configured.

You can configure an interface to convert the dynamic MAC addresses to sticky secure MAC addresses and add them to the running configuration by enabling sticky learning. To enable sticky learning, enter the **switchport port-security mac-address sticky** interface configuration command. When you enter this command, the interface converts all the dynamic secure MAC addresses, including those that were dynamically learned before sticky learning was enabled, to sticky secure MAC addresses.

The sticky secure MAC addresses do not automatically become part of the configuration file, which is the startup configuration that is used each time the switch restarts. If you save the sticky secure MAC addresses in the configuration file, when the switch restarts, the interface does not need to relearn these addresses. If you do not save the configuration, the MAC addresses are lost. If you have disabled sticky learning, the sticky secure MAC addresses are converted to dynamic secure addresses and are removed from the running configuration. A secure port can have from 1 to 132 associated secure addresses. The total number of available secure addresses on the switch is 1024.

The following lists the security violation situations:

- The maximum number of secure MAC addresses has been added to the address table, and a station whose MAC address is not in the address table attempts to access the interface.

- An address learned or configured on one secure interface is seen on another secure interface in the same VLAN.

Table 6-5 describes the various port security keyword options.

Table 6-5   Port Security Keyword Options

Command	Description
mac-address *mac-address*	(Optional) Specifies a secure MAC address for the port by entering a 48-bit MAC address. You can add additional secure MAC addresses up to the maximum value configured.
maximum *value*	(Optional) Sets the maximum number of secure MAC addresses for the interface. The range is from 1 to 132. The default is 1.
violation	(Optional) Sets the security violation mode or the action to be taken if port security is violated. The default is shutdown.
protect	Sets the security violation protect mode. When port secure MAC addresses reach the limit that is allowed on the port, packets with unknown source addresses are dropped until you remove enough secure MAC addresses to drop below the maximum value.
restrict	Sets the security violation restrict mode. In this mode, a port security violation causes a trap notification to be sent to the network management station.
shutdown	Sets the security violation shutdown mode. In this mode, a port security violation causes the interface to immediately become error disabled, and an SNMP trap notification is sent. When a secure port is in the error-disabled state, you can bring it out of this state by entering the **errdisable recovery cause psecure-violation** global configuration command, or you can manually re-enable it by entering the **shutdown** and **no shutdown** interface configuration commands.

An address violation occurs when a secured port receives a source address that has been assigned to another secured port or when a port tries to learn an address that exceeds its address table size limit, which is set with the **switchport port-security maximum** command. Table 6-5 lists the address violation keyword options **protect**, **restrict**, and **shutdown** for the **switchport port-security violation** command.

Example 6-17 illustrates a typical application of port security.

Example 6-17   Configuring Port Security

```
AccessSwitch(config)#interface f0/1
AccessSwitch(config-if)#switchport mode access
AccessSwitch(config-if)#switchport port-security
AccessSwitch(config-if)#switchport port-security maximum 1
AccessSwitch(config-if)#switchport port-security mac-address 0008.eeee.eeee
AccessSwitch(config-if)#switchport port-security violation shutdown
```

To verify port security settings for a particular interface, use the **show port-security interface** command. The options are illustrated in Table 6-6.

Table 6-6   **show port-security** Keyword Options

Command	Description
interface *interface-id*	(Optional) Displays the port security settings for the specified interface.
address	(Optional) Displays all the secure addresses on all ports.
begin	(Optional) Sets it so that the display begins with the line that matches the specified expression.
exclude	(Optional) Sets it so that the display excludes lines that match the specified expression.
include	(Optional) Sets it so that the display includes lines that match the specified expression.
expression	Enters the expression that will be used as a reference point in the output.

Use the **show port-security address** command to display the secure MAC addresses for all ports. Use the **show port-security** command without keywords to display the port security settings for the switch. Example 6-18 illustrates the verification of port security.

Example 6-18   Verifying Port Security

```
AccessSwitch#show run interface f0/9
Building configuration...

Current configuration : 317 bytes
!
interface FastEthernet0/9
 switchport mode access
 switchport port-security
```

Example 6-18   Verifying Port Security   *(continued)*

```
 switchport port-security maximum 3
 switchport port-security mac-address 0005.9a3c.7800
 switchport port-security mac-address 0040.9632.c466
 switchport port-security mac-address 0040.9646.80ae
 no ip address
 spanning-tree portfast
end
AccessSwitch#show port-security interface f0/9
Port Security : Enabled
Port status : SecureUp
Violation mode : Shutdown
Maximum MAC Addresses : 3
Total MAC Addresses : 3
Configured MAC Addresses : 3
Aging time : 0 mins
Aging type : Absolute
SecureStatic address aging : Disabled
Security Violation count : 0
AccessSwitch#show port-security address
          Secure Mac Address Table
-------------------------------------------------------------------
Vlan    Mac Address       Type              Ports    Remaining Age
                                                       (mins)
----    -----------       ----              -----    -------------
   1    0005.9a3c.7800    SecureConfigured  Fa0/9      -
   1    0040.9632.c466    SecureConfigured  Fa0/9      -
   1    0040.9646.80ae    SecureConfigured  Fa0/9      -
-------------------------------------------------------------------
Total Addresses in System : 3
Max Addresses limit in System : 1024
AccessSwitch#show port-security
Secure Port     MaxSecureAddr  CurrentAddr  SecurityViolation  Security Action
                   (Count)       (Count)       (Count)
-------------------------------------------------------------------
    Fa0/9            3             3             0              Shutdown
-------------------------------------------------------------------
Total Addresses in System : 3
Max Addresses limit in System : 1024
```

Lab 6.2.5   Configuring Port Security

In this lab, you configure port security on individual FastEthernet ports.

Executing Adds, Moves, and Changes

The following lists the steps for adding a new MAC address on an access switch that connects a workstation to the network:

 Step 1 Configure port security.

Step 2 Configure the MAC address to the port allocated for the new interface so that the first MAC address you see on the port is the only address permitted.

To delete a MAC address on an access switch that connects a workstation to the network, remove the MAC address restrictions from the port.

To move a MAC address from one access switch to another, delete the MAC address from one physical segment/logical network and assign it to a new physical segment. The following lists the steps for doing this:

 Step 1 Add the MAC address to the new physical port.

Step 2 On the new access switch, configure port security.

Step 3 On the new access switch, configure the MAC address to the port allocated for the new user.

Step 4 When all security is in place for the new location, shut down the old port and remove any MAC restrictions. Remove any old access lists from the original access switch.

If an Ethernet NIC fails, that MAC address is no longer valid because MAC addresses are unique. Installing a new Ethernet NIC does not permit the affected workstation to have access to the network because the security policy is based on the old MAC address. In this case, the only changes that you need to make are to the switch itself to remove the old MAC address from the security on the port and to add the new MAC address to the security on the port.

To add a new switch to a network, perform the following steps:

 Step 1 Configure the switch name, IP address, and default gateway to be used for management purposes.

Step 2 Configure administrative access for the console, auxiliary, and VTY interfaces, as appropriate.

Step 3 Configure security for the device. You should consider two levels of security: the user EXEC level and the privileged EXEC level.

Step 4 Configure the access switch ports as necessary to support single workstations, IP phones, and trunking to upstream/downstream switches.

To ensure that the new switch does not become the root of the spanning tree (see Chapter 7, "Spanning Tree Protocol"), increase the priority value. Connect the switch into the existing infrastructure only after you have completed all the switch configuration steps.

To move equipment from one location to another, treat the process as both a removal and an addition of equipment, depending on the number of configuration changes required. If the administrative and interface changes are minimal, you can overwrite those specific configuration parameters. If the equipment is being moved to a site that has few or no similar configuration settings, you should erase the configuration and proceed as if you are adding a new network device.

 Lab 6.2.6   Add, Move, and Change MAC Addresses

In this lab, you add a MAC address to the switch, then move the address and change it.

Managing Switch Configuration Files

First, recall that the switch configuration file is erased using the **erase startup-config** privileged EXEC command. This command clears the *non-volatile RAM (NVRAM)* for the switch. NVRAM is RAM that retains its contents when a unit is powered off.

Network administrators should document and maintain the operational configuration files for network devices. Back up the most current configuration file on a server or disc. This is not only essential for documentation, but it is also useful if you need to restore a configuration file.

You can use the **copy** command to copy a configuration from or to a file server. On the Catalyst 2950 series, use the **copy nvram:startup-config tftp:** command to upload the startup configuration in NVRAM to a TFTP server.

The following lists the steps to upload a configuration file from a switch to a TFTP server for storage:

 Step 1 Verify that the TFTP server is accessible and properly configured.

Step 2 Log into the switch through the console port or a Telnet session.

Step 3 Upload the switch configuration to the TFTP server. Specify the IP address or hostname of the TFTP server and the destination filename.

Use one of these privileged EXEC commands:

```
copy system:running-config tftp:[[[//location]/directory]/filename]
copy nvram:startup-config tftp:[[[//location]/directory]/filename]
```

Example 6-19 illustrates the use of the **copy** command to upload the running-config file to a TFTP server.

Example 6-19   Saving Configuration Files

```
AccessSwitch#copy nvram:startup-config tftp://192.168.1.3/AccessSwitch.cfg
Address or name of remote host [192.168.1.3]?
Destination filename [AccessSwitch]?
!!
1189 bytes copied in .068 secs (17485 bytes/sec)
```

Lab 6.2.7a   Managing Switch Operating System Files

In this lab, you create and verify a basic switch configuration, back up the switch IOS to a TFTP server, and then restore it.

Lab 6.2.7b   Managing Switch Startup Configuration Files

In this lab, you create and verify a basic switch configuration, back up the switch start-up configuration file to a TFTP server, and then restore it.

Password Recovery

For security and management purposes, you must set passwords on the console and VTY lines. You also must set an enable password and an enable secret password. These practices help ensure that only authorized users have access to the user and privileged EXEC modes of the switch.

Sometimes, you can achieve physical access to the switch, but you cannot gain access to the user or privileged EXEC mode because you do not know the passwords or you have forgotten them.

In these circumstances, you need to follow a password recovery procedure. You can find password recovery procedures for most Cisco devices at www.cisco.com/en/US/products/sw/ioss-wrel/ps1831/products_tech_note09186a00801746e6.shtml.

Lab 6.2.8   Password Recovery Procedure on a Catalyst 2950 Series Switch

In this lab, you reset the console password and recover access to the switch.

Upgrading the Cisco IOS Image

IOS images are periodically released with bug fixes, new features, and performance improvements. If you can make the network more secure or operate it more efficiently with a new version of the IOS, you should upgrade the IOS.

To upgrade the IOS, log onto Cisco.com and download a copy of the new image to a local server. For example, you can download Catalyst 2950 images and associated web-based GUI software at http://www.cisco.com/cgi-bin/Software/Iosplanner/Planner-tool/iosplanner.cgi?get_crypto=&data_from=&hardware_name=CAT2950&software_name=&release_name=&majorRel=&state=:HW&type=.

You can find instructions for installing the images at http://www.cisco.com/univercd/cc/td/doc/product/lan/cat2950/12122ea5/2950scg/swiosfs.htm.

Lab 6.2.9   Firmware Upgrade of a Catalyst 2950 Series Switch

In this lab, you create and verify a basic switch configuration and then upgrade the IOS and HTML files from a file that the instructor supplies.

Chapter Summary

Switches are similar to routers. They have basic computer components, including CPU, RAM, and an operating system. Several ports are used to connect hosts and for management. LEDs on the front of the switch show the system status, RPS, port mode, and port status. When powered on, a switch performs POST automatically to verify that the switch functions correctly. You can use HyperTerminal to configure or check the status of a switch.

Another similarity to Cisco routers is the CLI. When you enter a question mark (**?**) to access help, a list of available commands appears. Switches provide word help and command syntax help.

Switches and routers have the same command modes. User EXEC is the default and is indicated by the greater-than character (>). The **enable** command changes user EXEC to privileged EXEC, as indicated by the pound sign (#). Password-protect access to privileged EXEC mode to prevent unauthorized use. The **configure** command enables you to access other command modes.

Default data is provided when you power up the switch for the first time. You can use **show running-config** and **show interfaces** commands to view factory default settings. For management purposes, a switch is assigned an IP address. Use the **show version** command to verify the IOS version and the configuration register settings.

After you have configured a switch with an IP address and gateway, you can access it through a web-based interface. This allows you to configure and manage the switch. You can access this service through a web browser with the IP address and port 80, which is the default port for HTTP.

You use the **duplex** command to configure interface duplex options. As often as not, troubleshooting issues with switches pertain to speed or duplex misconfigurations.

A switch dynamically learns and maintains thousands of MAC addresses. If frames associated with a previously learned MAC address are not received, the MAC address entry is automatically discarded or aged out after 300 seconds. You can enter the command **clear mac-address-table** in the privileged EXEC mode to manually clear address tables.

A permanent MAC address assigned to an interface ensures that the switch will not automatically age out the MAC address and that security will be enhanced. You can use the command **mac address-table static** *mac-addr* **vlan** *vlan-id* **interface** *interface-id* to configure a static MAC address. Use the **no** form of the command to remove it. Port security provides a basic level of security at the access layer. Port security commands restrict network access based on allowable MAC addresses or a maximum number of MAC addresses. Use the commands **show port security**, **show port security address**, and **show port security interface** to verify port security.

Configure the switch name, IP address, default gateway, and line passwords on a new switch that you add to a network. When you move or switch a host from one port to another, you should remove configurations that can cause unexpected behavior. Maintain documentation for the current configuration, and periodically perform backups to a server.

Check Your Understanding

Complete all the review questions listed here to test your understanding of the topics and concepts in this chapter. Answers are listed in Appendix A, "Answers to Check Your Understanding and Challenge Questions and Activities."

1. Which CLI prompt indicates that you are working in privileged EXEC mode?

   A. Switch#

   B. Switch>

   C. Switch-exec>

   D. Switch-config

2. Which command would you enter in the privileged EXEC mode to list the command options?

   A. **?**

   B. **init**

   C. **help**

   D. **login**

3. How do you start a Catalyst 2950 series switch?

   A. Press the on/off switch.

   B. Power up the redundant power supply.

   C. Connect a network cable to another switch on the network.

   D. Attach the power cable plug to the switch power supply.

4. What color will the Catalyst 2950 series switch RPS LED be if the RPS is plugged in but not functioning correctly?

   A. Green

   B. Amber

   C. Flashing green

   D. Flashing amber

5. If the POST tests complete successfully on a Catalyst switch, what display could you see on the console?

   A. The > prompt

   B. The privileged EXEC prompt

   C. The Management Console Logon screen

   D. A list of commands available on the switch

6. What CLI command should you enter to display a list of commands that begin with the letter C on a Catalyst switch?

   A. **c?**

   B. **c ?**

   C. **help c**

   D. **help c***

7. What CLI command should you enter to display the command syntax help so that you can learn how to complete a command that begins with config?

   A. **config?**

   B. **config ?**

   C. **help config**

   D. **help config***

8. Which Cisco IOS command correctly configures an IP address and subnet mask on a switch?

   A. **ip address**

   B. **ip address 196.125.243.10**

   C. **196.125.243.10 ip address**

   D. **ip address 196.125.243.10 255.255.255.0**

9. Which configuration mode will you use to configure a particular port on a switch?

   A. User mode

   B. Global configuration mode

   C. Interface configuration mode

   D. Controller configuration mode

10. When you use the **show interfaces** command to display the status and statistics for the interfaces configured on a Catalyst switch, which output field indicates the MAC address that identifies the interface hardware?

    A. MTU 1500 bytes

    B. Hardware is ... 10BASET

    C. Address is 0050.BD73.E2C1

    D. 802.1d STP State: Forwarding

11. Which **show** command requires that you have privileged EXEC mode access?

   A. **show ip**

   B. **show version**

   C. **show running**

   D. **show interfaces**

12. What does the **duplex full** command do?

   A. Sets full-duplex mode for the switch

   B. Sets full-duplex mode for an interface

   C. Sets full-duplex mode with flow control for the switch

   D. Sets full-duplex mode with flow control for an interface

13. Which command restricts port usage to no more than ten devices?

   A. **switchport secure 10**

   B. **switchport max-mac-count 10**

   C. **switchport port-security maximum 10**

   D. **switchport port-security 10 max-mac**

14. What does the **erase startup-config** command do on a Catalyst 2950 series switch?

   A. Deletes the MAC address table on the switch

   B. Resets the switch configuration to the factory defaults

   C. Resets the switch configuration to the last-saved version

   D. Deletes all configuration information on the switch, including all the defaults

   E. Resets the switch configuration to the factory defaults and erases all VLAN information

15. Which command will display the switch IOS version and the configuration register settings?

   A. Switch# **show configuration-register**

   B. Switch# **show running-configuration**

   C. Switch# **show startup-configuration**

   D. Switch# **show version**

   E. Switch# **show env-vars**

16. What is configured with an IP address and gateway so that you can manage a switch from a host on the network?

A. Port 1

B. Console

C. VLAN1

D. AUX

E. CLI

17. What information should an administrator keep backed up as a text file or printed copy to document the network and ensure easy switch recovery?

A. The current running-config

B. The VLAN.dat file

C. The IOS image

D. The MAC address database

E. The switch help file

Challenge Questions and Activities

These questions and activities are purposefully designed to be similar to the more complex styles of questions you might see on the CCNA exam. Answers are listed in Appendix A.

1. An offsite location has received a Cisco Catalyst switch. You are to reconfigure the switch for use at a different facility. What should you do before reconfiguring the switch? (Choose two.)

   A. Clear the current configuration by holding down the reset button while powering on the switch.

   B. Erase previously configured VLAN information by deleting the vlan.dat file in flash.

   C. Remove the current configuration file with the **erase startup-config** command.

   D. Delete the IOS image from the flash memory.

   E. Power cycle the switch and enter setup mode.

   F. Clear the HTML directory in flash of previously saved files.

2. What basic settings should you configure on a new switch when you first add it to a network? (Choose three.)

   A. The switch name

   B. The IP configuration for the management interface

   C. VLANs

   D. Port security

   E. Static MAC addresses

   F. Line passwords

3. What does a green system LED tell you about a switch? (Choose two.)

   A. The switch has power.

   B. The switch is working properly.

   C. The switch is not working properly.

   D. The switch is going through POST.

   E. The switch is initializing.

4. A user is having problems communicating on the network. A network technician finds the connecting switch mode LED indicating STAT and the switch port of the suspect connection displaying a solid amber light. What could this mean? (Choose three.)

   A. A link is not detected.

   B. The port has an address violation.

   C. The port is sending or receiving data.

   D. The port is administratively disabled.

   E. Spanning Tree Protocol is blocking the port.

   F. The switch and host duplex modes do not match.

5. What can you do in user EXEC mode of the switch CLI? (Choose three.)

   A. Access configuration mode.

   B. Change the terminal settings.

   C. Display system information.

   D. Change LAN interface settings.

   E. Display the contents of the MAC address table.

CHAPTER 7

Spanning Tree Protocol

Objectives

Upon completion of this chapter, you should be able to answer the following questions:

- What problems can occur with redundant switched topologies?

- How are broadcast storms created?

- How do multiple frame transmissions occur?

- How does MAC database instability occur?

- What is the purpose of STP?

- What process does STP follow when maintaining a loop-free network topology?

- How does STP select the root bridge?

- How do spanning-tree port states function?

- What is spanning-tree path cost?

- How does STP recalculate port states to accommodate topology changes?

- What is the function of RSTP?

Key Terms

This chapter uses the following key terms. You can find the definitions in the Glossary.

Redundancy is desirable in a campus or enterprise network. Redundancy helps to minimize network downtime. The downside of redundancy is the increased likelihood of Layer 2 or Layer 3 loops.

The features of redundant switched topologies are described in this chapter as well as the problems associated with broadcast storms, multiple frame transmissions, and Media Access Control (MAC) address table instability.

Spanning Tree Protocol (STP) was invented to address issues caused by physical redundancy in a switched topology. There are two major spanning-tree solutions: IEEE 802.1d and IEEE 802.1w. IEEE 802.1d is the original IEEE standard for spanning tree. IEEE 802.1d introduced five STP states. IEEE 802.1w is an evolved form of 802.1d, with significant enhancements, including consolidating some of the 802.1d states. 802.1w is fast becoming the standard in switched networks.

Redundant Topologies

Redundancy in a network is critical. It allows networks to be fault tolerant. Redundant topologies protect against network downtime, or nonavailability. The failure of a single link, port, or network device can cause downtime. Network engineers are often required to balance the cost of redundancy with the need for network availability.

Redundant topologies based on switches and bridges are susceptible to broadcast storms, multiple frame transmissions, and MAC address database instability. These problems can make a network unusable. Therefore, you should carefully plan and monitor redundancy.

Switched networks bestow the benefits of smaller collision domains, microsegmentation, and full duplex operation. Switched networks provide better performance.

Redundancy in a network is required to protect against loss of connectivity because of a failed individual component. However, this provision can result in physical topologies with loops. Physical layer loops can cause serious problems in switched networks.

Redundancy

Many companies and organizations increasingly rely on computer networks for their operations. Access to file servers, databases, the Internet, intranets, and extranets is critical for successful businesses. If the network is down, productivity and customer satisfaction decline.

Increasingly, companies require continuous network availability, or uptime. Uptime of 100 percent is perhaps impossible, but many organizations try to achieve 99.999 percent, or "five nines," uptime. Extremely reliable networks are required to achieve this goal. This is interpreted to mean about one hour of downtime, on average, for every 4000 days, or approximately 5.25 minutes of downtime per year. Achieving such a goal requires extremely reliable networks.

Network reliability is achieved through reliable equipment and network designs that are tolerant to failures and faults. You should design networks to reconverge rapidly so that you can bypass the fault.

As an illustration, assume that you must use a car to get to work. If the car has a fault that makes it unusable, it is impossible to use the car to go to work until you get it repaired. On average, if the car is unusable because of failure one day out of ten, the car has 90 percent usage. Therefore, reliability is also 90 percent. A second car improves matters. You do not need two cars just to get to work, but a second car provides redundancy, or backup, if the primary vehicle fails. The ability to get to work no longer depends on a single car. Both cars might become unusable simultaneously, 1 day in every 100. The second car raises reliability to 99 percent.

A goal of redundant topologies is to eliminate network outages caused by a single point of failure. All networks need redundancy for enhanced reliability. A network of roads is one way of thinking of a redundant topology. If one road is closed for repair, an alternate route to the destination is likely available. Consider a river that separates the community from the town center. If only one bridge crosses the river, people have only one way into town. The topology has no redundancy. If the bridge is flooded or damaged by an accident, travel to the town center across the bridge is impossible. A second bridge across the river creates a redundant topology. The suburb is not cut off from the town center if one bridge is impassable.

Redundant Switched Topologies

Although redundant designs, as in Figure 7-1, might eliminate the possibility that a single point of failure problem will result in loss of function for the entire switched or bridged network, you must take into account problems that redundant designs can cause.

Figure 7-1   A Redundant Switched Topology Can Be a Source of Layer 2 Problems

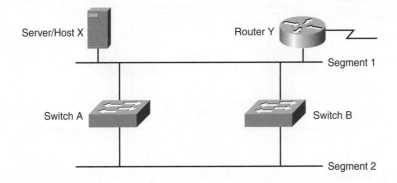

The following lists some of the problems that can occur with redundant links and devices in switched or bridged networks:

- *Broadcast storms*—Without a loop-avoidance process in operation, each switch or bridge floods broadcasts endlessly. This situation is commonly called a broadcast storm.

- **Multiple frame transmission**—Multiple copies of unicast frames can be delivered to destination stations. Many protocols expect to receive only a single copy of each transmission. Multiple copies of the same frame can cause unrecoverable errors.

■ **MAC database instability**—Instability in the MAC address table content results from copies of the same frame being received on different ports of the switch. Data forwarding can be impaired if the switch consumes the resources that are coping with instability in the MAC address table.

Layer 2 LAN protocols, such as Ethernet, lack a mechanism to recognize and eliminate end-lessly looping frames. Some Layer 3 protocols implement a Time to Live (TTL) mechanism that limits the number of times a packet can be retransmitted by a Layer 3 networking device. Lacking such a mechanism, Layer 2 devices continue to retransmit looping traffic indefinitely.

A loop-avoidance mechanism is required to solve each of these problems. This chapter will discuss each of these issues in greater detail.

Broadcast Storms

Broadcasts and multicasts can cause problems in a switched network. Without specialized switch configurations, switches treat multicasts the same as broadcasts. Broadcast and multicast frames are flooded out all ports, except the one on which the frame was received. Figure 7-2 illustrates a broadcast storm. Broadcast storms are not as prevalent as in the past due to the shift toward Layer 3 switching.

Figure 7-2   Broadcast Storm

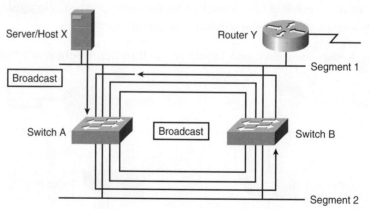

The following example, based on Figure 7-2, helps to illustrate how broadcast storms can occur:

1. When host X sends a broadcast frame, such as an Address Resolution Protocol (ARP) for its default gateway (router Y), switch A receives the frame.

2. Switch A examines the Destination Address field in the frame and determines that the frame must be flooded onto the bottom Ethernet link, segment 2.

3. When this copy of the frame arrives at switch B, the process repeats and a copy of the frame is transmitted onto the top Ethernet, segment 1 near switch B.

4. Because the original copy of the frame also arrives at switch B via the top Ethernet, these frames travel around the loop in both directions, even after the destination station has received a copy of the frame.

A broadcast storm can disrupt normal traffic flow. It can also disrupt all the devices on the switched or bridged network because the CPU must process broadcasts in each device on the segment; thus, a broadcast storm can lock up the user PCs and servers that are trying to process all the broadcast frames.

A loop-avoidance mechanism eliminates this problem by preventing one of the four interfaces from transmitting frames during normal operation, therefore breaking the loop. This mechanism is called spanning tree and is discussed later in this chapter.

Multiple Frame Transmissions

In a redundant topology, multiple copies of the same frame can arrive at the intended host, potentially causing problems with the receiving protocol. Most protocols are designed not to recognize or cope with duplicate transmissions. In general, protocols that use a sequence numbering mechanism assume that many transmissions have failed and that the sequence number has recycled. Other protocols attempt to hand the duplicate transmission to the appropriate upper-layer protocol, with unpredictable results.

An example helps to illustrate how multiple frame transmissions can occur. See Figure 7-3.

Figure 7-3   Multiple Frame Transmissions Can Occur in Redundant Switched Topologies

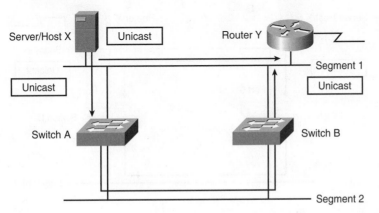

The following lists the sequence of events describing how multiple copies of the same frame can arrive at the intended host:

1. When host X sends a unicast frame to router Y, one copy is received over the direct Ethernet connection, segment 1. At more or less the same time, switch A receives a copy of the frame and puts it into the switch A buffers.

2. If switch A examines the Destination Address field in the frame and finds no entry in the MAC address table for router Y, switch A floods the frame on all ports except the originating port.

3. When switch B receives a copy of the frame through switch A on segment 2, switch B also forwards a copy of the frame onto segment 1 if the MAC address table has no entry for router Y.

4. Router Y receives a copy of the same frame for the second time.

STP, discussed later in this chapter, eliminates this problem by preventing one of the four interfaces from transmitting frames during normal operation, therefore breaking the loop.

MAC Database Instability

MAC database instability results when multiple copies of a frame arrive on different ports of a switch.

An example helps to illustrate how MAC database instability comes occurs. See Figure 7-4.

Figure 7-4   MAC Database Instability Can Also Occur in Redundant Switched
Topologies

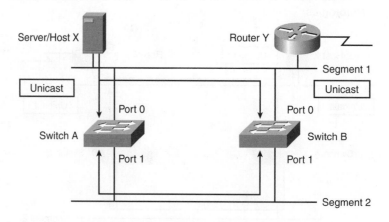

Multiple copies of the same frame can arrive at the intended host.

In Figure 7-4, switch B installs a database entry, mapping the MAC address of host X to port 0. Port 0 connects to segment 1 when the first frame arrives. Sometime later, when the copy of the frame transmitted through switch A arrives at port 1 of switch B, switch B must remove the first entry and install one that incorrectly maps the MAC address of host X to the port 1 that connects to segment 2.

Depending on the internal architecture of the switch in question, it might or might not cope well with rapid changes in its MAC database. Again, STP eliminates this problem by preventing one of the four interfaces from transmitting frames during normal operation, therefore breaking the loop.

Spanning Tree Protocol

Redundancy in a network is required to protect against loss of connectivity because of a failed individual component. However, this provision can result in physical topologies with loops. Physical layer loops can cause serious problems in switched networks.

You use the *Spanning Tree Protocol (STP)* in switched networks to create a loop-free logical topology from a looped physical topology. Links, ports, and switches that are not part of the active loop-free topology do not forward data frames. STP is a powerful tool that gives network administrators the security of a redundant topology without the risk of problems that switching loops cause.

STP Background

STP was originally developed by the Digital Equipment Corporation. The IEEE 802 committee subsequently revised the Digital Equipment spanning-tree algorithm in the *IEEE 802.1d* specification. The Digital Equipment algorithm and the IEEE 802.1d algorithm are not the same and are not compatible. Cisco switches, such as the Catalyst 2950 series, use the IEEE 802.1d STP. STP is enabled by default on Catalyst switches.

The purpose of STP is to maintain a loop-free network topology. A loop-free topology occurs when the switch or bridge recognizes a loop in the topology and logically blocks one or more redundant ports automatically, as illustrated in Figure 7-5.

Figure 7-5   STP Intelligently Blocks Selected Ports to Logically Solve Problems That Physical Loops Cause

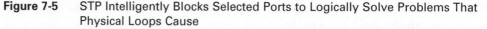
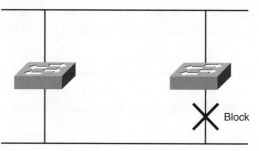

STP continually probes the network so that it can detect the failure or addition of a link, switch, or bridge. When the network topology changes, the switches and bridges that are running STP automatically reconfigure their ports to avoid the creation of loops or the loss of connectivity.

Spanning-Tree Operation

Convergence in STP is a state in which all the switch and bridge ports have transitioned to either the forwarding or the blocking state. See the section "Spanning-Tree Port States" for more information on states. Convergence is necessary for normal network operations. For a switched or bridged network, a key issue is the amount of time required for convergence when the network topology changes. Fast convergence is a desirable network feature because it reduces the time that bridges and switches have ports in transitional states without sending user traffic. The normal convergence time with IEEE 802.1d STP is 30 to 50 seconds.

STP uses two key concepts when converging to a loop-free logical topology: bridge ID (BID) and path cost. Bridge ID will be explored in the next section, "Selecting the Root Bridge."

STP depends on the concept of path cost; the shortest path is based on cumulative link costs. Link costs are based on the speed of the link. The spanning-tree *path cost* is an accumulated total path cost based on the bandwidth of all the links in the path. Table 7-1 shows some of the path costs specified in the IEEE 802.1d specification. The IEEE 802.1d specification has been revised; in the older specification, the cost was calculated based on a bandwidth of 1000 Mbps. The calculation of the new specification uses a nonlinear scale to accommodate higher-speed interfaces. Most Catalyst switches incorporate the revised cost calculations. A key point to remember about STP cost is that lower costs are better.

Table 7-1   Spanning-Tree Path Costs for the Revised and Previous IEEE Specification

Link Speed	Cost (Revised IEEE Specification)	Cost (Previous IEEE Specification)
10 Gbps	2	1
1 Gbps	4	1
100 Mbps	19	10
10 Mbps	100	100

STP performs three steps when it initially converges on a logically loop-free network topology:

1. **Elects one root bridge**—STP has a process to elect a root bridge. Only one bridge can act as the root bridge in a given network. On the *root bridge*, all ports are *designated ports*. Designated ports are normally in the forwarding state. In the forwarding state, a port can send and receive traffic. In Figure 7-6, switch X is elected as the root bridge.

Note

For more detailed information on spanning-tree operation, refer to *CCNP 3: Multilayer Switching Companion Guide*, Second Edition.

Figure 7-6   Various Spanning-Tree Parameters Include Designated Ports, Nondesignated Ports, and Root Ports

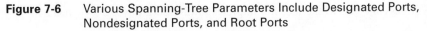
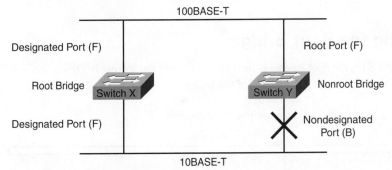

2. **Selects the root port on the nonroot bridge**—STP establishes one *root port* on the *nonroot bridge* (any bridge that is not the root bridge is a non-root bridge). The root port is the lowest-cost path from the nonroot bridge to the root bridge. Root ports are normally in the forwarding state. Spanning-tree path cost is an accumulated cost calculated on the bandwidth. In Figure 7-6, the lowest-cost path to the root bridge is from switch Y through the 100BASE-T Fast Ethernet link.

3. **Selects the designated port on each segment**—On each segment, STP establishes one designated port. The designated port is selected on the bridge that has the lowest-cost path to the root bridge. Designated ports are normally in the forwarding state, forwarding traffic for the segment. In Figure 7-6, the designated port for both segments is on the root bridge because the root bridge is directly connected to both segments. The 10BASE-T Ethernet

port on switch Y is a *nondesignated port* because each segment has only one designated port. Nondesignated ports are normally in the blocking state to logically break the loop topology. When a port is in the blocking state, it is not forwarding traffic but can still receive traffic.

As a result, for every switched network, the following elements exist:

- One root bridge per network

- One root port per nonroot bridge

- One designated port per segment

- Unused, or nondesignated ports

Root ports and designated ports are used for forwarding (F) data traffic. Nondesignated ports discard data traffic. These ports are called blocking (B) or discarding ports.

If all this seems excessively complicated, you can be comforted by the fact that switched networks rely on STP less and less as the industry migrates toward pure Layer 3 switched solutions.

Selecting the Root Bridge

When you use STP, the root bridge is the bridge that has the lowest BID. The *bridge ID* includes the priority and MAC address of the bridge, as illustrated in Figure 7-7.

Figure 7-7   Bridge ID Determines the Root Bridge

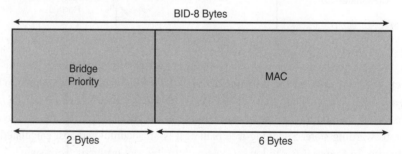

Switches and bridges that run the spanning-tree algorithm exchange configuration messages with other switches and bridges at regular intervals (every 2 seconds by default). Switches and bridges exchange these messages using a multicast frame called the *bridge protocol data unit (BPDU)*. One of the pieces of information included in the BPDU is the BID.

STP calls for you to assign each switch or bridge a unique BID. The BID is made up of a priority value (2 bytes) and the bridge MAC address (6 bytes). The default priority, in accordance with

IEEE 802.1d, is 32,768 (1000 0000 0000 0000 in binary, or 0x8000 in hex), which is the midrange value. The root bridge is the bridge that has the lowest BID. For the bridge MAC address used in the BID, a Cisco Catalyst switch uses a MAC address from a pool of MAC addresses that are assigned to the backplane of the switch.

In Figure 7-8, both switches use the same default priority. The switch that has the lowest MAC address will be the root bridge. In this example, switch X is the root bridge, with a BID of 0x8000-0c00.1111.1111.

Figure 7-8   Root Bridge Selection Relies on BPDUs

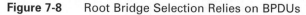
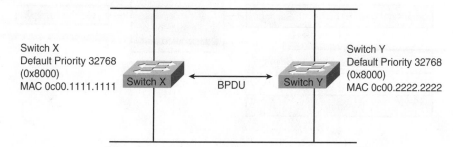

Network engineers can set the switch priority to a smaller value than the default, which makes the BID smaller. They should only do this when the traffic flow on the network is well understood.

Lab 7.2.4   Selecting the Root Bridge

In this lab, you create a basic switch configuration, verify it, and determine which switch is selected as the root switch with factory default settings.

Spanning-Tree Port States

With STP, ports transition through four states: *blocking*, *listening*, *learning*, and *forwarding*. See Figure 7-9. When STP is enabled, every bridge in the network goes through the blocking state and the transitory states of listening and learning at power-up. If properly configured, the ports then stabilize to the forwarding or blocking state. Forwarding ports provide the lowest-cost path to the root bridge. During a topology change, a port temporarily implements the listening and learning states.

the transitional listening state, it can send and receive BPDUs to determine the active topology.

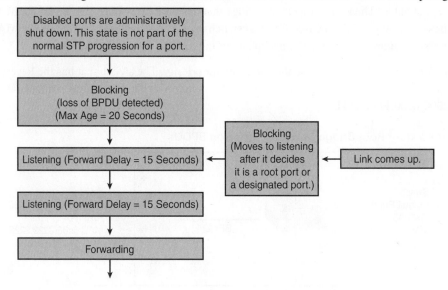

At this point, no user data is passed. During the listening state, the bridge selects the root bridge, selects the root ports on the nonroot bridges, and selects the designated ports on each segment.

The time it takes for a port to transition from the listening state to the learning state or from the learning state to the forwarding state is called the *forward delay*. The forward delay has a default value of 15 seconds.

The learning state reduces the amount of flooding required when data forwarding begins. If a port is still a designated or root port at the end of the learning state, the port transitions to the forwarding state. In the forwarding state, a port can send and receive user data. Ports that are not the designated or root ports transition back to the blocking state.

Normally, a port transitions from the blocking state to the forwarding state in 30 to 50 seconds. You can tune spanning-tree timers to adjust the timing, but normally, you should set these timers to the default value. The default values are put in place to give the network enough time to gather all the correct information about the network topology.

If a switch port is connected only to end-user stations (not connected to another switch or bridge), you should enable a Catalyst switch feature called *PortFast* on those end-user ports. With PortFast, when such an end-user port first comes up, it automatically transitions from the blocking state to the forwarding state. This is acceptable because no loops can be formed through the port, a result of no other switches or bridges being connected to it.

If a switch port is connected only to end-user stations (not connected to another switch or bridge), you should enable a Catalyst switch feature called *PortFast* on those end-user ports. With PortFast, when such an end-user port first comes up, it automatically transitions from the blocking state to the forwarding state. This is acceptable because no loops can be formed through the port, a result of no other switches or bridges being connected to it.

An example helps to illustrate STP port states. See Figure 7-10.

Figure 7-10   Nondesignated Ports Are Blocking and Others Are Forwarding

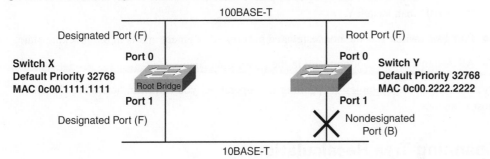

The following list describes the ports in Figure 7-10:

- The ports on switch X, the root bridge, are the designated ports (forwarding).

- The Fast Ethernet port, port 0, on switch Y is the root port (forwarding). The Fast Ethernet port has a lower-cost path to the root bridge than the Ethernet port.

- The Standard Ethernet port, port 1, on switch Y is the nondesignated port (blocking). Each segment has only one designated port.

The STP operation results in a logical loop-free topology.

As another example of spanning-tree operation, see Figure 7-11.

Figure 7-11   Spanning-Tree Operation with Three Switches

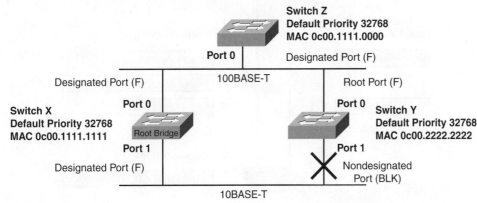

The following list describes the ports in Figure 7-11:

- The root bridge is switch Z, which has the lowest BID.

- The root port is port 0 on switches X and Y. Port 0 is the lowest-cost path to the root on both switches.

- The designated port is port 0 of switch Z. All ports on the root are designated ports. Port 1 of switch X is a designated port. Because both switch X and switch Y have the same path cost to the root bridge, the designated port is selected to be on switch X because it has a lower BID than switch Y.

- Port 1 on switch Y is the nondesignated port on the segment and is in the blocking state.

- All designated and root ports are in the forwarding state.

By reviewing a few examples of spanning-tree operation, you can learn how STP will act in most situations.

Spanning-Tree Recalculation

When the network topology changes, switches must recompute STP. That disrupts user traffic.

A switched internetwork has converged when all the switch and bridge ports are in either the forwarding or blocking state. Forwarding ports send and receive data traffic and BPDUs. Blocking ports receive only BPDUs.

When the network topology changes, switches and bridges recompute the spanning tree and disrupt network traffic. Figure 7-12 illustrates a converged STP topology. Figure 7-13 illustrates the immediate behavior of STP after port 1/2 fails on switch Cat-A. Figure 7-14 illustrates a reconverged STP topology.

Figure 7-12   STP Has Converged

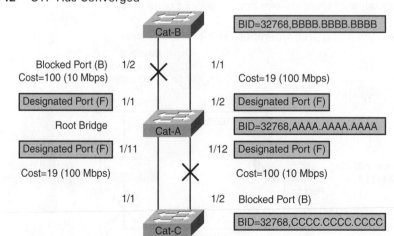

Figure 7-13   Port 1/2 Fails, Resulting in STP Recalculation

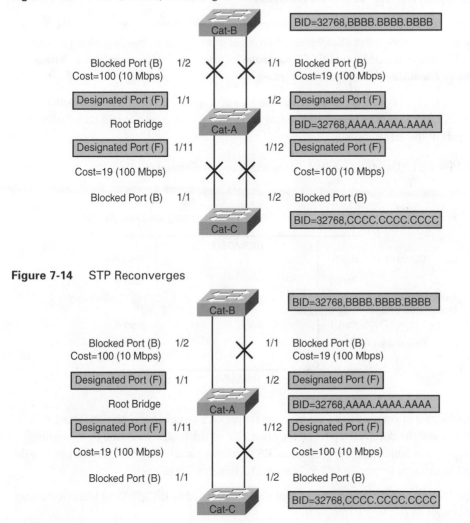

Figure 7-14   STP Reconverges

Convergence on a new spanning-tree topology that uses the IEEE 802.1d standard can take up to 50 seconds. This convergence is made up of the max_age of 20 seconds, the listening forward delay of 15 seconds, and the learning forward delay of 15 seconds.

Lab 7.2.6   Spanning-Tree Recalculation

In this lab, you create a basic switch configuration, verify it, and observe the behavior of the spanning-tree algorithm in the presence of switched network topology changes.

Note

The behind-the-scenes operations involved with STP reconvergence are beyond the scope of this book. Refer to *CCNP 3: Multilayer Switching Companion Guide*, Second Edition, for more detail.

Rapid Spanning Tree Protocol

Rapid Spanning Tree Protocol (RSTP) significantly reduces the time to reconverge the active topology of the network when changes to the physical topology or its configuration parameters occur. RSTP defines the additional *RSTP port roles* of *alternate* and *backup*, and it defines port states as *discarding*, learning, or forwarding.

See Figure 7-15. RSTP selects one switch as the root of a spanning tree–connected active topology. RSTP assigns port roles to individual ports on the switch, depending on whether the ports are part of the active topology.

Figure 7-15   RSTP Defines Five Port Roles (Backup not Shown)

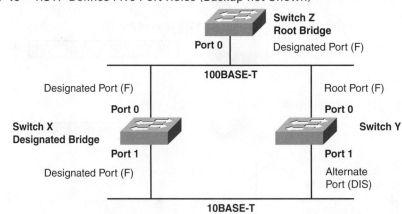

RSTP provides rapid connectivity following the failure of a switch, a switch port, or a LAN. A new root port and the designated port on the other side of the bridge transition to forwarding through an explicit handshake between them. RSTP allows switch port configuration so that the ports can transition to forwarding directly when the switch reinitializes.

RSTP, specified in *IEEE 802.1w*, supersedes STP as specified in IEEE 802.1d while remaining compatible with STP.

The following are the definitions that RSTP uses for port roles:

- **Root**—A forwarding port elected for the spanning tree topology.
- **Designated**—A forwarding port elected for every switched LAN segment.
- **Alternate**—An alternate path to the root bridge, which is different from the path that the root port takes.
- **Backup**—A backup path that provides a redundant (but less desirable) connection to a segment where another switch port already connects. Backup ports can exist only where two ports are connected in a loopback by a point-to-point link or bridge with two or more connections to a shared LAN segment.
- **Disabled**—A port that has no role within the operation of spanning tree.

Root and designated port roles include the port in the active topology. Alternate and backup port roles exclude the port from the active topology.

RSTP also has a different set of port states. The *RSTP port state* controls the forwarding and learning processes and provides the values of discarding, learning, and forwarding. Table 7-2 compares STP port states with RSTP port states.

Table 7-2   RSTP Port States

Operational Status	STP Port State	RSTP Port State	Port Included in Active Topology
Enabled	Blocking	Discarding	No
Enabled	Listening	Discarding	No
Enabled	Learning	Learning	Yes
Enabled	Forwarding	Forwarding	Yes
Disabled	Disabled	Discarding	No

In a stable topology, RSTP ensures that every root port and designated port transitions to forwarding while all alternate ports and backup ports are always in the discarding state.

The rapid transition is the most important feature introduced with IEEE 802.1w. Prior to the introduction of 802.1w, the spanning-tree algorithm waited passively for the network to converge before transitioning a port to the forwarding state. The new RSTP actively confirms that a port can safely transition to forwarding without relying on a timer configuration. To achieve fast convergence on a port, the protocol relies on two new variables: the edge ports and the point-to-point (pt-pt) links. See Figure 7-16.

Figure 7-16   RSTP Incorporates the Concepts of Edge Ports and Point-to-Point Links

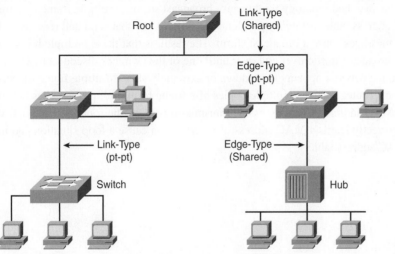

With *edge ports*, no ports that are directly connected to end stations can create bridging loops in the network. Edge ports can go directly to forwarding, skipping the listening and learning stages. An edge port does not generate topology changes when its link toggles.

RSTP can achieve rapid transition to forwarding only on edge ports, new root ports, and *point-to-point links*:

- **Edge ports**—If you configure a port as an edge port on an RSTP switch by using the spanning-tree portfast interface configuration command, the edge port immediately transitions to the forwarding state. An edge port is the same as a PortFast-enabled port. You should enable it only on ports that connect to a single end station.

- **Root ports**—If RSTP selects a new root port, it blocks the old one and immediately transitions the new root port to the forwarding state.

- **Point-to-point links**—If you connect one port to another through a point-to-point link and the local port becomes designated, it negotiates a rapid transition with the other port.

The link-type variable is automatically derived from the duplex mode of a port. A port operating in full-duplex mode is point-to-point, whereas a port operating in half-duplex mode is considered shared by default. You can override the automatic link-type setting with an explicit configuration.

Figure 7-16 does not represent a preferred design. It is simply an example of link types.

Chapter Summary

Redundancy is defined as a duplication of components that allows continued functionality despite the failure of an individual component. In a network, redundancy means having a backup method to connect all devices. Redundant topologies increase network reliability and decrease downtime caused by a single point of failure.

A redundant switched topology might cause broadcast storms, multiple frame transmissions, and MAC address table instability problems. Multiple hosts that send and receive multiple broadcast messages cause a broadcast storm. The result is that these multiple hosts continue to propagate broadcast traffic over and over until one of the switches disconnects. During a broadcast storm, the network appears to be down or extremely slow. Multiple frame transmissions occur when a router receives multiple copies of a frame from multiple switches because of an unknown MAC address. These excessive transmissions cause the router to time out. When a switch incorrectly learns a MAC address of a port, it can cause a loop situation and instability for the MAC address table.

Because switches operate at Layer 2 of the OSI model, all forwarding decisions are made at this level. Layer 2 does not provide a TTL value, which is the set amount of time that a packet is provided to reach a destination. The problem is that physical topologies contain switching or bridging loops necessary for reliability, but a switched network cannot have loops. The solution is to allow physical loops but create a loop-free logical topology.

The loop-free logical topology that is created is called a spanning tree. The topology is a star or extended star that spans the tree of the network. All devices are reachable or spanned. The algorithm that you use to create this loop-free logical topology is the spanning-tree algorithm.

STP establishes a root node, called the root bridge. The STP constructs a topology that has one path for every node on the network. This results in a tree that originates from the root bridge. Redundant links that are not part of the shortest path tree are blocked. A loop-free topology is possible because certain paths are blocked. Data frames received on blocked links are dropped.

Switches send messages called bridge protocol data units (BPDU) to allow loop-free logical topology to be formed. Blocked ports continue to receive BPDUs. BPDUs contain information that allows switches to perform specific actions:

- Select a single switch that will act as the root of the spanning tree.

- Calculate the shortest path from itself to the root switch.

- Designate one of the switches as the designated switch (designated bridge).

- Choose one of its ports as its root port, for each nonroot switch.

- Select ports that are part of the spanning tree. These ports are called designated ports.

The IEEE 802.1w LAN standard defines the RSTP. It clarifies port states and roles, defines a set of link types, and allows switches in a converged network to generate BPDUs rather than use the root bridge BPDUs. The blocking state of a port is renamed as the discarding state. The role of a discarding port is that of an alternate port. The discarding port can become the designated port if the designated port of the segment fails.

Check Your Understanding

Complete all the review questions listed here to test your understanding of the topics and concepts in this chapter. Answers are listed in Appendix A, "Answers to Check Your Understanding and Challenge Questions and Activities."

1. Which three frame types are flooded to all ports except the source port on a switch? (Choose three.)

   A. Unicast frames

   B. Multicast frames

   C. Broadcast frames

   D. Frames with a known destination address

   E. Frames with an unknown destination address

2. Which term commonly describes the endless flooding or looping of frames?

   A. Flood storm

   B. Loop overload

   C. Broadcast storm

   D. Broadcast overload

3. Which term describes multiple copies of a frame arriving on different ports of a switch?

   A. Flood storm

   B. Multiple frame transmission

   C. MAC database instability

   D. Loop overload

4. When does the STP automatically reconfigure switch or bridge ports?

   A. When the network topology changes

   B. When the forward delay timer expires

   C. When an administrator specifies a recalculation

   D. When a new BPDU is not received within the forward delay

5. How does the STP provide a loop-free network?

   A. By placing all ports in the blocking state

   B. By placing all bridges in the blocking state

   C. By placing some ports in the blocking state

   D. By placing some bridges in the blocking state

6. Which port has the lowest-cost path from the nonroot bridge to the root bridge?

A. Root

B. Blocking

C. Designated

D. Nondesignated

7. With STP, how is the designated port selected on a segment?

A. Lowest-cost path to the root bridge

B. Highest-cost path to the root bridge

C. Lowest-cost path to the closest nonroot bridge

D. Highest-cost path to the closest nonroot bridge

8. Which statement is true of a port in the listening state?

A. It can check for BPDUs and populate the MAC table.

B. It can check for BPDUs but not populate its MAC table.

C. It can populate its MAC table but not forward user frames.

D. It can forward user frames but not populate its MAC table.

9. In which state is a nondesignated port, typically?

A. Blocking

B. Learning

C. Listening

D. Forwarding

10. In which state is a root port, typically?

A. Blocking

B. Learning

C. Listening

D. Forwarding

11. On which STP bridge are all ports designated ports?

A. Root bridge

B. Nonroot bridge

C. Bridge with the lowest priority

D. Bridge with the highest bridge ID

12. Which of the following is required for STP to detect a topology change?

    A. When a BPDU is not received within 2 seconds

    B. When a device does not respond to a handshake message

    C. When the max_age timer has expired without receiving a BPDU

    D. When a device does not respond quickly enough to a handshake request

13. Which switched network issue does RSTP address?

    A. Network security

    B. Size of the network

    C. Redundant topology

    D. Speed of convergence

14. What is the RSTP equivalent to the STP listening state?

    A. Blocking

    B. Listening

    C. Discarding

    D. Forwarding

15. With RSTP, which two port roles are included in the active topology?

    A. Root and alternate

    B. Root and designated

    C. Alternate and backup

    D. Designated and backup

16. What must a switch running spanning tree do when it is first turned on?

    A. Adjust its bridge priority value

    B. Learn the BIDs of all other switches in the network

    C. Request the MAC address of all connected hosts

    D. Select the BPDU with the greatest MAC address

    E. Adjust its bridge priority value to network conditions

17. A network engineer installs a device that has a reliability rating of 90 percent. What will the overall reliability be if the engineer adds a redundant device that also has a 90 percent reliability rating?

    A. 90 percent

    B. 92 percent

    C. 95 percent

D. 99 percent

E. 99.999 percent

F. 100 percent

Challenge Questions and Activities

These questions and activities are purposefully designed to be similar to the more complex styles of questions that you might see on the CCNA exam. Answers are listed in Appendix A.

1. Which of the following are problems associated with redundant switched Ethernet topologies? (Choose two.)

   A. Broadcast storms

   B. Routing loops

   C. Multiple frame copies

   D. Load balancing

   E. Incorrect frame addressing

   F. Unicast frame flooding

2. Which of the following ports discard data traffic during STP operation? (Choose three.)

   A. Blocking ports

   B. Disabled ports

   C. Designated ports

   D. Root ports

   E. Forwarding ports

   F. Listening ports

3. The network shown in Figure 7-17 is not running spanning-tree algorithm. What would be the result if the workstation sent an ARP request?

Figure 7-17 Switched Topology Without Spanning Tree

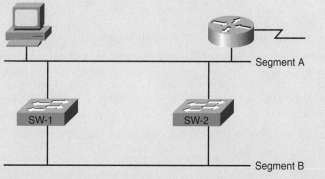
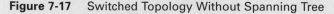

A. The frame will loop between SW-1 and SW-2 until the TTL field drops to zero.

B. The frame will loop until the TTL field reaches the default maximum value.

C. The frame will be prevented by the router from traveling the network.

D. The frame will continuously loop between SW-1 and SW-2.

4. List the IEEE 802.1d spanning-tree states in order.

A. Learning, listening, disabled, forwarding, blocking

B. Disabled, listening, learning, forwarding, blocking

C. Listening, learning, disabled, forwarding, blocking

D. Disabled, blocking, listening, learning, forwarding

5. Categorize each of the following options as either STP or RSTP.

A. IEEE 802.1d

B. Discarding ports

C. Some ports go to forwarding immediately

D. IEEE 802.1w

E. May take 50 seconds to converge

F. Blocking ports

G. Default: all ports must listen and learn before forwarding

H. Point-to-point, edge, and shared link types

6. How will spanning tree prevent switching loops in the network shown in Figure 7-18?

Figure 7-18   STP with Redundant Uplinks

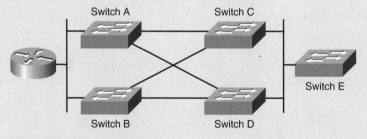

A. Traffic will be load-balanced between all switches.

B. A single switch will be elected as the root switch, and redundant paths to this switch will be blocked.

C. Two of the switches will be elected root bridges, thus blocking traffic between the other two switches.

D. Two of the switches will be elected designated switches, thus blocking traffic between the other two switches.

E. Either switch A or switch B will be elected as the root switch, and switch C or switch D will become the designated switch.

7. What will be the result of the spanning-tree root bridge selection process in the network shown in Figure 7-19?

Figure 7-19 Fundamental STP Operation

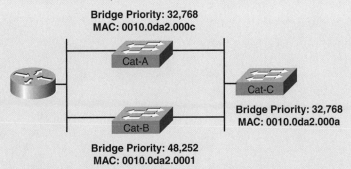

A. Cat-A will be the root bridge.

B. Cat-B will be the root bridge.

C. Cat-C will be the root bridge.

D. Cat-A and Cat-B will be the root bridges.

E. Cat-A and Cat-C will be the root bridges.

8. Why does a network engineer want to build redundancy into a network? (Choose two.)

A. Eliminate excessive personnel.

B. Provide multiple paths for connectivity in the event of link failure.

C. Provide multiple paths for concurrent data transfer.

D. Eliminate outages.

E. Eliminate multiple instances of spanning tree.

CHAPTER 8

Virtual LANs

Objectives

Upon completion of this chapter, you should be able to answer the following questions:

- What are the basic features of a VLAN?

- How do Catalyst switches support VLAN functionality?

- What are the VLAN membership modes?

- How do you change the name of a VLAN?

- How do you assign switch ports to a VLAN?

- How do you interpret the output of **show** commands to verify VLAN configuration?

- How do you modify a VLAN?

- How do you troubleshoot common VLAN problems?

Key Terms

This chapter uses the following key terms. You can find the definitions in the Glossary:

virtual LAN (VLAN)   *page 218*

inter-VLAN routing   *page 218*

Layer 3 switches   *page 218*

multilayer switches   *page 218*

application-specific integrated circuits (ASIC)
  page 220

trunk   *page 221*

VLAN Management Policy Server (VMPS)   *page 222*

CatOS   *page 222*

VLAN Trunking Protocol (VTP)   *page 223*

Cisco Discovery Protocol (CDP)   *page 223*

Dynamic Host Configuration Protocol (DHCP)
  page 232

An important feature of Ethernet switching is the ability to create virtual LANs (VLAN). A *VLAN* is a logical broadcast domain that can span multiple physical LAN segments. You can group VLANs by job functions or departments, regardless of the physical location of the users; however, modern VLAN implementations typically incorporate VLANs in a localized manner, spanning only one or two switches. Traffic between VLANs is restricted. Switches and bridges forward unicast, multicast, and broadcast traffic only on LAN segments that serve the VLAN to which the traffic belongs. Devices on a VLAN communicate only with devices that are on the same VLAN unless a router on the network is configured to enable *inter-VLAN routing*. It is common now for switches with Layer 3 functionality, sometimes called *Layer 3 switches or multilayer switches*, to perform inter-VLAN routing.

VLANs were traditionally used to increase overall network performance by logically grouping users and resources. Businesses often used VLANs as a way of ensuring that a particular set of users were logically grouped regardless of their physical location. Organizations used VLANs to group users in the same department. For example, users in the marketing department were placed in the Marketing VLAN, whereas users in the engineering department were placed in the Engineering VLAN. Although you can still see this type of VLAN implementation in switched networks, newer implementations often restrict a VLAN to one access layer switch and use distribution layer switches to handle traffic flow among access layer switches via inter-VLAN routing; this model is feasible because inter-VLAN routing via Layer 3 switching is now just as fast as traditional Layer 2 switching.

Properly designed and configured VLANs are powerful tools for network engineers, providing segmentation, flexibility, and security. VLANs simplify tasks when additions, moves, and changes to a network are necessary. VLANs improve network security and help control Layer 3 broadcasts.

VLAN Concepts

VLANs allow almost complete independence of the physical and logical topologies. Administrators can use VLANs to define groupings of workstations, even if they are separated by switches and on different LAN segments, as one broadcast domain. A VLAN is a logical group of network stations, services, and devices that is not restricted to a physical LAN segment, as illustrated in Figure 8-1.

VLANs facilitate easy administration of logical groups of stations and servers that can communicate as if they were on the same physical LAN segment. They also facilitate easier administration of moves, adds, and changes in members of these groups.

VLANs often logically segmented switched networks based on job functions, departments, or project teams, regardless of the physical location of users or physical connections to the network. All workstations and servers that a particular workgroup used shared the same VLAN, regardless of the physical connection or location.

Figure 8-1   Traditional VLAN Implementation

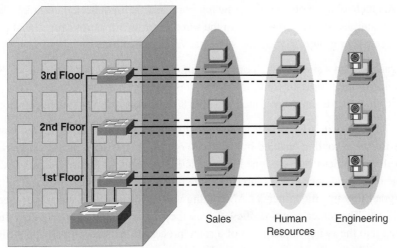

Sales   Human   Engineering
              Resources

You configure or reconfigure VLANs manually using the Catalyst switch CLI or via centralized network management software. You do not need to physically move or connect network equipment to configure VLANs. You can group switch ports into a single VLAN.

A workstation in a VLAN group is restricted to communicating with file servers in the same VLAN group (minus the intervention of a router). VLANs logically segment the network into different broadcast domains so that packets are only switched between ports that are assigned to the same VLAN.

The original purpose of VLANs was to supply segmentation services traditionally provided by physical routers in LAN configurations. Although there has been a dramatic shift in switched network design with respect to VLAN implementation, the original functionality has not changed.

VLANs offer segmentation, flexibility, and security. Routers in VLAN topologies provide broadcast filtering, security, and traffic management. Switches do not bridge traffic between VLANs, because this violates the integrity of the VLAN broadcast domain. You should route traffic only between VLANs.

Broadcast Domains with VLANs and Routers

A VLAN is a logical broadcast domain that can span multiple physical LAN segments; this logical broadcast domain is also an IP subnet. Within a switched network, VLANs offer segmentation and organizational flexibility. You can design a VLAN to establish stations that are segmented logically by functions, project teams, and applications without regard to the physical location of users. You can assign each switch port to only one VLAN, thereby adding a layer of security. Ports in a VLAN share broadcasts; ports in different VLANs do not share broadcasts. Containing broadcasts within a VLAN improves the overall performance of the network.

Within the switched internetwork, VLANs provide segmentation and organizational flexibility. Using VLAN technology, you can group switch ports and their connected users into logically defined communities, such as coworkers in the same department, a cross-functional product team, or diverse user groups sharing the same network application.

A VLAN can exist on a single switch or span multiple switches. VLANs can include stations in a single building or multiple-building infrastructures. VLANs can also connect across WANs using service provider technologies such as IEEE 802.1Q-in-Q VLAN Tag Termination.

Routing or Layer 3 switching enables data traffic to flow between VLANs; Layer 3 switching is basically wire-speed routing enabled by dedicated *application-specific integrated circuits (ASIC)*. ASICs are microchips designed for a specific function. In Figure 8-2, a VLAN is created with one router and one switch. Three separate broadcast domains exist. In the figure, you see the original way in which inter-VLAN routing was handled, with a separate router interface for each VLAN. The router routes traffic between the VLANs; in a Layer 3 switch, the router is incorporated into the switch in the form of a route processor, with accompanying ASICs. A router is required for traffic to flow between VLANs.

Figure 8-2   Inter-VLAN Routing Requires a Router

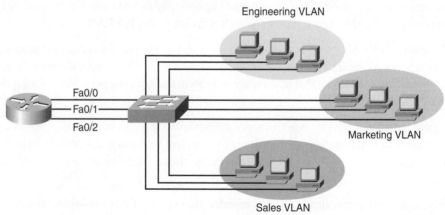

The switch in Figure 8-2 forwards frames to the router interfaces if certain circumstances exist:

- If the frame is a broadcast frame

- If the destination of the frame is one of the MAC addresses on the router

If workstation 1 on the Engineering VLAN wants to send frames to workstation 2 on the Sales VLAN, it sends the frames to the Fa0/0 MAC address of the router. Routing occurs via the IP address on the Fa0/0 router interface for the Engineering VLAN.

If workstation 1 on the Engineering VLAN wants to send a frame to workstation 3 on the same VLAN, the destination MAC address of the frame is that of workstation 3.

VLAN implementation on a switch causes certain actions to occur:

- The switch maintains a separate bridging table for each VLAN.

- If the frame comes in on a port in VLAN 1, the switch searches the bridging table for VLAN 1.

- When the frame is received, the switch adds the source address to the bridging table if it is currently unknown.

- The destination is checked so that a forwarding decision can be made.

- For learning and forwarding, the search is made against the address table for that VLAN only.

If the destination IP address of an IP packet is on a different VLAN (subnet), a router or Layer 3 switch must route the packet.

VLAN Operation

A Cisco Catalyst switch operates in a network like a traditional bridge. Each VLAN that is configured on the switch implements address learning, forwarding and filtering decisions, and loop avoidance mechanisms as if the VLAN were a separate physical bridge.

Internally, the Catalyst switch implements VLANs by restricting data forwarding to destination ports that are in the same VLAN as originating ports. That is, when a frame arrives on a switch port, the Catalyst must retransmit the frame only to ports that belong to the same VLAN. The implication is that a VLAN that is operating on a Catalyst switch limits transmission of unicast, multicast, and broadcast traffic. Traffic originating from a particular VLAN only floods other ports that are in that VLAN.

Normally, a port carries traffic only for the single VLAN to which it belongs. For a VLAN to span across multiple switches, a *trunk* is required to connect two switches, as displayed in Figure 8-3.

Figure 8-3   Trunk Carrying Traffic for Three VLANs over the Same Link

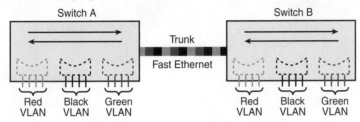

A trunk can carry traffic for multiple VLANs. VLAN operations are summarized as follows:

- Each logical VLAN is like a separate physical bridge.

- VLANs can span across multiple switches.

- Trunks carry traffic for multiple VLANs.

- Trunks use special encapsulation to distinguish between different VLANs.

Chapter 9, "VLAN Trunking Protocol," explores VLAN trunks in detail.

Switch ports belonging to a VLAN are configured with a membership mode that determines to which VLAN they belong. The following are the VLAN membership modes to which Catalyst switch ports can belong:

- **Static**—An administrator statically configures the assignment of VLANs to ports.

- **Dynamic**—The Catalyst switches support dynamic VLANs by using a *VLAN Management Policy Server (VMPS)*, which we should point out is not a widely deployed technology. The VMPS can be a Catalyst switch running the *CatOS* operating system. The 2950 series cannot operate as the VMPS. The VMPS contains a database that maps MAC addresses to VLAN assignments. When a frame arrives on a dynamic port at the Catalyst access switch, the Catalyst switch queries the VMPS for the VLAN assignment based on the source MAC address of the arriving frame.

Figure 8-4 illustrates these VLAN membership modes.

Figure 8-4   Static and Dynamic VLAN Membership Modes

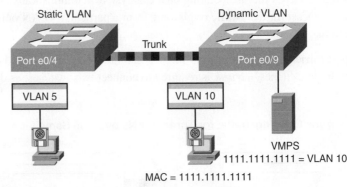

A dynamic port can belong to only one VLAN at a time. Multiple hosts can be active on a dynamic port only if they all belong to the same VLAN. The use of dynamic port assignments with VMPS appears to be losing support as a recommended solution.

VLAN Configuration

It is useful to know some preliminary information prior to configuring VLANs on Catalyst switches.

Before you create VLANs, you must decide whether to use the optional *VLAN Trunking Protocol (VTP)* to maintain global VLAN configuration information for your network. Chapter 9, "VLAN Trunking Protocol," explores VTP. Here we focus on basic VLAN configuration.

Most Catalyst desktop switches support a maximum of 64 active VLANs. Catalyst 2950 series switches running the standard image can support up to 250 VLANs; those running support up to 4094 VLANs. On Catalyst switches, the default configuration is for a separate instance of spanning tree to run on each VLAN.

Catalyst switches have a factory default configuration such that various default VLANs are pre-configured to support various media and protocol types. The default Ethernet VLAN is VLAN 1. *Cisco Discovery Protocol (CDP)* and VTP advertisements are sent on VLAN 1. CDP is a proprietary Layer 2 protocol used to discover basic information about neighboring Cisco devices.

For you to be able to communicate with the Catalyst switch remotely for management purposes, the switch must have an IP address. This IP address must be in the management VLAN, which by default is VLAN 1. Before you can create a VLAN, the switch must be in VTP server mode or VTP transparent mode. The default mode on a Catalyst switch is VTP server mode. Chapter 9 explores VTP modes.

Configuring Static VLANs

By far, the most common method of configuring VLANs is to manually assign port-to-VLAN mappings on each switch. Here, we discuss the methods of adding VLANs, naming VLANs, and assigning ports to VLANs.

One pervasive switch configuration requirement is the creation of VLANs. The **vlan** command in global configuration mode is used for this purpose. Example 8-1 illustrates the addition of

Example 8-1 Adding a VLAN

```
Switch#configure terminal
Switch(config)#vlan 10
Switch(config-vlan)#name VLAN10
Switch(config-vlan)#?
VLAN configuration commands:
  are       Maximum number of All Route Explorer hops for this VLAN (or zero
            if none specified)
  backupcrf Backup CRF mode of the VLAN
  bridge    Bridging characteristics of the VLAN
  exit      Apply changes, bump revision number, and exit mode
  media     Media type of the VLAN
  mtu       VLAN Maximum Transmission Unit
  name      Ascii name of the VLAN
  no        Negate a command or set its defaults
  parent    ID number of the Parent VLAN of FDDI or Token Ring type VLANs
  ring      Ring number of FDDI or Token Ring type VLANs
  said      IEEE 802.10 SAID
  shutdown  Shutdown VLAN switching
  state     Operational state of the VLAN
  ste       Maximumn number of Spanning Tree Explorer hops for this VLAN (or
            zero if none specified)
  stp       Spanning tree characteristics of the VLAN
  tb-vlan1  ID number of the first translational VLAN for this VLAN (or zero
            if none)
  tb-vlan2  ID number of the second translational VLAN for this VLAN (or zero
            if none)
```

VLAN 10 on a Catalyst 2950 switch.

Table 8-1 lists the commands to use when adding a VLAN.

Table 8-1 Adding a VLAN

Command/Variable	Description
vlan *vlan-id*	Configures the ID of the VLAN to be added and configured. For *vlan-id*, the range is 1 to 4094 when the enhanced software image is installed and 1 to 1005 when the standard software image is installed. Do not enter leading zeros. You can enter a single VLAN ID, a series of VLAN IDs separated by commas, or a range of VLAN IDs separated by hyphens.
name *vlan-name*	(Optional) Specifies the VLAN name, which is an ASCII string from 1 to 32 characters that must be unique within the administrative domain.

By default, a switch is in VTP server mode so that you can add, change, or delete VLANs. If the switch is set to VTP client mode, you cannot add, change, or delete VLANs.

For the Catalyst 2950 series switch, use the **vlan** global configuration command to enter the config-vlan configuration mode. Use the **no** form of this command to delete the VLAN.

In config-vlan mode, you can name the VLAN. You can see other options in config-vlan mode, such as spanning-tree options, by entering the **?** command.

Each VLAN has a unique, four-digit ID that is a number from 0001 to 1005. To add a VLAN to the VLAN database, assign a number and name to the VLAN. VLAN 1 (including VLAN1002, VLAN1003, VLAN1004, and VLAN1005) is the factory-default VLAN.

To add an Ethernet VLAN, you must specify at least a VLAN number. If you do not enter a name for the VLAN, the default is to append the VLAN number to the word VLAN. For example, VLAN0004 would be the default name for VLAN 4 if you do not specify a name.

To modify an existing VLAN name or number, use the same command syntax that you use to add a VLAN. In Example 8-2, the VLAN name for VLAN 10 is changed to SwitchLab10.

Example 8-2   Changing the Name of a VLAN

```
Switch#configure terminal
Switch(config)#vlan 10
Switch(config-vlan)#name SwitchLab10
```

After you create a VLAN, you can manually assign a port or a number of ports to it. A port can belong to only one VLAN at a time. When you assign a switch port to a VLAN using this method, it is known as a static-access port.

On a Catalyst 2950 series switch, configure the VLAN port assignment from the interface configuration mode using the **switchport access** command. Use the **vlan** *vlan-number* option to set static-access membership. Use the **dynamic** option to have a VMPS server control and assign the VLAN. Example 8-3 shows a sample of VLAN port assignment.

Example 8-3   Assigning Ports to a VLAN

```
Switch#configure terminal
Switch(config)#interface fastethernet 0/2
Switch(config-if)#switchport access vlan ?
  <1-4094>  VLAN ID of the VLAN when this port is in access mode
  dynamic   When in access mode, this interfaces VLAN is controlled by VMPS
Switch(config-if)#switchport access vlan
Switch(config-if)#switchport access vlan 10
Switch(config-if)#end
Switch#show vlan
```

continues

Example 8-3   Assigning Ports to a VLAN   *(continued)*

```
VLAN Name                             Status   Ports
___ _____   ____. _____.
1    default                          active   Fa0/1, Fa0/3, Fa0/4, Fa0/5
                                               Fa0/6, Fa0/7, Fa0/8, Fa0/9
                                               Fa0/10, Fa0/11, Fa0/12, Gi0/1
                                               Gi0/2
10   VLAN10                           active   Fa0/2
1002 fddi-default                     active
1003 token-ring-default               active
1004 fddinet-default                  active
1005 trnet-default                    active


VLAN Type  SAID   MTU   Parent RingNo BridgeNo Stp  BrdgMode Trans1 Trans2
___ ___. _____ __. ___ ___ ____ __ ____ ___ ___
1    enet  100001 1500  -      -      -        -    -        0      0
10   enet  100010 1500  -      -      -        -    -        0      0
1002 fddi  101002 1500  -      -      -        -    -        0      0
1003 tr    101003 1500  -      -      -        -    -        0      0
1004 fdnet 101004 1500  -      -      -        ieee -        0      0
1005 trnet 101005 1500  -      -      -        ibm  -        0      0
```

By default, all ports are members of VLAN 1.

Lab 8.2.3   Configuring Static VLANs

In this lab, you create static VLANs.

Verifying VLAN Configuration

On a Catalyst 2950 series switch, use the **show vtp status** command to verify a recent configuration change or to view the VTP configuration information. The command output displays the VTP mode. In Example 8-4, the switch is in server mode. Chapter 9 discusses detailed VTP information. Recall that the switch must be in server or transparent mode to add, change, or delete VLANs.

Example 8-4   Displaying VTP Status

```
Switch#show vtp status
VTP Version                    : 2
Configuration Revision         : 4
Maximum VLANs supported locally : 250
Number of existing VLANs       : 6
VTP Operating Mode             : Server
VTP Domain Name                :
VTP Pruning Mode               : Disabled
VTP V2 Mode                    : Disabled
VTP Traps Generation           : Disabled
MD5 digest                     : 0x97 0x59 0xCE 0x69 0x3E 0xD4 0x91 0xD5
Configuration last modified by 10.10.10.50 at 11-9-93 05:33:42
Local updater ID is 10.10.10.50 on interface Vl1
     (lowest numbered VLAN interface found)
```

To verify a trunk configuration on a Catalyst 2950 series switch, use the **show interfaces** *interfaces* **switchport** and the **show interfaces** *interfaces* **trunk** command to display the trunk parameters and VLAN information of the port. Chapter 9 discusses detailed information on trunking. Example 8-5 illustrates these commands. The Catalyst 2950 series switch supports trunking on each of its Fast Ethernet and Gigabit Ethernet ports.

Example 8-5   Verifying VLAN Trunking Information

```
Switch#show interfaces ?
  FastEthernet     FastEthernet IEEE 802.3
  GE-WAN           GigabitEthernetWAN IEEE 802.3z
  GigabitEthernet  GigabitEthernet IEEE 802.3z
  Null             Null interface
  Vlan             Catalyst Vlans
<output omitted>
  stats            Show interface packets & octets, in & out, by switching path
  status           Show interface line status
  switchport       Show interface switchport information
  trunk            Show interface trunk information
  |                Output modifiers
  <cr>
Switch#show interfaces gigabitethernet0/1 switchport
Name: Gi0/1
Switchport:Enabled
Administrative Mode:dynamic desirable
Operational Mode:static access
Administrative Trunking Encapsulation:negotiate
```

continues

Example 8-5   Verifying VLAN Trunking Information   *(continued)*

```
Negotiation of Trunking:On
Access Mode VLAN:1 (default)
Trunking Native Mode VLAN:1 (default)
Voice VLAN:none
Administrative private-vlan host-association:none
Administrative private-vlan mapping:none
Operational private-vlan:none
Trunking VLANs Enabled:ALL
Pruning VLANs Enabled:2-1001
Capture Mode: Disabled
Capture VLANs Allowed:ALL

Protected:true
Unknown unicast blocked:disabled
Unknown multicast blocked:disabled

Voice VLAN:none (Inactive)
Appliance trust:none
Switch#show interfaces fastethernet0/1 trunk

Port        Mode            Encapsulation  Status          Native vlan
Fa0/1       desirable       802.1q         trunking        1

Port        Vlans allowed on trunk
Fa0/1       1-4094

Port        Vlans allowed and active in management domain
Fa0/1       1,4,196,306

Port        Vlans in spanning tree forwarding state and not pruned
Fa0/1       1,306
```

After you have configured the VLAN, you should validate its parameters. Use the **show vlan id** *vlan-id* or the **show vlan name** *vlan-name* command to display information about a particular VLAN. These commands are illustrated in Example 8-6.

Example 8-6   Validating VLAN Parameters

```
Switch#show vlan ?
  brief     VTP all VLAN status in brief
  id        VTP VLAN status by VLAN id
  internal  VLAN internal usage
  name      VTP VLAN status by VLAN name
  summary   VLAN summary information
```

Example 8-6   Validating VLAN Parameters   *(continued)*

```
|         Output modifiers
  <cr>

Switch#show vlan id 10

VLAN Name                             Status    Ports
-- -------------------- ------- ------------------.

10   VLAN10                           active    Fa0/2

VLAN Type  SAID      MTU   Parent RingNo BridgeNo Stp  BrdgMode Trans1 Trans2
-- ---. ------ --. --- --- ---- -- ---- --- ---

10   enet  100010    1500  -      .      .       -    .        0      0
Switch#show vlan name VLAN10

VLAN Name                             Status    Ports
-- -------------------- ------. ------------------.

10   VLAN10                           active    Fa0/2

VLAN Type  SAID      MTU   Parent RingNo BridgeNo Stp  BrdgMode Trans1 Trans2
-- ---. ------ --. --- --- ---- -- ---- --- ---

10   enet  100010    1500  -      .      .       -    .        0      0
```

Use the **show vlan brief** command to display one line for each VLAN that shows the VLAN
name, the status, and the switch ports. The output displays the VLAN assignment and membership type for all switch ports. Example 8-7 displays output from the **show vlan brief** command.

Example 8-7   Verifying VLAN Information with **show vlan brief**

```
Switch#show vlan brief

VLAN Name                             Status    Ports
-- -------------------- ------. ------------------.

1    default                          active    Fa0/1, Fa0/3, Fa0/4, Fa0/5
                                                Fa0/6, Fa0/7, Fa0/8, Fa0/9
                                                Fa0/10, Fa0/11, Fa0/12, Gi0/1
                                                Gi0/2
10   VLAN10                           active    Fa0/2
1002 fddi-default                     active
1003 token-ring-default               active
1004 fddinet-default                  active
1005 trnet-default                    active
```

Use the **show vlan** command to display information on all configured VLANs. This command displays the switch ports assigned to each VLAN. Other VLAN parameters that are displayed include the type (the default is Ethernet); the security association ID (SAID), used for the FDDI trunk; the MTU (the default is 1500 for Ethernet VLAN); the STP in use; and other parameters used for Token Ring or FDDI VLANs. Example 8-8 displays sample output from the **show vlan** command.

Example 8-8   Verifying VLAN Information with show vlan

```
Switch#show vlan

VLAN Name                             Status    Ports
---- -------------------------------- --------- -------------------------------
1    default                          active    Fa0/1, Fa0/3, Fa0/4, Fa0/5
                                                Fa0/6, Fa0/7, Fa0/8, Fa0/9
                                                Fa0/10, Fa0/11, Fa0/12, Gi0/1
                                                Gi0/2
10   VLAN10                           active    Fa0/2
1002 fddi-default                     active
1003 token-ring-default               active
1004 fddinet-default                  active
1005 trnet-default                    active


VLAN Type  SAID   MTU    Parent RingNo BridgeNo Stp  BrdgMode Trans1 Trans2
---- ----- ------ ------ ------ ------ -------- ---- -------- ------ ------
1    enet  100001 1500   -      -      -        -    -        0      0
10   enet  100010 1500   -      -      -        -    -        0      0
1002 fddi  101002 1500   -      -      -        -    -        0      0
1003 tr    101003 1500   -      -      -        -    -        0      0
1004 fdnet 101004 1500   -      -      -        ieee -        0      0
1005 trnet 101005 1500   -      -      -        ibm  -        0      0
```

Again, to reiterate an important **show** command on Catalyst switches, use the **show interfaces** *interfaces* **switchport** command to display the VLAN information for a particular interface. Example 8-9 shows additional sample output for this command.

On the Catalyst 2950 series switch, use the **show spanning-tree vlan** command to display the STP configuration for a particular VLAN.

Example 8-10 shows spanning-tree information for VLAN 1 on a Catalyst 2950 series switch. The switch is the root bridge for VLAN 1. Therefore, all active ports are designated ports for VLAN 1. The bridge priority is 32769, with a MAC address of 0009.e8a1.5880. The switch is running the IEEE 802.1d STP.

Example 8-9 Verifying VLAN Information for a Particular Interface

```
Switch#show interfaces f0/2 switchport
Name: Fa0/2
Switchport: Enabled
Administrative Mode: dynamic desirable
Operational Mode: down
Administrative Trunking Encapsulation: dot1q
Negotiation of Trunking: On
Access Mode VLAN: 10 (VLAN10)
Trunking Native Mode VLAN: 1 (default)
Trunking VLANs Enabled: ALL
Pruning VLANs Enabled: 2-1001


Protected: false


Voice VLAN: none (Inactive)
Appliance trust: none
```

Example 8-10 Verifying Spanning Tree Information for a Particular VLAN

```
Switch#show spanning-tree ?
  active             Report on active interfaces only
  backbonefast       Show spanning tree backbonefast status
  blockedports       Show blocked ports
  bridge             Status and configuration of this bridge
  detail             Detailed information
  inconsistentports  Show inconsistent ports
  interface          Spanning Tree interface status and configuration
  mst                Multiple spanning trees
  pathcost           Show Spanning pathcost options
  root               Status and configuration of the root bridge
  summary            Summary of port states
  uplinkfast         Show spanning tree uplinkfast status
  vlan               VLAN Switch Spanning Trees
  |                  Output modifiers
  <cr>
Switch#show spanning-tree vlan ?
  <1-4094>  VLAN id

Switch#show spanning-tree vlan 1


VLAN0001
  Spanning tree enabled protocol ieee
  Root ID    Priority    32769
             Address     0009.e8a1.5880
```

Example 8-10   Verifying Spanning Tree Information for a Particular VLAN   *(continued)*

```
                   This bridge is the root
                   Hello Time   2 sec  Max Age 20 sec  Forward Delay 15 sec

    Bridge ID  Priority    32769  (priority 32768 sys-id-ext 1)
                   Address       0009.e8a1.5880
                   Hello Time   2 sec  Max Age 20 sec  Forward Delay 15 sec
                   Aging Time 300


Interface        Port ID                        Designated                Port ID
Name             Prio.Nbr      Cost Sts      Cost Bridge ID              Prio.Nbr
--------------  ----  ----- --- ----- ------------------ ----
Fa0/1            128.1          19 FWD          0 32769 0009.e8a1.5880 128.1
Fa0/5            128.5          19 FWD          0 32769 0009.e8a1.5880 128.5
Fa0/9            128.9          19 FWD          0 32769 0009.e8a1.5880 128.9
Fa0/12           128.12         19 FWD          0 32769 0009.e8a1.5880 128.12
Gi0/2            128.14          4 FWD          0 32769 0009.e8a1.5880 128.14
```

Recall that a Catalyst switch can support a separate spanning tree for each VLAN, allowing for load balancing between switches. For example, one switch can be the root for VLAN 1, and another switch can be the root for VLAN 2. (This idea is explained in great detail in *CCNP 3: Multilayer Switching Companion Guide*, Second Edition, from Cisco Press.)

 Lab 8.2.4   Verifying VLAN Configurations

In this lab, you create and name two VLANs, assign ports, and move hosts.

Adding, Changing, and Deleting VLANs

To add, change, or delete VLANs, put the switch in VTP server or transparent mode. When you make VLAN changes from a switch that is in VTP server mode, the change is automatically propagated to other switches in the VTP domain. VLAN changes made from a switch in VTP transparent mode impact the local switch only; changes are not propagated to the domain. Chapter 9 discusses these VTP considerations in detail.

After you create a new VLAN (refer to Example 8-1), be sure to make the necessary changes to VLAN port assignments (refer to Example 8-3). Separate VLANs typically imply separate IP networks. Be sure to plan the new IP addressing scheme and its deployment to stations before moving users to the new VLAN. Separate VLANs also require inter-VLAN routing so that users in the new VLAN can communicate with other VLANs. Inter-VLAN routing consists of setting up the appropriate IP parameters and services, including default gateway and *Dynamic Host Configuration Protocol (DHCP)*. DHCP is a protocol used for the purpose of dynamically assigning IP addresses to hosts.

To modify VLAN attributes, such as VLAN name, use the **vlan** *vlan-id* global configuration command, as in Example 8-1. You cannot change the VLAN number. To use a different VLAN number, create a new VLAN using a new number, and then reassign all ports to this VLAN.

To move a port into a different VLAN, use the same commands that you used to make the original assignments. For the Catalyst 2950 series switch, use the **switchport access** interface configuration command to perform this function, as illustrated in Example 8-3.

You do not need to remove a port from a VLAN to make this change. After you reassign a port to a new VLAN, that port is automatically removed from its previous VLAN.

When you delete a VLAN from a switch that is in VTP server mode, the VLAN is removed from all switches in the VTP domain. When you delete a VLAN from a switch that is in VTP transparent mode, the VLAN is deleted on that specific switch only. Use the **no vlan** *vlan-id* command to remove a VLAN that is in VLAN configuration mode.

Before deleting a VLAN, be sure to reassign all member ports to a different VLAN. If you fail to move a port to an active VLAN, it will be unable to communicate with other stations.

To reassign a port to the default VLAN (VLAN 1), use the **no switchport access vlan** command in interface configuration mode.

Lab 8.2.6   Deleting VLAN Configurations

The purpose of this exercise is to delete VLAN settings.

Troubleshooting VLANs

VLANs are now common in campus networks. They give network engineers flexibility in designing and implementing networks. VLANs also enable broadcast containment, security, and geographically disparate communities of interest. However, as with basic LAN switching, problems can occur when you implement VLANs. This section explores some of the more common problems that can occur with VLANs and provides several tools and techniques for troubleshooting.

Figure 8-5 illustrates the general troubleshooting methodology for switched LANs. VLAN troubleshooting is the last step of the switched LAN troubleshooting process.

Misconfiguration of a VLAN is one of the most common errors in switched networks. Recognizing the symptoms of the problem and identifying an action plan can help you identify and solve the problem.

Figure 8-5   Switched LAN Troubleshooting Process

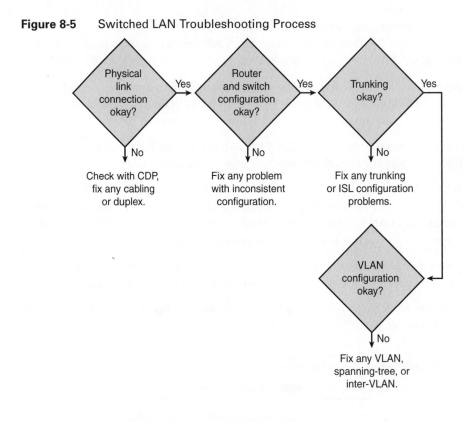

Troubleshooting VLAN Problems

This section examines VLAN problems that can occur with a router or switch.

When you are faced with poor throughput problems, check to see what type of errors exist. The adapter card might be bad. Combinations of FCS and alignment errors and runts generally point to a duplex mismatch. The usual culprit is the auto-negotiation between devices or a mismatched setting between the two sides of a link. Consider these questions:

- Is the problem on the local side or the remote side of the link?

- What path is the packet taking? Is it going across trunks or non-trunks to other switches?

The answers to these questions point the network engineer in the direction of a solution for the particular problem at hand.

If you see that the number of collisions in output from a **show interfaces** command is increasing rapidly, the problem might be an overloaded link or a duplex mismatch.

Some believe that switched Ethernet eliminates collisions. In truth, switches minimize the number of collisions, but if they are running in half-duplex mode, the collisions will still occur because two devices can attempt to communicate at the same time.

An example of collisions in half-duplex mode is a news server that has many clients attempting to communicate at the same time. The traffic comes through the router and switch to the directly connected server. At the same time, the server attempts to communicate back to these clients. But as the server is answering one client, another client sends a request. A collision is possible as a result. The only cure for collisions on Ethernet is to run in full-duplex mode (which is almost always done nowadays).

Table 8-2 summarizes VLAN-related problems and suggested solutions.

Table 8-2   VLAN Problems and Solutions

Problem Facts	Possible Problem Causes and Action Plans
Performance on the VLAN is slow or unreliable.	■ Bad adapter in a device. Check hardware. ■ Incorrect full-duplex or half-duplex Ethernet settings. ■ Change duplex setting as appropriate. ■ Cabling problem. Check connected LED; check for correct cable and proper attachment; and check cable length to be sure it does not exceed maximum cable distance.
Attached terminal or modem connection cannot communicate with router or switch.	■ Misconfigured terminal and console port. Check that the baud rate and character format match. ■ Check to see if a default route is needed on the router to reach a switch on a different IP subnet. If so, add the route.
Local VLAN devices cannot communicate with remote devices on a VLAN beyond the router.	■ Misconfigured IP addressing or mask. Check using CDP and **show interface** commands. ■ Default gateway not specified or incorrect. Check router, switch, servers, and clients. ■ VLAN misconfigured. Check port assignments. Eliminate unnecessary connections between VLANs if a port belongs to multiple VLANs. ■ VLAN inconsistency problem. Make sure the VLANs match on both sides of a trunk. See Chapter 9. ■ Trunking problem. Make sure that there is proper trunking, that VLAN 1 is being used, and that no valid VTP server information update has occurred. See Chapter 9.

The next section looks at some specific troubleshooting scenarios involving VLANs.

VLAN Troubleshooting Scenarios

This section explores three VLAN-related troubleshooting scenarios:

- One device cannot communicate with another device.

- A device cannot establish a connection across a trunk link.

- VTP is not updating the configuration on other switches when the VLAN configuration changes.

Scenario 1: One Device Cannot Communicate with Another Device

The following are some suggested solutions when one device cannot communicate with another device:

- Make sure that the IP address, subnet mask, and VLAN membership of the switch interface is correct by using the **show interfaces** command. To prevent conflicts, ensure that the interfaces are configured with IP addresses and subnet masks in different subnets.

- If the host is in the same subnet as the switch interface, make sure that the switch interface and the switch port to which the host is connected are assigned to the same VLAN. Use the **show interfaces** and **show vlan** commands.

- If the host is in a different subnet, ensure that the default gateway (default route) on the switch is configured with the address of a router in the same subnet as the switch interface. Use the **show ip route** command.

- Check the spanning-tree state on the port using the **show spanning-tree** interface configuration command. If the port is in listening or learning mode, wait until the port is in forwarding mode and try to connect to the host again.

- Check that the speed and duplex settings on the host and the appropriate switch ports are correct. Use the **show interfaces** command.

- If the connected device is an end station, do the following:

  — Enable spanning-tree PortFast on the port. Use the **spanning-tree portfast** interface configuration command. PortFast places the port in forwarding mode immediately, bypassing listening and learning modes. (Do not use this feature for connections to non–end station devices.)

  — Disable trunking on the port. Use the **no switchport mode trunk** interface command.

  — Disable channeling on the port. Use the **no channel-group** interface configuration command.

- Make sure that the switch is learning the MAC address of the host. Use the **show mac-address-table dynamic** command.

Scenario 2: A Device Cannot Establish a Connection Across a Trunk Link

Chapter 9 explores VLAN trunking in detail. The following are some suggested solutions when a device cannot establish a connection across a trunk link:

- Make sure that the trunking mode that is configured on both ends of the link is valid. The trunking mode should be on or desirable on one end and on, desirable, or auto on the other end. Use the **show interfaces trunk** command.

- Make sure that the trunk encapsulation type that is configured on both ends of the link is valid. Use the **show interfaces** *interface-id* [**switchport** | **trunk**] command.

- On IEEE 802.1Q trunks, check that the native VLAN is the same on both ends of the trunk. Use the **show interfaces** *interface-id* [**switchport** | **trunk**] command.

Scenario 3: VTP Is Not Updating the Configuration on Other Switches When the VLAN Configuration Changes

Chapter 9 explores VTP in detail. The following are some suggested solutions when VTP is not updating the configuration on other switches when the VLAN configuration changes:

- Make sure that the switches are connected through trunk links. VTP updates are exchanged only over trunk links. Use the **show interfaces trunk** command.

- Ensure that the VTP domain name is the same on the appropriate switches. VTP updates are exchanged only between switches in the same VTP domain. Use the **show vtp status** command.

- Check to see if the switch is in VTP transparent mode. Only switches in VTP server or VTP client mode update their VLAN configuration based on VTP updates from other switches. Use the **show vtp status** command.

- If you are using VTP passwords, you must configure the same password on all switches in the VTP domain. To change or set the VTP password, use the **vtp password** global configuration command. To clear an existing VTP password, use the **no vtp password** global configuration command. You will examine VTP passwords in Chapter 9.

This completes the analysis of VLAN troubleshooting.

Chapter Summary

A VLAN is a set of network services, comprising a single broadcast domain, and not restricted to a physical segment or LAN switch. You configure or reconfigure VLANs through software that makes it unnecessary to physically connect or move cables and equipment. VLANs provide segmentation, flexibility, and security. Routers in VLAN topologies provide broadcast filtering, security, and traffic management. You should only route traffic between VLANs. Switches cannot bridge traffic between VLANs because this violates the integrity of the VLAN broadcast domain.

The primary benefit of VLANs is that they permit the network engineer to organize the LAN logically instead of physically. This includes the ability to move workstations on the LAN, add workstations to the LAN, change the LAN configuration, control network traffic, and enhance security via segmentation.

A VLAN is a broadcast domain that one or more switches create. You use VLANs to create broadcast domains and improve the overall performance of the network. Implementing VLANs on a switch causes the switch to maintain a separate bridging table for each VLAN. If the frame comes in on a port in VLAN 1, the switch searches the bridging table for VLAN 1. When the switch receives the frame, it adds the source address to the bridging table if it is currently unknown. The switch then checks the destination so that it can make a forwarding decision. For learning and forwarding, the search is made against the address table for that VLAN only.

Static VLANs consist of ports on a switch that you manually assign to a VLAN by using a VLAN management application or via the switch operating system. These ports maintain their assigned VLAN configuration until you change them manually. Dynamic VLANs do not rely on ports that you assign to a specific VLAN.

Use the **show vtp status**, **show vlan**, **show vlan brief**, **show vlan id** *vlan-id*, **show vlan name** *vlan-name*, **show interfaces switchport**, **show interfaces trunk**, and **show spanning-tree vlan** commands to verify VLAN configuration.

You use a systematic approach to troubleshoot issues on a VLAN. To isolate a problem, first check the physical indications, such as LED status, and then proceed to Layer 2 and Layer 3 problem isolation.

Check Your Understanding

Complete all the review questions listed here to test your understanding of the topics and concepts in this chapter. Answers are listed in Appendix A, "Answers to Check Your Understanding and Challenge Questions and Activities."

1. Which feature is required for a VLAN to span two switches?

   A. A trunk to connect the switches

   B. A router to connect the switches

   C. A bridge to connect the switches

   D. A VLAN configured between the switches

2. What does a VLAN Membership Policy Server (VMPS) map to VLAN assignments?

   A. Host IDs

   B. Usernames

   C. IP addresses

   D. MAC addresses

3. What is the default VTP mode on a Catalyst switch?

   A. Off

   B. Client

   C. Server

   D. Transparent

4. What is the logical sequence for configuring a Catalyst switch port to be in VLAN 3?

   A. Create the VLAN, and then assign the port to the VLAN.

   B. Assign the port to the VLAN; all VLANs are created by default.

   C. Create the VLAN, assign ports to it, and then configure VTP.

   D. Assign the port to the VLAN; this also creates the VLAN with a default name.

5. How many VLANs can a port belong to at one time?

   A. Only one VLAN

   B. Up to 64 VLANs

   C. Up to 128 VLANs

   D. One or two VLANs

6. Which of the following best describes what the **show vlan** command displays?

   A. VTP domain parameters

   B. VMPS server configuration parameters

   C. The ports that are members of each VLAN

   D. Names of the VLANs and the ports assigned to them

7. Which command displays the spanning-tree configuration status of the ports on a Catalyst 2950 series switch?

   A. **show vlan**

   B. **show trunk**

   C. **show spanning-tree**

   D. **show spantree config**

8. How do VLANs help the network administrator organize the network? (Choose three.)

   A. They allow the administrator to change LAN configurations easily.

   B. They allow the administrator to place enterprise servers anywhere in the network.

   C. They allow the administrator to add or move workstations easily.

   D. VLANs allow for scalability by allowing an infinite number of subnets.

   E. They allow the administrator to group users by function rather than by location.

   F. VLANs eliminate the need for cumbersome and perplexing IP subnet schemes.

9. Which of the following can assist a network engineer in troubleshooting a problem on a switched network? (Choose two.)

   A. Start with the network as a whole and work inward.

   B. Determine if the problem is isolated or recurring.

   C. Check the link to the router and the IP addressing scheme.

   D. Check the switchport LED status for physical indications of problems.

   E. Verify that 80 percent of network traffic is flowing over the campus backbone.

10. Which of the following are characteristics of static VLANs? (Choose three.)

   A. Each port is associated with a specific VLAN.

   B. Ports work out their own configuration.

   C. Manual configuration of port assignments is required.

   D. Less administrative overhead is involved when users are moved.

   E. Static VLANs require administrator interaction when users are moved.

   F. The configuration is based on a database.

Challenge Questions and Activities

These questions and activities are purposefully designed to be similar to the more complex styles of questions you might see on the CCNA exam. Answers are listed in Appendix A.

1. If a device on a VLAN cannot establish a connection across a trunk link, which three actions should you take to resolve the problem? (Choose three.)

   A. Make sure that the trunking mode that is configured on both ends of the link is valid.

   B. Make sure that the trunk encapsulation type that is configured on both ends of the link is valid.

   C. Make sure that the port is connected and is not receiving physical-layer (alignment or FCS) errors.

   D. Make sure that the port is trunking and that the allowed VLAN list permits the desired VLAN range to pass through.

   E. If the host is on the same subnet as the switch interface, make sure that the switch interface and the switch port to which the host is connected are assigned to the same VLAN.

2. How many broadcast domains exist in the scenario presented in Figure 8-6?

Figure 8-6   VLANs and Broadcast Domains

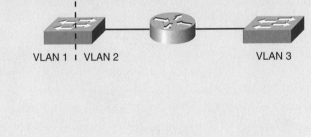

VLAN 1 ı VLAN 2   VLAN 3

   A. 1

   B. 2

   C. 3

   D. 4

   E. 5

VLAN Trunking Protocol

Objectives

Upon completion of this chapter, you should be able to answer the following questions:

- What are the basic features of a VLAN?

- What functionality is provided by 802.1Q trunking?

- What is the ISL protocol and how does it work?

- What are the features of VTP?

- What are the modes in which VTP operates?

- How does VTP operate in a management domain?

- How does the VTP pruning of VLANs work?

- How do you configure VTP?

- How do you configure 802.1Q trunking?

- How do you configure ISL trunking?

- How does inter-VLAN routing work?

- How do you configure router-on-a-stick?

Key Terms

This chapter uses the following key terms. You can find the definitions in the Glossary:

VLAN Trunking Protocol (VTP)   page 244

Inter-Switch Link (ISL)   page 246

IEEE 802.1Q   page 246

native VLAN   page 247

mono spanning tree (MST)   page 248

Per VLAN Spanning Tree + (PVST+)   page 249

maximum transmission unit (MTU)   page 251

Dynamic Trunk Protocol (DTP)   page 253

VTP domain   page 256

VTP server   page 256

VTP pruning   page 258

inter-VLAN routing   page 261

router-on-a-stick   page 261

Early virtual local-area networks (VLAN) were difficult to implement across networks. Each VLAN was manually configured on each switch. VLAN management over an extended network was a complicated task. To further complicate matters, each switch manufacturer had different VLAN capability methods. To solve these problems, VLAN trunking was developed.

VLAN trunking allows many VLANs to be defined throughout an organization by the addition of special tags to frames that identify the VLANs to which the frames belong. This tagging allows many VLANs to be carried throughout a large switched network over a common backbone or trunk. VLAN trunking is standards-based, with the IEEE 802.1Q trunking protocol now widely implemented. Inter-Switch Link (ISL) is a Cisco proprietary trunking protocol that can be implemented in Cisco networks.

Cisco created *VLAN Trunking Protocol (VTP)* to automate many VLAN configuration tasks, so that configurations on a VTP server are propagated automatically to other switches in the VTP domain.

VLAN technology provides network engineers with many advantages. Among other things, VLANs help control Layer 3 broadcasts, improve network security, and logically group network users. However, VLANs have an important limitation: They operate at Layer 2, which means that devices on different VLANs cannot communicate without the use of routers and network layer addresses. Routers and route processors enable inter-VLAN routing.

This chapter explains VLAN trunking, VTP implementation, and inter-VLAN routing in a switched network.

Trunking

In general, the history of trunking goes back to the origins of radio and telephone switching technologies. In radio technology, a trunk is a single communications line that carries multiple channels of radio signals.

In the telephony industry, the trunking concept is associated with the telephone communication path or channel between two points, as shown in Figure 9-1. A key concept regarding a trunk is that it simultaneously carries multiple lines of communication. Central offices (CO) are interconnected by trunks, thus forming an end-to-end solution for analog telephones.

Shared trunks are created for redundancy between COs. Multiplexers combine several voice signals into a single trunk link and demultiplex the signals at the other end (see Figure 9-2).

Figure 9-1   Traditional Telephone Trunk Line Carries Multiple Simultaneous Conversations

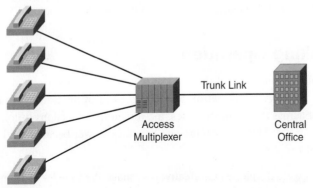

Figure 9-2   Shared Telephone Trunks Between COs Provide Redundancy

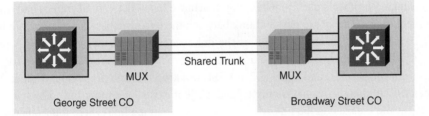

The concept used by the radio and telephone industries was then adopted to data communications. An example of this in a communications network is a backbone link between a main distribution frame (MDF) and an intermediate distribution frame (IDF). A backbone is composed of several trunks.

The same principle of trunking is now applied to network switching technologies. A trunk is a physical and logical connection between two switches across which network traffic travels, as Figure 9-3 illustrates.

Figure 9-3   VLAN Trunking

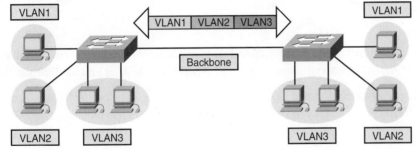

A trunk is a single transmission channel between two points. In a switched network, a trunk is a point-to-point link that supports several VLANs, as Figure 9-3 shows. A trunk's purpose is to conserve ports when a link is created between two devices that implement VLANs.

VLAN Trunking Operation

The switching tables at both ends of the trunk can be used to make forwarding decisions based on the destination Media Access Control (MAC) addresses of the frames. As the number of VLANs that travel across the trunk increases, the forwarding decisions become slower and more difficult to manage. The decision process becomes slower because the larger switching tables take longer to process.

Trunking protocols were developed to effectively manage the transfer of frames from different VLANs on a single physical line. Trunking protocols enable the distribution of frames to the associated ports at both ends of the trunk.

Modern trunking protocols use frame tagging to achieve faster delivery of frames and make management easier. The single physical link between the two switches can carry traffic for any VLAN. To achieve this, each frame sent on the link is tagged to identify which VLAN to which it belongs. Different tagging schemes exist. The two most common tagging schemes for Ethernet segments are ISL and IEEE 802.1Q. ISL trunking is Cisco proprietary. Figure 9-4 illustrates ISL trunking. A frame is only tagged while it exists on a trunk link. The frame carries no tag while it exists on the link where it originates and the link where it terminates. The initial switch along the path adds the tag and the final switch along the path strips the tag.

Figure 9-4   ISL Trunking

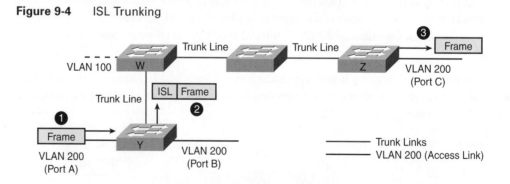

With *ISL*, an Ethernet frame is encapsulated with an additional header that contains a VLAN ID. With *IEEE 802.1Q*, a tag containing the VLAN ID is embedded into the Ethernet frame.

It is important to understand that a trunk link does not belong to a specific VLAN. A trunk link is a conduit for VLANs between switches and routers, as Figure 9-5 illustrates.

Figure 9-5   VLAN Trunking Multiplexing Data from Multiple VLANs onto a Single Link

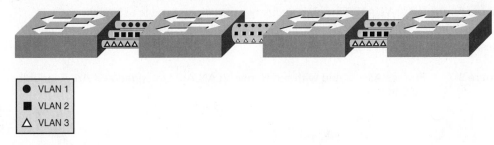

IEEE 802.1Q Trunking

The IEEE 802.1Q protocol interconnects multiple switches and routers and defines VLAN topologies. Cisco supports IEEE 802.1Q for Fast Ethernet and Gigabit Ethernet interfaces. The IEEE 802.1Q protocol carries traffic for multiple VLANs over a single link on a multivendor network.

IEEE 802.1Q extends IP routing capabilities to include support for routing IP frame types in VLAN configurations using the IEEE 802.1Q encapsulation.

The two ports on either end of an 802.1Q trunk are assigned to a *native VLAN* (VLAN 1 by default, but configurable to another VLAN). All untagged frames are assigned to the native VLAN.

Figure 9-6 illustrates 802.1Q trunking between various types of Cisco Catalyst switches.

Figure 9-6   IEEE 802.1Q Trunking

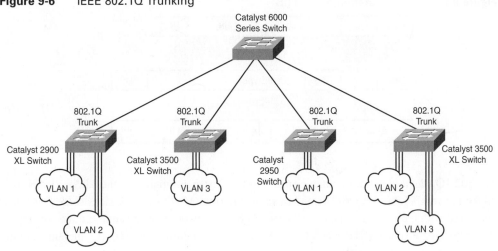

An 802.1Q trunk and its associated trunk ports have a native VLAN value. 802.1Q does not tag frames for the native VLAN. Therefore, ordinary end stations are able to read the native untagged frames, but can not read any other frame because the frames are tagged. Figure 9-7 illustrates native VLANs and untagged frames.

Figure 9-7   Frames Associated with the Native VLAN Are Untagged and Are Readable by End Stations

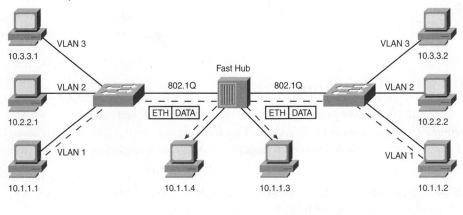

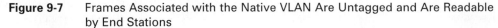

Figure 9-8 shows how adding a tag in a frame results in recomputation of the frame check sequence (FCS). A recomputation of the FCS is required because the embedded tag increases the size of the Ethernet frame.

Figure 9-8   Recomputation of the FCS

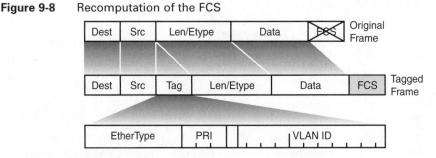

The 802.1Q standard defines a unique spanning-tree instance running on the native VLAN for all the network VLANs. An 802.1Q *mono spanning tree (MST)* network lacks some flexibility compared with a per-VLAN spanning tree + (PVST+) network that runs one instance of Spanning Tree Protocol (STP) per VLAN. A mono spanning tree is an 802.1Q implementation of spanning tree in which only one instance of spanning tree is used for all VLANs.

Per-VLAN spanning tree (PVST) maintains a spanning tree instance for each VLAN configured in the network. It uses ISL trunking and allows a VLAN trunk to be forwarding for some VLANs while blocking for other VLANs. Cisco developed *PVST+* to enable the running of several STP instances and allow interconnection of an MST zone, typically the 802.1Q-based network of another vendor, to a PVST zone. No specific configuration is needed to achieve this connection. Ideally, a mixed environment looks like the one shown in Figure 9-9.

Figure 9-9   Cisco PVST+ Interoperates with Other Vendors' STP Implementations

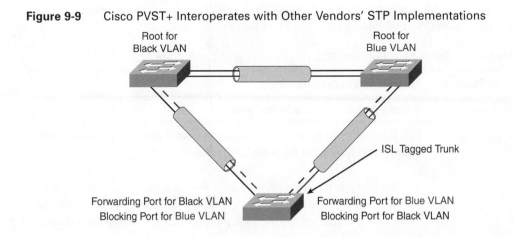

PVST+ provides support for 802.1Q trunks and the mapping of multiple spanning trees to the single spanning tree of 802.1Q switches. PVST+ networks must be in a treelike structure for proper STP operation. Providing different STP root switches per VLAN creates a more redundant network.

The PVST+ architecture distinguishes three types of regions:

- PVST region

- PVST+ region

- MST region

Each region consists of a homogeneous switch. You can connect a PVST region to a PVST+ region by connecting two ISL ports. Similarly, you can connect a PVST+ region to an MST region by connecting two 802.1Q ports.

To support the IEEE 802.1Q standard, the Cisco existing STP implementation was extended to become PVST+ by adding support for tunneling across an IEEE 802.1Q MST region. Tunneling means that the bridge protocol data units (BPDU) are flooded through the MST region along the single spanning tree present in the MST region. Therefore, PVST+ is compatible with both the 802.1Q MST and Cisco PVST protocols without requiring extra commands for configuration. In addition, PVST+ adds verification mechanisms to ensure that there is no inconsistent configuration of port trunking and VLAN IDs across switches.

IEEE 802.1Q trunks impose some limitations on the trunking strategy for a network:

- Make sure that the native VLAN for an 802.1Q trunk is the same on both ends of the trunk link. If they are different, spanning-tree loops might result.

- Make sure that your network is loop-free before you disable STP.

Table 9-1 shows how IEEE 802.1Q trunking interacts with other switch features. Port groups and EtherChannel technology is explored in detail in *CCNP 3: Multilayer Switching Companion Guide*, Second Edition (published by Cisco Press).

Table 9-1   Interaction Between 802.1Q Features and Trunk Ports

Switch Feature	Trunk Port Interaction
Secure ports	A trunk port cannot be a secure port.
Port grouping	802.1Q trunks can be grouped into EtherChannel port groups, but all trunks in the group must have the same configuration. When a group is first created, all ports follow the parameters that are set for the first port to be added to the group. If you change the configuration of one of these parameters, the switch propagates the setting that you enter to all ports in the group. The settings include the following: • Allowed VLAN list • STP path cost for each VLAN • STP port priority for each VLAN • STP PortFast setting • Trunk status (if one port in a port group ceases to be a trunk, all ports cease to be trunks)

ISL Trunking

ISL is a Cisco proprietary protocol that interconnects multiple switches and maintains VLAN information as traffic travels between switches. ISL provides VLAN capabilities while maintaining full wire-speed performance over Fast Ethernet links in full- or half-duplex mode.

Running a trunk in full-duplex mode is efficient and highly recommended. ISL operates in a point-to-point environment. The ISL frame tagging that the Catalyst series of switches uses is a low-latency mechanism to multiplex traffic from multiple VLANs on a single physical path. It has been implemented for connections among switches, routers, and network interface cards (NIC) that are used on nodes, such as servers. To support the ISL feature, each connecting device must be ISL-configured. An ISL-configured router allows inter-VLAN communications. A non-ISL device that receives ISL-encapsulated Ethernet frames might consider them to be protocol errors if the size of the header plus data frame exceeds the *maximum transmission unit (MTU)*, the largest IP packet size allowed to be sent out a particular interface. Ethernet interfaces default to an MTU of 1500 because the data field of an Ethernet frame must be limited to 1500 bytes, and the IP packet sits inside the data field of the Ethernet frame.

ISL functions at Layer 2 by encapsulating a data frame with a new header and a cyclic redundancy check (CRC), a type of hash function that produces a checksum against a block of data for the purposes of detecting and correcting errors. ISL is protocol-independent because the data frame can carry any upper-layer protocol. Administrators use ISL to maintain redundant links and load balance traffic between parallel links using the STP. Figure 9-10 illustrates ISL trunking.

Figure 9-10 ISL Trunking with VLAN Tags

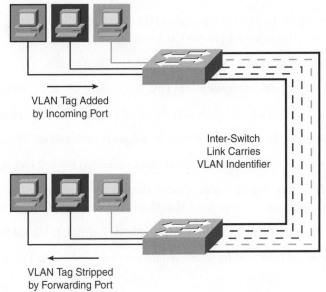

VLAN Tag Added
by Incoming Port

Inter-Switch
Link Carries
VLAN Indentifier

VLAN Tag Stripped
by Forwarding Port

Ports configured as ISL trunk ports encapsulate each frame with a 26-byte ISL header and a 4-byte CRC before sending it out the trunk port, as shown in Figure 9-11. Because ISL technology is implemented in application-specific integrated circuits (ASIC), frames are tagged at wire-speed performance. The number of VLANs supported by a switch depends on the switch hardware.

Figure 9-11   ISL Header and CRC Added to Ethernet Frames on ISL Trunks

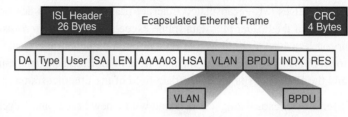

The following describes the information contained in the ISL frame header:

- **DA**—40-bit multicast destination address.

- **Type**—4-bit descriptor of the encapsulated frame types: Ethernet (0000), Token Ring (0001), Fiber Distributed Data Interface (FDDI) (0010), and ATM (0011).

- **User**—4-bit descriptor used as the type field extension or to define Ethernet priorities. It is a binary value from 0 (the lowest priority) to 3 (the highest priority).

- **SA**—48-bit source MAC address of the transmitting Catalyst switch.

- **LEN**—16-bit frame-length descriptor minus DA, Type, User, SA, LEN, and CRC.

- **AAAA03**—Standard Subnetwork Access Protocol (SNAP) 802.2 LLC header.

- **HSA**—First 3 bytes of the SA (manufacturer or unique organizational ID).

- **VLAN ID**—15-bit VLAN ID; only the lower 10 bits are used for 1024 VLANs.

- **BPDU**—1-bit descriptor that identifies whether the frame is a spanning-tree BPDU. It also identifies if the encapsulated frame is a Cisco Discovery Protocol (CDP) frame.

- **INDX**—16-bit descriptor that identifies the transmitting port ID. It is used for diagnostics.

- **RES**—16-bit reserved field used for additional information, such as the FDDI frame control field.

Configuring VLAN Trunking

It is becoming less common to use ISL trunking and more common to use 802.1Q trunking with Cisco Catalyst switches. Older Catalyst switches supported ISL or both ISL and 802.1Q trunking. Newer Catalyst switches support ISL and 802.1Q trunking or 802.1Q trunking alone. For example, the Catalyst 3750 switch supports both ISL and 802.1Q, but the Catalyst 2950 switch supports only 802.1Q encapsulation.

802.1Q Trunk Configuration

On a Catalyst 2950 switch, 802.1Q is configured automatically when trunking is enabled on the interface using the **switchport mode trunk** command. The full syntax for the **switchport mode** command is **switchport mode {access | dynamic {auto | desirable} | trunk}**.

Use the switchport mode interface configuration command to set a Fast Ethernet or Gigabit Ethernet port to trunk mode. The Catalyst 2950 series switches support the *Dynamic Trunk Protocol (DTP)*, which manages automatic trunk negotiation.

The **switchport mode** command has four options:

- **trunk**—Configures the port into permanent 802.1Q trunk mode and negotiates with the connected device to convert the link to trunk mode.

- **access**—Disables port trunk mode and negotiates with the connected device to convert the link to nontrunk.

- **dynamic desirable**—Triggers the port to negotiate the link from nontrunk to trunk mode. The port negotiates to a trunk port if the connected device is in either trunk state, desirable state, or auto state. Otherwise, the port becomes a nontrunk port, which is the default mode for all Ethernet interfaces. This is the default switch port mode for all Ethernet interfaces.

- **dynamic auto**—Enables a port to become a trunk only if the connected device has the state set to trunk or desirable. Otherwise, the port becomes a nontrunk port.

The **switchport nonnegotiate** interface command, which is introduced in Catalyst 2950 Release 12.1(6)EA2, specifies that Dynamic Trunking Protocol (DTP) negotiation packets are not sent on the Layer 2 interface. The switch does not engage in DTP negotiation on this interface. This command is valid only when the interface switchport mode is access or trunk (configured by using the **switchport mode access** or the **switchport mode trunk** interface configuration command). The **switchport nonnegotiate** command returns an error if you attempt to execute it in dynamic (auto or desirable) mode. Use the **no** form of this command to return to the default setting.

Table 9-2 shows the steps to configure a port as an 802.1Q trunk port, beginning in global configuration mode.

Table 9-2   Steps to Configure a Switch Port as a Trunk Port

Step	Action	Notes
1.	Enter the interface configuration mode and the port to be configured for trunking: AccessSwitch(config)#**interface** *interface*	After the interface configuration is entered, the prompt changes from (config)# to (config-if)#.
2.	Configure the port as a VLAN trunk: AccessSwitch(config-if)#**switchport mode trunk**.	Enable trunking on the selected interface.
3.	Specify the default VLAN: AccessSwitch(config-if)# **switchport access vlan** *vlan-id*	(Optional) Specifies the default VLAN used if the interface stops trunking.
4.	Specify the native VLAN: AccessSwitch(config-if)# **switchport trunk native vlan** *vlan-id*	Required for the native VLAN. If the native VLAN is 1, this step is not necessary.

On a Catalyst 2950 switch, use the **switchport trunk native vlan** *vlan-id* command to set the native VLAN for sending and receiving untagged traffic on an 802.1Q trunk.

 Lab 9.1.5b   Trunking with 802.1Q

In this lab, you create an 802.1Q trunk link between the two switches to allow communication between paired VLANs.

ISL Trunk Configuration

This section covers how to configure ISL trunks using the IOS on Catalyst switches supporting ISL, such as the Catalyst 2900XL, 3500XL, 3550, 3560, 3750, 4000, 4500, 5000, 5500, 6000, and 6500 switches.

Use the **switchport trunk encapsulation** interface configuration command to set a Catalyst switch that supports both 802.1Q and ISL (such as a Catalyst 4000) to encapsulate with ISL. Then, use the **switchport mode trunk** interface configuration command to configure the interface as a Layer 2 trunk.

The encapsulation types supported on the Catalyst switches vary, but the following three are common on Catalyst switches that support DTP and both 802.1Q and ISL:

- **dot1q**—The interface uses only 802.1Q trunking encapsulation when trunking.

- **isl**—The interface uses only ISL trunking encapsulation when trunking.

- **negotiate**—The device negotiates trunking encapsulation with a peer on the interface. This is the default mode on most Catalyst switches.

Catalyst 2950 series switches do not support ISL encapsulation. Check your device to determine which encapsulation type it supports: ISL, dot1q, or both.

Example 9-1 illustrates the configuration of ISL trunking on a Catalyst 4000 switch.

Example 9-1   Configuring ISL Trunking

```
Switch#configure terminal
Switch(config)#interface GigabitEthernet 2/24
Switch(config)#shutdown
Switch(config)#switchport trunk encapsulation isl
Switch(config)#switchport mode trunk
Switch(config)#no shutdown
```

By shutting down the interface, traffic flow is prevented until the configuration is complete.

Lab 9.1.5a   Trunking with ISL

In this lab, you create an ISL trunk link between the two switches to allow communication between paired VLANs.

VTP

Cisco created VLAN Trunking Protocol (VTP) to solve operational problems in a switched network with VLANs. VTP is a Cisco proprietary protocol.

Consider the example of a domain with several interconnected switches that support several VLANs. A domain is a logical group of users and resources under the control of one server, which is called the primary domain controller. To maintain connectivity within VLANs, each VLAN must be manually configured on each switch. As the organization grows and additional switches are added to the network, each new switch must be manually configured with VLAN information. A single incorrect VLAN assignment can cause cross-connected VLANs due to VLAN configuration inconsistencies.

With VTP, VLAN configuration is consistently maintained across a common administrative domain. Additionally, VTP reduces management and monitoring complexities of networks with VLANs.

VTP Concepts

VTP is a Layer 2 messaging protocol that maintains VLAN configuration consistency by managing the additions, deletions, and name changes of VLANs across networks. VTP minimizes misconfigurations and configuration inconsistencies that can cause problems, such as duplicate VLAN names or incorrect VLAN-type specifications.

A *VTP domain* is an administrative domain consisting of one switch or several interconnected switches that share the same VTP environment. You can configure a switch to be in only one VTP domain. Figure 9-12 shows a VTP domain. VTP messages ensure that VLAN information is synchronized across a VTP domain. When a VLAN is added, for example, that information is propagated across the VTP domain, and other switches synchronize the added VLAN information with their existing VLAN information.

Figure 9-12   VTP Domain

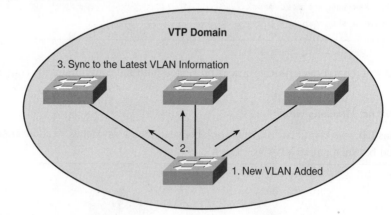

By default, a Catalyst switch is in the no-management–domain state until it receives an advertisement for a domain over a trunk link or until you configure a management domain. Configurations are made to a single *VTP server*. A VTP server is a Catalyst switch on which configuration changes are propagated across links to all connected switches in the VTP domain. VTP sends advertisements on trunk ports only.

VTP Operations

VTP operates in one of three modes: server mode, transparent mode, or client mode. You can complete different tasks depending on the VTP operation mode. The following describes the characteristics of the three modes:

- **Server mode**—The default VTP mode is server mode, but VLANs are not propagated over the network until a management domain name is specified or learned. When you create, modify, or delete a VLAN on a VTP server, the change is propagated to all switches in the VTP domain. VTP messages are transmitted out all trunk connections. VTP advertisements are both originated and forwarded. VLAN information is synchronized with other VTP servers and clients. VLAN information is saved in nonvolatile random-access memory (NVRAM).

- **Transparent mode**—When you create, modify, or delete a VLAN in VTP transparent mode, the change affects only the local switch and does not propagate to other switches in the VTP domain. VTP advertisements are forwarded, but not originated on the switch. The VLAN information is not synchronized with other switches. The VLAN information is saved in NVRAM.

- **Client mode**—You cannot create, change, or delete VLANs when in VTP client mode. VTP advertisements are forwarded in VTP client mode. VLAN information is synchronized with other VTP clients and servers. VLAN information is not saved in NVRAM.

VTP advertisements are flooded throughout the management domain. VTP advertisements are sent every 5 minutes or whenever a change occurs in VLAN configurations. Advertisements are transmitted over the default VLAN (VLAN 1) using a multicast frame. A configuration revision number is included in each VTP advertisement. A higher configuration revision number indicates that the VLAN information being advertised is more current than the stored information.

One of the most critical components of VTP is the configuration revision number. Each time a VTP server modifies its VLAN information, the VTP server increments the configuration revision number by one. The server then sends out a VTP advertisement with the new configuration revision number. If the configuration revision number being advertised is higher than the number stored on the other switches in the VTP domain, the switches overwrite their VLAN configurations with the new information being advertised, as Figure 9-13 shows. The configuration revision number in VTP transparent mode is always 0.

Figure 9-13   VTP Messages Synchronizing VLAN Information Within a VTP (Management) Domain

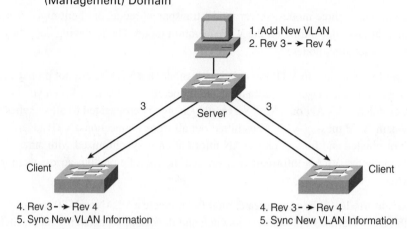

1. Add New VLAN
2. Rev 3 - ➤ Rev 4

3

Server

3

Client

Client

4. Rev 3 - ➤ Rev 4
5. Sync New VLAN Information

4. Rev 3 - ➤ Rev 4
5. Sync New VLAN Information

Caution

An important consideration is that, in the overwrite process, if the VTP server deleted all VLANs and has the higher revision number, the other devices in the VTP domain also delete their VLANs.

A device that receives VTP advertisements must check various parameters before incorporating the received VLAN information. First, the management domain name and password in the advertisement must match those configured in the local switch. Next, if the configuration revision number indicates that the message was created after the configuration currently in use, the switch incorporates the advertised VLAN information. To reset the configuration revision number on a Catalyst switch, use the **delete vtp** privileged EXEC command. This command was introduced to Catalyst 2950 switches in Release 12.0(5.2)WC(1).

The last operational consideration for VTP is that of VTP pruning. *VTP pruning* uses VLAN advertisements to determine when a trunk connection is needlessly flooding traffic. VTP pruning is a technology that results in the prevention of unnecessary traffic on switch segments.

By default, a trunk connection carries traffic for all VLANs in the VTP management domain. Commonly, some switches in an enterprise network do not have local ports configured in each VLAN.

Figure 9-14 shows a switched network with VTP pruning enabled. Only switches 1 and 4 support ports configured in the blue VLAN. The broadcast traffic from station A is not forwarded to switches 3, 5, and 6 because traffic for the blue VLAN has been pruned on the links indicated on switches 2 and 4.

VTP pruning increases available bandwidth by restricting flooded traffic to those trunk links that the traffic must use to access the appropriate network devices. Note that VTP pruning can only be enabled on VTP servers, not on VTP clients.

Note that VTP is not as widely deployed as in the past. If VTP is not to be deployed, all switches should be placed in transparent mode.

Figure 9-14   VTP Pruning Preventing Unnecessary VLAN Traffic in a VTP Domain

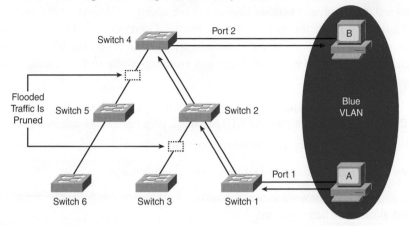

Configuring VTP

When creating VLANs, you must decide whether to use VTP in your network. With VTP, you can make configuration changes on one or more switches, and those changes are automatically communicated to all other switches in the same VTP domain.

Default VTP configuration values depend on the switch model and the software version. The following lists the default values for the Catalyst 2950 series switches:

- **VTP domain name**—None

- **VTP mode**—Server

- **VTP password**—None

- **VTP pruning**—Disabled

- **VTP version**—1

- **VTP trap**—Disabled

The VTP domain name can be specified or learned. By default, the domain name is not set. You can optionally set a password for the VTP management domain. However, if you do not assign the same password for each switch in the domain, VTP does not function properly.

VTP pruning eligibility is one VLAN parameter that the VTP protocol advertises. Enabling or disabling VTP pruning on a VTP server propagates the change throughout the management domain.

Use the **vtp** global configuration command to modify the VTP configuration, including the storage filename, domain name, interface, and mode:

```
vtp {domain domain-name | file filename | interface name | mode
    {client | server | transparent} | password password | pruning |
    version number}
```

The **domain** and **mode** keywords were added to Catalyst 2950 switches in Release 12.1(9)EA1. The **password**, **pruning**, and **version** keywords were added to Catalyst 2950 switches in Release 12.1(11)EA1. Use the **no** form of this command to remove the filename or to return to the default settings. When the VTP mode is transparent, you can save the VTP configuration in the switch configuration file by entering the **copy running-config startup-config** privileged EXEC command.

Alternately, you can use the **vtp** privileged EXEC command, introduced in Release 12.1(9)EA1 on Catalyst 2950 switches, to configure the VTP password, pruning, and the administrative version:

```
Switch# vtp {password password | pruning | version number}
```

Use the **no** form of this command to return to the default settings.

The domain name and password are case sensitive. A domain name cannot be removed after it is assigned; it can only be reassigned.

Example 9-2 illustrates VTP configuration and the resulting output of the **show vtp status** command.

```
Example 9-2    Configuring VTP
AccessSwitch#configure terminal
AccessSwitch(config)#vtp domain hawaii
AccessSwitch(config)#vtp mode transparent
AccessSwitch(config)#vtp password cisco
AccessSwitch(config)#vtp pruning
AccessSwitch(config)#end
AccessSwitch#show vtp status
VTP Version                     : 2
Configuration Revision          : 0
Maximum VLANs supported locally : 250
Number of existing VLANs        : 6
VTP Operating Mode              : Transparent
VTP Domain Name                 : hawaii
VTP Pruning Mode                : Enabled
VTP V2 Mode                     : Disabled
VTP Traps Generation            : Disabled
MD5 digest                      : 0xA6 0xE8 0x48 0x78 0x2F 0x5F 0x1A 0x71
Configuration last modified by 10.10.10.50 at 1-1-06 14:38:06
Local updater ID is 10.10.10.50 on interface Vl1 (lowest numbered VLAN interface
  found)
```

The following lists the characteristics of the switch in Example 9-2:

- The configuration revision number is 0.

- The switch is transparent in the VTP domain.

- The VTP domain name is hawaii.

- Pruning is enabled.

- The VTP version is 1 (default setting).

- A VTP password is configured.

> **Lab 9.2.5   VTP Client and Server Configurations**
>
> In this lab, you configure VTP to establish server and client switches.

Inter-VLAN Routing Overview

Inter-VLAN communication occurs between broadcast domains through a Layer 3 device. In a VLAN environment, frames are switched only between ports within the same broadcast domain. VLANs perform network partitioning and traffic separation at Layer 2. Inter-VLAN communication cannot occur without a Layer 3 device, such as a router. Use ISL or IEEE 802.1Q to enable trunking on a router subinterface. *Inter-VLAN routing* is routing between VLANs on a router or Layer 3 switch.

Router-on-a-Stick

Figure 9-15 illustrates a router attached to a core switch. The configuration between a router and a core switch is sometimes referred to as a *router-on-a-stick*. The router can receive packets on one VLAN and forward them to another VLAN. To perform inter-VLAN routing functions, the router must know how to reach all VLANs being interconnected. There must be a separate logical connection on the router for each VLAN, and you must enable ISL or 802.1Q trunking on a single physical connection. The router already knows about directly connected networks; it must learn routes to networks not connected directly to it.

To support ISL or 802.1Q trunking, you must subdivide the physical Fast Ethernet interface of the router into multiple, logical, addressable interfaces, one per VLAN, as shown in Figure 9-16. The resulting logical interfaces are called subinterfaces. Without this subdivision, a separate physical interface would have to be dedicated to each VLAN.

Figure 9-15   Router-on-a-Stick Employing a Layer 2 Switch Trunked to a Router

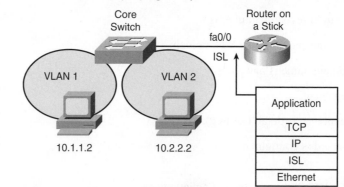

Figure 9-16   Logical Subinterfaces on the Router End of a Trunk Link in a Router-on-a-Stick Topology

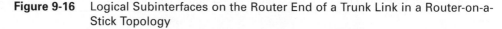

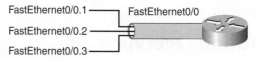

In Figure 9-16, the FastEthernet0/0 interface is divided into multiple subinterfaces: FastEthernet0/0.1, FastEthernet0/0.2, and FastEthernet0/0.3 for three separate VLANs.

Configuring Inter-VLAN Routing

Configuring inter-VLAN routing is a methodical process. This book focuses on the router-on-a-stick topology for inter-VLAN routing. For other types of inter-VLAN routing configuration, such as using switch virtual interfaces on multilayer switches, read *CCNP 3: Multilayer Switching Companion Guide*, Second Edition (published by Cisco Press). The router-on-a-stick solution is somewhat dated because of the advent of multilayer switches; router-on-a-stick is only used in a network with only Layer 2 switches.

Before going any further, each router and switch need to be checked to see which VLAN encapsulations they support. Catalyst 2950 switches have supported 802.1Q trunking since the release of Cisco IOS Release 12.0(5.2)WC(1), but they do not support ISL trunking. For inter-VLAN routing to work properly, all the routers and switches involved must support the same encapsulation. Figure 9-17 illustrates the router-on-a-stick topology.

On a router, an interface can be logically divided into multiple, virtual subinterfaces. Subinterfaces provide a flexible solution for routing multiple data streams through a single physical interface. To define subinterfaces on a physical interface, perform the following tasks:

- Identify the interface.

- Define the VLAN encapsulation.

- Assign an IP address to the interface.

Figure 9-17   One Router with Three Subinterfaces Corresponding to Three VLANs in the
Router-on-a-Stick Topology

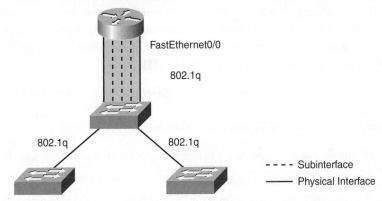

To identify the interface, use the **interface** command in global configuration mode:

```
Router(config)#interface fastethernet port-number subinterface-number
```

port-number identifies the physical interface, and *subinterface-number identifies* the virtual
interface. Figure 9-18 illustrates the subinterfaces and associated VLANs.

Figure 9-18   A Fast Ethernet Interface Can Be Subdivided into Logical Subinterfaces
Associated in a One-to-One Fashion with VLANs

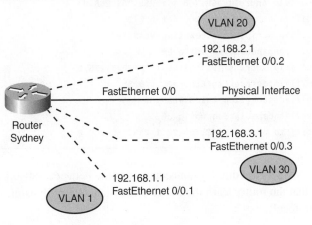

The router must be able to talk to the switch by using a standardized trunking protocol. This
means that both devices that are connected must understand each other. To define the VLAN
encapsulation, enter the appropriate **encapsulation** command in interface configuration mode:

```
Router(config-if)#encapsulation isl vlan-id
Router(config-if)#encapsulation dot1q vlan-id [native]
```

vlan-id identifies the VLAN for which the subinterface carries traffic. A VLAN ID is added to the frame only when the frame is destined for a nonlocal network. Each VLAN packet carries the VLAN ID within the packet header. With 802.1Q encapsulation, do not configure encapsulation on the native VLAN of an IEEE 802.1Q trunk without using the **native** keyword. (Always use the **native** keyword when *vlan-id* is the ID of the IEEE 802.1Q native VLAN.) The **native** keyword was added in IOS Release 12.1(3)T.

To assign the IP address to the interface, enter the following command in interface configuration mode:

```
Router(config-if)#ip address ip-address subnet-mask
```

ip-address and *subnet-mask* are the 32-bit network address and mask of the specific interface. Recall that each VLAN is its own IP subnet.

In Example 9-3, the router has three subinterfaces configured on Fast Ethernet interface 0/0. These three interfaces are identified as 0/0.1, 0/0.2, and 0/0.3, as shown in Figure 9-18. All interfaces are encapsulated for 802.1Q. Interface 0/0.1 routes packets for VLAN 1, whereas interface 0/0.2 routes packets for VLAN 20, and 0/0.3 routes packets for VLAN 30.

Example 9-3   Configuring Inter-VLAN Routing
```
Router(config)#interface FastEthernet 0/0.1
Router(config-subif)#description Management VLAN 1
Router(config-subif)#encapsulation dot1q 1 native
Router(config-subif)#ip address 192.168.1.1 255.255.255.0
Router(config-subif)#interface FastEthernet 0/0.2
Router(config-subif)#description Accounting VLAN 20
Router(config-subif)#encapsulation dot1q 20
Router(config-subif)#ip address 192.168.20.1 255.255.255.0
Router(config-subif)#interface FastEthernet 0/0.3
Router(config-subif)#description Sales VLAN 30
Router(config-subif)#encapsulation dot1q 30
Router(config-subif)#ip address 192.168.30.1 255.255.255.0
```

In Example 9-3, the VLANs are directly connected. Routing between networks not directly connected requires that the router learn the routes either statically or dynamically (such as through a routing protocol).

If the trunk encapsulation were ISL, as might be the case if connecting to a Catalyst 2900XL switch (for example), the procedure is exactly the same, except that no native VLAN concept (or associated configuration) exists, and all instances of **dot1q** are replaced with **isl** in the router configuration. On the switch side, the configuration would not have any native VLAN options configured, but entering the additional **switchport trunk encapsulation isl** command is needed prior to entering the **switchport mode trunk** command.

In summary, to configure router-on-a-stick for inter-VLAN routing, complete the following tasks:

Step 1 Enable the trunk encapsulation on the switch port connecting to the router. (802.1Q is the only option on Catalyst 2950 switches, so no configuration is required for this step.)

Step 2 Enable trunking on the switch port connecting to the router.

Step 3 Specify the native VLAN on the switch port. (This is required only if you use 802.1Q trunking with a native VLAN other than VLAN 1.) An error will result from a native VLAN mismatch on either end of a trunk.

Step 4 Enable the trunk encapsulation on the Fast Ethernet subinterface of the router. (Add the native option if you use 802.1Q trunking and the subinterface is associated with the native VLAN.)

Step 5 Assign a network layer address to each subinterface.

Lab 9.3.6   Configuring Inter-VLAN Routing

In this lab, you create a basic configuration on a router and test the routing functionality.

Chapter Summary

A trunk is a physical and logical connection between two switches across which network traffic travels. The concept of trunking goes back to the origins of radio and telephone switching technologies. In the context of a LAN switching environment, a trunk is a point-to-point link that supports several VLANs.

A trunk's purpose is to conserve ports when creating a link between two devices implementing VLANs. Trunking bundles multiple virtual links over one physical link by allowing the traffic for several VLANs to travel over a single cable between the switches.

To effectively manage the transfer of frames from different VLANs on a single physical line, trunking protocols were developed. Trunking protocols establish agreement for the distribution of frames to the associated ports at both ends of the trunk.

Trunking protocols use a frame tagging mechanism to assign an identifier to the frames. This provides better management and faster delivery. Frame tagging functions at Layer 2 and requires little processing or administrative overhead. ISL (the Cisco proprietary Inter-Switch Link protocol) and 802.1Q (the IEEE standard) are the most common tagging schemes for Ethernet segments.

VTP was created to solve operational problems in a switched network with VLANs, such as cross-connected VLANs caused by configuration inconsistencies.

With VTP, VLAN configuration is consistently maintained across a common administrative domain. A VTP domain is made up of one or more interconnected devices that share the same VTP domain name. A switch can only be in one VTP domain. When transmitting VTP messages to other switches in the network, the VTP message is encapsulated in a trunking protocol frame, such as ISL or IEEE 802.1Q. VTP switches operate in one of three modes: server, client, or transparent.

With VTP, each switch advertises the following on its trunk ports: its management domain, the configuration revision number, the VLANs that it knows about, and certain parameters for each known VLAN.

By default, server and client Catalyst switches issue VTP advertisements every 5 minutes. Servers inform neighbor switches what they believe to be the current VTP revision number. The configuration revision number is compared and, if differences exist, the switches request new VLAN information and increment the number.

Before configuring VTP and VLAN on a network, determine the version number of VTP, if a new domain needs to be created, and the VTP mode. At least one server needs to be in the VTP domain.

Before adding a VTP client, use the **show vtp status** command to verify that the VTP configuration revision number is lower than the configuration revision number on the other switches in the VTP domain.

When a host in one broadcast domain wants to communicate with a host in another broadcast domain, a router must be involved to facilitate inter-VLAN routing. On a router, an interface can be logically divided into multiple virtual subinterfaces. Subinterfaces provide a flexible solution for routing multiple data streams through a single physical interface.

Check Your Understanding

Complete all the review questions listed here to test your understanding of the topics and concepts in this chapter. Answers are listed in Appendix A, "Answers to Check Your Understanding and Challenge Questions and Activities."

1. Which feature is required for a VLAN to span two switches?

   A. A trunk to connect the switches

   B. A router to connect the switches

   C. A bridge to connect the switches

   D. A VLAN configured between the switches

2. What are two reasons that network administrators use ISL? (Choose two.)

   A. To maintain redundant links

   B. To allow clients to see the ISL header

   C. To provide inter-VLAN communications over a bridge

   D. To provide trunking between Cisco switches and other vendor switches

   E. To load balance traffic between parallel links using STP

3. What is required to support the ISL feature between two devices?

   A. Being ISL-capable

   B. Running Cisco IOS

   C. Being VLAN-capable

   D. Being 802.1Q-capable

4. What primary benefit does VTP offer?

   A. Allows trunking to provide redundancy

   B. Minimizes redundancy on a switched network

   C. Allows you to run several VLANs over a single trunk

   D. Minimizes misconfigurations and configuration inconsistencies

5. How many VTP domains can you configure for a switch?

   A. One

   B. Two

   C. Four

   D. Eight

6. What command correctly configures a switch for transparent mode in the VTP domain "AccessSwitch?"

   A. **vtp mode trunk on**

   B. **vtp mode transparent**

   C. **vtp domain AccessSwitch**

   D. **vtp domain AccessSwitch transparent**

7. What is the default VTP mode on a Catalyst switch?

   A. Off

   B. Client

   C. Server

   D. Transparent

8. If you group 802.1Q trunks into EtherChannel port groups, what guideline must you follow?

   A. Each port in the group must be a secure port.

   B. Each trunk in the group can have its own configuration.

   C. All ports must follow the parameters set for the first port that is added to the group.

   D. All trunks must follow the parameters set for the first trunk that is added to the group.

9. When you are deleting a VLAN from a VTP domain, where must the change be performed?

   A. On a switch in VTP server mode

   B. On every switch in VTP client mode

   C. On a switch in VTP transparent mode

   D. On every switch, regardless of VTP mode

10. What precaution must you take when redeploying a switch to a new VTP domain in the network?

    A. Set a unique VTP password on the switch for security.

    B. Preconfigure all VLANs in the new VTP domain on the switch.

    C. Verify that the VTP revision number is lower than the existing domain.

    D. Configure the switch to VTP transparent mode to minimize impact.

11. Suppose that the VTP is not updating the configuration on other switches when the VLAN configuration changes. Which command do you use to determine if the switch is in VTP transparent mode?

    A. **show trunk**

    B. **show spantree**

C. **show interfaces**

D. **show vtp status**

12. What command correctly assigns a subinterface to VLAN 50 using 802.1Q trunking?

   A. Router(config)#**encapsulation 50 dot1Q**

   B. Router(config)#**encapsulation 802.1Q 50**

   C. Router(config-if)#**encapsulation dot1Q 50**

   D. Router(config-if)#**encapsulation 50 802.1Q**

13. In which mode is a VTP switch operating if it has been configured to only forward VTP advertisements?

   A. Client

   B. Root

   C. Server

   D. Transparent

   E. Nontransparent

14. Two hosts are connected to the same switch, but are on different VLANs. Which of the following statements is true regarding communication between two hosts?

   A. A bridge can connect the two hosts to allow them to communicate.

   B. A router is required for communication between the hosts.

   C. The hosts must be connected to two different switches in order for communication to be established between them.

   D. The hosts should be able to communicate without additional intervention.

   E. The VLANs must be connected with a VLAN network.

15. What must be used to provide routed communication between multiple VLANs over a single router interface?

   A. A single logical interface

   B. Logical subinterfaces

   C. A NIC that supports trunking

   D. A multiport transceiver

   E. Multiple physical interfaces

   F. Multiple switched links to the router

Challenge Questions and Activities

These questions and activities are purposefully designed to be similar to the more complex styles of questions you might see on the CCNA exam. Answers are listed in Appendix A.

1. The switches in Figure 9-19 are interconnected by trunk links and are configured for VTP as shown. A new VLAN is added to Switch1. Which of the following actions will occur? (Choose four.)

Figure 9-19   VTP Mode Effect

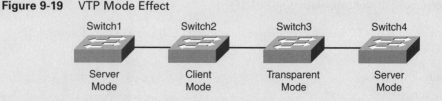

A. Switch1 will send a VTP update to Switch2.

B. Switch2 will add the VLAN to its database and pass the update to Switch3.

C. Switch3 will pass the VTP update to Switch4.

D. Switch3 will add the VLAN to its database.

E. Switch4 will add the VLAN to its database.

F. Switch4 will not receive the update.

2. Put the following in order to indicate the steps to configure a switch port as a trunk.

A. Verify trunk settings.

B. Configure the switch port mode to trunk.

C. Determine the encapsulations that the port will support.

D. Set the trunking protocol if necessary.

E. Set the native VLAN if necessary.

3. Two of the following relate to ISL and two of the following relate to IEEE 802.1Q. Indicate the correct associations.

A. Shares switching table information between switches

B. Distributes VLAN membership information from a central server

C. Industry standard

D. Frame tagging by encapsulation

E. Frame tagging by insertion

F. Cisco proprietary

Answers to Check Your Understanding and Challenge Questions and Activities

Chapter 1

Check Your Understanding

1. D

   A is wrong because the mask of 10.1.1.3 is unknown based on reading this command. B is wrong because 186.157.5.0 is the destination network. C is wrong because it has nothing to do with tracing a route. D is right because it explains the syntax of the displayed command correctly.

2. A

   A is right because it describes the result of the routing algorithm that a Cisco router uses. B, C, and D do not accurately reflect the behavior of a Cisco router in this scenario.

3. C

   C is right because 30 seconds is the timer used for RIP updates.

4. B

   B is right because 15 is the maximum hop count that RIP permits.

5. B

   B is right because it displays the correct syntax for enabling RIP. RIP does not use an AS number, as in C and D.

6. D

   D is right because it displays the correct default value for the holddown timer that RIP uses.

7. A

   A is right because Cisco engineers designed the **debug** output such that the contents of the parenthetical expression indicate the source address of the update.

8. A

   Cisco engineers designed the **debug ip rip** output to use this message to indicate the receipt of a malformed RIP packet.

9. C

   C is right because $28 - 20 = 8$, and $2^8 = 256$.

10. C

C is right because $2^7 - 2 = 128 - 2 = 126$.

11. B

B is right because $32 - 30 = 2$, and $2^2 - 2 = 4 - 2 = 2$.

12. C

$2^4 = 16$, which is the least power of 2 greater than 9, and $2^4 = 16$, which is the least power of 2 greater than 12. Therefore, 4 bits are borrowed for subnetting and 4 bits are dedicated for hosts on each subnet. With 4 bits borrowed in the fourth octet, the subnet mask is 255.255.255.240.

13. C

The second octet of private Class B networks ranges from 16 to 31, which is 00010000 to 00011111 in binary. These binary values have the first four bits in common, so the summary address is 172.16.0.0/12.

14. D

Multicast addresses range from 224.0.0.0 to 239.255.255.255, or equivalently, IPv4 addresses with 1110 in the first octet. Therefore, 224.0.0.0/4 represents all multicast addresses.

Challenge Questions and Activities

1. F

192.168.16.128/27 takes the address space through 192.168.16.159, leaving C and F as possible answers, but C is a network address.

2. B, C, D

0.0 is a wire address, 1.255 is a broadcast address, and 2.182 is out of range.

Chapter 2

Check Your Understanding

1. D

A, B, and C are incorrect because they do not overtly limit the scope of route changes.

2. A

LSAs permit link-state synchronization. Specifying the cost and determining the best path are functions that follow link-state synchronization, so B and C are incorrect. D is handled through the hello protocol, not LSAs.

3. A, C

B is incorrect because OSPF is not proprietary. D and E are wrong because OSPF is nothing like RIP and it is not a distance vector protocol.

4. D

A, B, and C are too restrictive. D is the optimal answer.

5. B

A and C are too restrictive. D doesn't make sense.

6. A

Root cost, link state, and hop count are not inversely proportional to bandwidth.

7. A

The syntax is incorrect in B, and the mode is incorrect in C and D for enabling OSPF.

8. A

This is one case where the obvious guess is correct. B represents **show ip ospf**. C would be correct if the *interface-type* parameter was appended to the displayed command. D represents **show ip ospf neighbor**.

9. B

debug ip ospf events does not display information about OSPF packets. **debug ip ospf packet** displays information about every OSPF packet received, including packet length in bytes. **debug ip ospf packet size** is not a valid command. The command output of **debug ip ospf mpls traffic-eng advertisements** does not include OSPF packet length.

10. C

Forty is the default OSPF dead interval timer on a broadcast multiaccess link.

Challenge Questions and Activities

1. B, D

The syntax for enabling OSPF and adding interfaces to the OSPF process are given by B and D. A, C, and E provide the wrong syntax.

2. B

The correct syntax for the network statement utilizes an inverse mask, which is only reflected in B.

Chapter 3

Check Your Understanding

1. A

The parentheses indicate the source address.

2. A

This is indicated in the section, "RIP Troubleshooting." The output is specific to a malformed packet.

3. B

The **debug ip igrp events** command provides summary information, whereas the **debug ip igrp transactions** command provides detailed information, including metrics.

4. C

Data packet traffic is not directly affected by EIGRP. IGRP sends the entire routing table, but EIGRP sends routing table changes.

5. C

The mode and syntax are only correct in C. It must be in router configuration mode with the **network** command.

6. D

The show ip eigrp neighbors command provides detailed information regarding the EIGRP adjacency formed between two neighbor EIGRP routers, including when the adjacency formed.

7. B

The **debug ip ospf packet** command provides detailed information about the contents of OSPF packets propagated on the network. The **debug ip ospf events** command does not include OSPF packet length information.

8. B

The summarization is configured at the interface level and the syntax is correct on B. The syntax order in D is incorrectly permuted.

9. A

There are no LSA, LSU, or RTP EIGRP packets types.

10. B

The EIGRP database displays with the **show ip eigrp topology** command, which shows the active or passive state of each route.

Challenge Questions and Activities

1. D

EIGRP does support VLSM. Monitoring neighbor adjacency changes has nothing to do with functionality. Bandwidth has no effect on anything but the metric. The correct answer is D.

2. D, E

The summary address is being sent out the serial interface of Router A. The correct syntax is reflected in D with the inverse mask.

3. B

The topology table has all the EIGRP successor, feasible successor, and non-feasible successor routes from which to choose from.

Chapter 4

Check Your Understanding

1. C, D

A and E are routing functions; B is a QoS function, which is not always available on Layer 2 switches.

2. C

Switches increase available bandwidth by microsegmentation, or creating dedicated network segments.

3. A

A is correct because only the destination MAC address is read before forwarding the frame with cut-through switching.

4. B

Switches use buffer memory to allow frames to pass through the switch in a many-to-one fashion; otherwise, switches are constrained to permit only a single frame to pass through it at any given instant.

5. D

Source addresses are used to populate the CAM table; destination addresses are used for forwarding decisions.

6. C

There is no such thing as a broadcast port, so B is incorrect. It does not make sense for a switch to send a frame back to the source (A). Because the destination address is in the CAM table, the switch does not need to flood the frame.

7. B, C, E

Unicast frames might or might not get flooded. Frames with known destination address are not flooded because the "destination port" is known.

8. B, C, D

Hubs and repeaters increase the size of collision domains. Workstations have no impact on the size of a collision domain.

9. A, C, D

Asymmetric switching prevents bottlenecks between ports of unlike bandwidth.

10. B

MAC addresses are used at Layer 2.

Challenge Questions and Activities

1. A

The router creates broadcast domains.

2. D

According to the table, the destination is known to be associated with Interface1.

Chapter 5

Check Your Understanding

1. A, B

A and B are OSI Layers 2 and 3, respectively, which represent the exact two layers for which switching can occur at the core. The access layer is not an OSI layer.

2. E

Because it provides DNS for the entire network, the server is an "enterprise" server and would be located in the MDF.

3. D

D is correct because a router (or route processor) is required to interconnect VLANs.

4. E

This is the definition of scalability.

5. D

The TIA/EIA-568-A standard specifies wiring connectivity requirements.

6. C, D

This is the definition of the core layer.

7. D

These are the respective functions of the distribution, core, and access layers.

8. B

This is the definition of the access layer.

9. A, D

User applications, file sharing, and print sharing do not require enterprise, or system-wide, access.

10. A, E

Switches and bridges provide microsegmentation.

Chapter 6

Check Your Understanding

1. A

A is correct, just as with a Cisco router.

2. A

? lists all available commands.

3. D

There is no on/off switch.

4. B

Green indicates that the RPS is operational. Flashing green indicates that the RPS is connected but unavailable because it is providing power to another device. Flashing amber indicates that the internal power supply failed and the RPS is providing power to the switch.

5. A

The user EXEC mode is entered upon successful boot, indicated by the greater-than sign.

6. A

The **c** immediately followed by the **?** is the user's way of requesting a list of all commands beginning with the letter C in the particular mode that the user is in.

7. B

The space after **config** followed by **?** indicates that the user wants to see all the keywords associated with (and immediately following) the command **config**.

8. D

The IP address and subnet mask are configured just as on a Cisco router interface.

9. C

The same mode is used for a Catalyst switch as for a Cisco router.

10. C

A and D have nothing to do with MAC addresses. B lists the interface type.

11. C

You wouldn't want someone to be able to enter the **show running-config** command in user EXEC mode because its output includes all the detailed configurations for the switch.

12. B

The command has no secondary flow control result.

13. C

C displays the correct syntax.

14. B

It does not delete all configuration information; for example, VLAN information is not deleted by this command. A and C are false.

15. D

This command works just as it does on a Cisco router.

16. C

Interface VLAN 1 is an SVI used for managing the switch.

17. A

An administrator should back up the running-config file in case he needs to restore it for some reason. This file provides a description of how the device is configured.

Challenge Questions and Activities

1. B, C

These are the two steps performed religiously in switch labs to restore the switches to factory default settings.

2. A, B, F

You can configure VLANs, port security, and static MAC addresses later.

3. A, B

The green system LED indicates that the switch has power and is working properly.

4. B, D, E

This is what the "STAT"-switch mode and solid amber port LED indicates. It does not mean a link is not detected. It does not mean the port is sending or receiving data. It does not mean the switch and host duplex modes do not match.

5. B, C, E

You cannot access configuration or change LAN interface settings.

Chapter 7

Check Your Understanding

1. B, C, E

A is not true in general. D represents frames for which the CAM table has active entries.

2. C

C is the correct term.

3. C

B is when multiple copies of the same frame arrive at the intended host.

4. A

This is a fundamental concept in STP.

5. C

6. A

This is the definition of root port.

7. A

This is the definition of designated port.

8. B

This is the definition of the listening state.

9. A

After STP converges, a nondesignated port is set as blocking.

10. D

After STP converges, a root port is forwarding.

11. A

The ports on the root bridge have the lowest-path cost to the root bridge and so are designated ports. On all other bridges besides the root bridge, there will be ports that are not designated ports.

12. C

C describes a situation in which an STP recalculation is required. A does not force a recalculation. B and D do not relate to STP.

13. D

IEEE 802.1d can prevent loops, but it is too slow to converge.

14. C

A indicates no listening. B does not exist with RSTP.

15. B

This is similar to IEEE 802.1d STP.

16. B

This is critical for the correct operation of STP (selecting the root bridge first).

17. D

The chances of both of them failing simultaneously is 1/10 times 1/10, or 1/100.

Challenge Questions and Activities

1. A, C

   B pertains to routers. D is not a problem. E is not a common issue. F is not an issue after the switch learns the MAC-to-port association.

2. A, B, F

   This follows from the definitions of the various STP port states.

3. D

   This is exactly the type of situation that STP was designed to prevent.

4. D

5. A, E, F, and G refer to STP (IEEE 802.1d). The others refer to RSTP (IEEE 802.1w).

6. B

   With STP, everything else depends on the selection of a sole root bridge. E is not known without more information.

7. C

   Bridge priority takes precedence, followed by the MAC address.

8. B, D

   A is silly. C is load balancing. E refers to multiple spanning tree (MST).

Chapter 8

Check Your Understanding

1. A

   A trunk allows traffic from multiple VLANs to traverse a single link.

2. D

   VMPS relies on a database of MAC addresses to map to dynamic switch ports.

3. C

   Catalyst switches default to VTP server mode. VTP is Cisco-proprietary.

4. A

   It is important to create the VLAN first. After you've done that, you can associate interfaces with the VLAN.

5. A

A port can belong to only one VLAN.

6. D

Although C is technically correct, D better describes the output.

7. C

For a sample of output of the **show spanning-tree** command, see Example 8-10.

8. A, C, E

B is wrong because the administrator does not place enterprise servers at the access layer, for example. D is incorrect because there is only a finite number of subnets on the planet. F is wrong because IP network design can still be complex.

9. B, D

A and C don't make sense. E is wrong because there is no prescribed percentage of traffic that should cross the backbone.

10. A, C, E

B, D, and F describe dynamic VLANs.

Challenge Questions and Activities

1. A, B, D

C describes a physical layer problem, not a trunking problem. E doesn't make sense.

2. C

Each VLAN is a broadcast domain.

Chapter 9

Check Your Understanding

1. A

A trunk allows traffic from multiple VLANs to traverse a single link.

2. A, E

B is incorrect because clients can interpret ISL headers. C is incorrect because inter-VLAN communication requires a router. D is incorrect because ISL is used only among Cisco devices.

3. A

ISL capability is required to perform ISL trunking between two devices.

4. D

VTP synchronizes VLAN information.

5. A

Only one VTP domain is allowed per switch.

6. B

The name of the domain is not specified when configuring the VTP mode. There is no such command as answer A's choice.

7. C

Server is the default VTP mode on Catalyst switches.

8. C

The ports in the port group formed by the EtherChannel are required to have the same parameters when forming an IEEE 802.1Q trunk.

9. A

The server propagates the deletion to other VTP servers and clients.

10. C

This is one of the most important precautions a switch administrator must be aware of when deploying Catalyst switches. This prevents unintentional propagation of bad VLAN information.

11. D

D is the only command that displays VTP information.

12. C

C uses the correct syntax.

13. D

Transparent mode is where advertisements are forwarded but not originated.

14. B

Inter-VLAN routing requires a router.

15. B

One physical interface with multiple logical subinterfaces is used on a router in a router-on-a-stick topology.

Challenge Questions and Activities

1. A, B, C, E

Transparent mode switches do not add updates to their databases. Switch4 will receive the VTP update.

2. C, D, B, E, A

With ISL or when the native VLAN is 1, Step E is not needed. On a Catalyst 2950, Steps C and D are not needed.

3. ISL: D and F; IEEE 802.1Q: C and E

A describes frame filtering. B describes VMPS.

10 Gigabit Ethernet   Ethernet that transmits data at 10,000,000,000 (1 billion) bits per second.

1000BASE-T   An IEEE standard (802.3ab) for Gigabit Ethernet based on four-pair UTP cabling.

1000BASE-X   A term referring to all fiber-based Gigabit Ethernet standards.

access layer   An entry point to the network for user workstations and servers. In a campus LAN, the device used at the access layer is typically a Layer 2 switch.

access link   A term used in Cisco campus LAN design that refers to an Ethernet cable that connects an end-user device to an access layer switch.

access point (AP)   A wireless LAN device that allows computers with wireless NICs to communicate with the AP using radio waves. The AP also connects to the wired LAN, providing wireless users with access to the wired LAN.

access switch   A Cisco campus network design term that refers to typically small switches that sit in wiring closets near the end-user devices. The end-user devices connect to the access switch to gain entry to the network.

acknowledgment packet   An EIGRP RTP packet that indicates receipt of any EIGRP packet during a reliable exchange.

active state   If an EIGRP router loses a successor and cannot find a corresponding feasible successor for the route, DUAL places the route in the active state. A query is then multicast to all neighbors in an attempt to locate a successor to the destination network.

adjacency database   A database that lists all the relationships formed between neighboring routers for the purpose of exchanging routing information.

age time   The period of time that a dynamically discovered MAC address remains in the MAC address table.

algorithm   The logic or process that a computer program uses to make decisions. In networking, many protocols use algorithms, including Spanning Tree Protocol and all IP routing protocols.

alternate port   RSTP port role providing an alternate path to the root bridge, which is different from the path that the root port takes.

application-specific integrated circuit (ASIC)   A computer chip that is designed for a specific purpose, as opposed to general purposes. For example, LAN switches use ASICs to perform certain functions, like forwarding frames, so that the process works quickly.

area   OSPF areas comprise the hierarchical components of an OSPF routing domain. All the segmented areas are connected to the backbone area, area 0.

area border router (ABR)   ABRs attach to multiple areas, maintain separate link-state databases for each area they are connected to, and route traffic destined for or arriving from other areas.

asymmetric switching   A term referring to cases in which an Ethernet switch is forwarding a frame that enters the switch on an interface that uses one speed and exits the switch on an interface that uses a different speed.

automatic summarization   The propagation of routing updates consisting of classful networks, independent of the subnets defined on the routers originating the updates.

autonegotiation   A process defined by IEEE 802.3x that defines how Ethernet NICs and switch ports can automatically negotiate the speed and the duplex settings used on an Ethernet link.

autonomous system (AS)   A term used with routing protocols that refers to an internetwork that is in the control of one company, organization, school, or government division. For example, a single company typically would be a single AS, as would a school system.

autonomous system boundary router (ASBR)   An OSPF router that connects to an external routing domain, or AS.

availability   The usefulness of the network, measured largely by throughput, response time, and access to resources.

backbone area   OSPF area 0. This area connects to all other OSPF areas. Route summaries from each area are injected into the backbone area.

backbone link   In LANs, a link between two switches that forwards frames between major sections of the LAN.

backplane   A large circuit board that contains sockets for expansion cards.

backup   This is an RSTP port role. This port provides a backup path that offers a redundant (but less desirable) connection to a segment where another switch port already connects. Backup ports can exist only where two ports are connected in a loopback by a point-to-point link.

backup designated router (BDR)   Does the same thing as the DR but overtly performs the role of DR only after the DR fails.

bit-time   The time required to send a single bit over some transmission medium. You can calculate the time as 1/speed, where speed is the number of bits per second sent over the medium. Also known as slot time.

blocking state   An IEEE 802.1d STP state in which the interface does not send frames or process received frames.

Border Gateway Protocol (BGP)   A routing protocol designed to exchange routing information between different autonomous systems. As such, BGP is an exterior gateway protocol (EGP).

bridge   In Ethernet, a Layer 2 device that receives an electrical signal in one port, interprets the bits, and makes a filtering or forwarding decision about the frame. If it forwards, it sends a regenerated signal.

bridge ID   An ordered pair, consisting of the bridge priority setting and the MAC address of the bridge.

Bridge Protocol Data Units (BPDU)   A term referring to the messages defined by the IEEE 802.1D Spanning Tree Protocol (STP). STP was first created for use by LAN bridges.

bridging table   A general term for the table on a LAN bridge used to make forwarding/filtering decisions. The table holds a list of MAC addresses and the port out which the bridge should forward frames so that they reach the right destination.

broadcast   In Ethernet, a frame that is sent to the broadcast MAC address (FFFF.FFFF.FFFF).

broadcast address   A special Ethernet address, FFFF.FFFF.FFFF, used as a destination MAC address to cause a frame to be sent to all devices on an Ethernet LAN.

broadcast domain   In Ethernet, a set of devices for which a broadcast sent by any device is received by all other devices in the same group.

broadcast frames   In Ethernet, a frame sent to the broadcast MAC address of FFFF.FFFF.FFFF. A broadcast frame should be forwarded to all devices on the same LAN.

broadcast storm   An event in which LAN broadcasts are continually forwarded in loops throughout a LAN, consuming most if not all LAN bandwidth and making the LAN generally unusable.

buffer In cabling, the term *buffer* refers to a part of an optical cable that provides physical protection to the glass fibers inside the buffer.

buffering The process that a bridge or switch uses to prevent collisions. Bridges and switches store, or place into a buffer, each received LAN frame, waiting until the output interface is idle before forwarding the frame.

carrier sense multiple access with collision avoidance (CSMA/CA) A wireless LAN access mechanism that is similar to CSMA/CD but by which the devices first request the right to send, hopefully avoiding collisions.

CatOS Cisco Systems' legacy operating system for many of the older switches, such as the 1200, 4000, 5000, 5500, and 6000; it is still supported as an option on the 4500 and 6500 switches. CatOS is the XDI UNIX like kernel Cisco acquired during its acquisition of the switching company Crescendo.

Cisco Discovery Protocol (CDP) A proprietary Layer 2 protocol used to discover basic information about neighboring Cisco devices.

Cisco Virtual Switch Manager (CVSM) Web-based GUI used to configure and monitor Catalyst 2900XL/3500XL, 2940, 2950, 2960, 3550, 3560, 3750, and 3750 metro series switches.

classful routing protocol A routing protocol where the routing updates do not carry subnet information, and in turn does not support variable length subnet masks. This limitation makes it impossible to have different-sized subnets inside of the same network class.

classless addressing An unicast IP address that is considered to have two parts: a prefix and a host part. The term *classless* means that the classful network rules are not applied to the address.

classless inter-domain routing (CIDR) Replaces the old process of assigning IP addresses based on Class A, B, and C addresses with a generalized network prefix. Instead of being limited to prefix lengths of 8, 16, or 24 bits, CIDR uses prefix lengths with bit counts ranging within the 32-bit continuum of IPv4 addresses. Blocks of addresses can be assigned to networks containing 32 hosts or to those with more than 500,000 hosts. This allows for address assignments that more closely fit an organization's specific needs.

classless routing protocol A routing protocol where the routing updates carry subnet information, and in turn supports variable-length subnet masks. This makes it impossible to have different-sized subnets inside of the same network class.

Cluster Management Suite (CMS) A web-based GUI management interface that certain Catalyst switch series support.

collision In Ethernet LANs, an event in which two or more devices send a frame onto the same collision domain. The electrical signals of the multiple frames overlap, destroying any ability for other devices to interpret the bits of the frame correctly.

collision domain A set of LAN interfaces (including NICs and network device interfaces) in which a collision will occur when frames are sent from them simultaneously.

command-line interface (CLI) Method of interacting with a computer. Commands are entered as lines of text from a keyboard, and output is also received as text.

Content Addressable Memory (CAM) A term referring to the memory hosting the MAC address table of a Cisco switch. CAM is memory hardware that enables fast table lookups.

core layer High-speed switching backbone. This layer of the network design should not perform packet manipulation. A core infrastructure that has redundant alternate paths gives stability to the network in the event of a single device failure.

cut-through switching A method of internal processing by Cisco switches. The switch looks at the destination MAC address when that part of an incoming frame arrives and then starts sending the frame out the output interface, even before the whole frame is received on the input interface.

cyclic redundancy check (CRC)   Type of hash function that produces a checksum against a block of data used to detect and correct errors.

dead interval   The time interval that OSPF uses to measure how long a router should wait before declaring an OSPF link to be dead. By default, the dead interval is four times the hello interval.

default gateway   On a computer, a reference to an IP address on the same subnet, with that IP address being the IP address of a router. When the computer needs to send a packet to another subnet, it sends the packet to its default gateway. This is also known as a default router.

default route   Routing table entry that directs frames for which a next hop is not explicitly listed in the routing table.

delay   *See* latency.

designated port   On each segment, STP establishes one designated port. The designated port is selected on the bridge that has the lowest-cost path to the root bridge. Designated ports are normally in the forwarding state, forwarding traffic for that segment.

designated router (DR)   On multiaccess networks, a DR is elected to consolidate the generation of LSAs on the network, reducing routing update traffic and managing link-state synchronization.

destination Media Access Control (MAC) address   A term referring to the field in an Ethernet header that lists the MAC address to which a frame has been sent.

Diffusing Update Algorithm (DUAL)   An algorithm invented by J.J. Garcia-Luna-Aceves that guarantees loop-free operation at every instant throughout a route computation and allows all devices that are involved in a topology change to synchronize simultaneously. EIGRP uses DUAL.

Dijkstra, Edsger Wybe   Dutch computer scientist who formulated the shortest path algorithm, known as Dijkstra's algorithm.

Dijkstra algorithm   The algorithm used to build a complex database of topology information. It efficiently computes the shortest path between nodes on a graph. In the case of networking, routers are the nodes and links are the edges of the graph.

disabled state   IEEE 802.1d STP state in which the interface has failed or has been administratively disabled. No frames are received or forwarded on the interface, and it is not a candidate for placement into the forwarding state.

discarding   An RSTP port state that replaces the 802.1d blocking state. The role of a discarding port is that of an alternate port. The discarding port can become the designated port if the designated port of the segment fails.

discontiguous subnets   The result of a major network (or subnet thereof) separating subnets of a different major network.

distribution layer   Layer between the access and core layers that helps to define and separate the core. The purpose of this layer is to provide a boundary definition where packet manipulation can take place. The distribution layer segments networks into broadcast domains.

distribution switch   A Cisco campus network design term that refers to switches that do not attach to end-user devices, but instead distribute traffic between different access switches and the rest of the network.

DNS server   A server with a list of hostnames and corresponding IP addresses that is intended to receive requests from end-user devices and respond with the IP address corresponding to the name listed in the DNS request.

domain name   A name, as defined by DNS, that uniquely identifies a computer on the Internet. DNS servers can then respond to DNS requests by supplying the IP address that is used by the computer that has a particular domain name. This term also refers to the part of a domain name that identifies a single company or organization, such as ciscopress.com.

Domain Name System (DNS)   The Internet-wide system by which a hierarchical set of DNS servers collectively holds all the name-IP address mappings. DNS servers refer users to the correct DNS server to successfully resolve a DNS name.

Dynamic Host Configuration Protocol (DHCP)   A protocol used to dynamically assign IP addresses to hosts.

Dynamic Trunk Protocol (DTP)   A Cisco proprietary protocol that manages automatic trunk negotiation.

edge port   An RSTP port concept. With edge ports, no ports that are directly connected to end stations can create bridging loops in the network. Edge ports can go directly to forwarding, skipping the listening and learning stages. An edge port does not generate topology changes when its link toggles.

e-mail server   Software whose function is to interact with client e-mail software on end-user computers and other e-mail servers for the purpose of forwarding and holding e-mail. You can think of an e-mail server as a local post office to which you can send mail and that can hold letters or packages for you until you retrieve them.

Enhanced Interior Gateway Routing Protocol (EIGRP)   A popular Cisco-proprietary IP routing protocol that uses a robust metric, converges quickly, and is used inside a single organization.

enterprise network   A network created for and owned by a single autonomous entity, like a single corporation, governmental agency, or school system.

EtherChannel   The use of multiple Ethernet links between two switches, with the switches combining the links into a single logical link. The switches then load-balance traffic over the link. Without an EtherChannel, only one of the parallel links would be useable because of Spanning Tree Protocol.

Ethereal   A networking analysis tool from Ethereal Software, available for free download and use from http://www.ethereal.com.

Ethernet   A LAN standard created by Xerox and later standardized by IEEE 802.3, 802.2 and many other standards. It provides a vast array of speeds, media, and features.

Ethernet header   The overhead data that Ethernet adds to the beginning of a Layer 3 packet before sending a frame onto a network.

Fast Ethernet   A type of Ethernet that sends data faster than the original Ethernet (100 Mbps versus 10 Mbps). When it was created, it was named "fast" Ethernet.

feasible distance   The best EIGRP metric along a path to a destination network, including the metric to the neighbor advertising that path.

feasible successor   An EIGRP backup route. Backup routes are selected when the successors are identified; however, these routes are kept in a topology table. Multiple feasible successors for a destination can be retained.

filtering   In Ethernet, the process that a bridge or switch performs when it decides that it should not forward a frame out another port.

fixed-length subnet masking (FLSM)   The process of assigning all subnets of the same major network to the same subnet mask. This is the norm when performing subnetting while using classful routing protocols.

flooding   The process that a switch or bridge uses to forward broadcasts and unknown destination unicasts. The bridge/switch forwards these frames out all ports except the port on which the frame was received.

forward delay   The time it takes for a port to transition from the listening state to the learning state or from the learning state to the forwarding state. The forward delay has a default value of 15 seconds.

forwarding   IEEE 802.1d STP state in which the interface can freely send and receive Ethernet frames.

forwarding (Ethernet)   In Ethernet, the process that a bridge or switch performs when it decides that it should forward a frame out another port.

forwarding database   A data structure consisting of stripped-down associations between network prefixes and next hops. Also known as the forwarding table.

fragment-free switching   A method of internal processing by Cisco switches. The switch looks at the destination MAC address when that part of an incoming frame arrives and then starts sending the frame out the output interface even before the input interface receives the whole frame. Unlike cut-through switching, however, fragment-free waits until the first 64 bytes of a frame has arrived before forwarding the frame, which ensures that the frame does not experience normal collisions.

frame   A term referring to the bits sent over a network, specifically including the data link header, trailer, and any data that the header and trailer encapsulates.

frame check sequence (FCS)   A field in the trailer of many data link layer protocols, including Ethernet. The FCS field is used to determine, via a CRC, whether the frame experienced bit errors during transmission. If it did, the frame is discarded.

full duplex   Networking transmission logic in which the devices on either end of a transmission medium are allowed to send data at the same time.

Gigabit Ethernet   Ethernet that transmits data at 1,000,000,000 bits per second.

gigabit interface converter (GBIC)   A type of slot on Cisco routers and Catalyst switches that is designed to accommodate a variety of copper and fiber media options.

half duplex   Networking transmission logic in which the devices on either end of a transmission medium cannot send data at the same time.

header   The overhead bytes that a networking protocol adds to data so that it can perform its work by interacting with other computers and networking devices that implement that same protocol. The header is typically shown to the left of the end-user data so that English-language readers, reading from left to right, see the header first. The header is transmitted on the media before the end-user data.

hello interval   The time interval that OSPF uses to measure how frequently hello packets are sent between neighbor routers.

hello packet   Packet that is specific to OSPF, IS-IS, and EIGRP containing basic information needed to establish formal neighbor relationships upon which actual routing information exchanges take place.

horizontal cross-connect (HCC)   In the IDF, this connects the Layer 1 horizontal cabling with the Layer 2 LAN switch ports and occasionally the Layer 3 router ports.

hostname   A text name, useful for end users, that represents an IP address. DNS servers can be used to resolve the name into the IP address it represents.

hub   In Ethernet, a Layer 1 device that receives an electrical signal in one port, interprets the bits, and regenerates a clean signal that it sends out all other ports of the hub. It also typically supplies several ports, which are often RJ-45 jacks.

HyperTerminal   A terminal emulator from Hillgraeve Inc. (www.hillgraeve.com), that was formerly shipped as part of most Microsoft operating systems. HyperTerminal is available for free download and can be used to access routers and switches via their console ports.

IEEE 802.1d   The original IEEE standard for Spanning Tree Protocol (STP).

IEEE 802.1Q   The IEEE standard for VLAN tagging of frames on a trunk link. With IEEE 802.1Q, a tag containing the VLAN ID is embedded into the Ethernet frame.

IEEE 802.1w   The IEEE standard specifying Rapid Spanning Tree Protocol (RSTP).

IEEE 802.3   The original IEEE standard for Ethernet, based mostly on DIX V2, but with some changes to the Ethernet header.

IEEE 802.3ab   The IEEE standard for Gigabit Ethernet using UTP cabling.

IEEE 802.3ae   The IEEE standard for 10 Gigabit Ethernet using optical cabling.

IEEE 802.3z   The IEEE standard for Gigabit Ethernet using optical cabling.

IEEE (Institute of Electrical and Electronics Engineers) An organization of professionals that does many things, including the definition of LAN standards.

Interior Gateway Protocol (IGP)   Any routing protocol designed to be used between routers inside the same autonomous system. RIP, IGRP, EIGRP, and OSPF are all IGPs.

Interior Gateway Routing Protocol (IGRP)   A Cisco-proprietary IP routing protocol that uses a robust metric and distance vector logic. It has been superseded by the much faster converging EIGRP.

Intermediate System-to-Intermediate System (IS-IS)   A routing protocol created for the OSI networking model. It was later expanded to exchange both OSI and IP routes.

International Organization for Standardization (ISO) An international body that defines many networking standards. This organization created the Open Systems Interconnect (OSI) model.

Internet   The entity that combines enterprise networks, individual users, and Internet service providers (ISP) into a single global IP network.

Internet Activities Board (IAB)   The organization that oversees the development of the TCP/IP protocol model.

Internet Assigned Numbers Authority (IANA)   The organization that assigns important numbers—including globally unique IP addresses—to the proper operation of the TCP/IP protocol and the Internet.

Internet Engineering Task Force (IETF)   The body that is responsible for the development and approval of TCP/IP standards.

Internet Protocol (IP)   One of the protocols of the TCP/IP network model that defines the concepts of logical addressing and routing.

Internet service provider (ISP)   A company that helps to create the Internet by providing connectivity to enterprises and individuals and interconnecting to other ISPs to create connectivity to all other ISPs.

internetwork   A combination of many IP subnets and networks, as created by building a network using routers. The term is used to avoid confusion with the term *network*, because an internetwork can include several IP networks.

Inter-Switch Link (ISL)   A Cisco proprietary protocol for VLAN tagging of frames on a trunk link. ISL functions at Layer 2 by encapsulating a data frame with a new header and a CRC.

inter-VLAN routing   Routing between VLANs on a router or Layer 3 switch.

IPv4   *See* IP version 4.

IPv6   *See* IP version 6.

IP version 4 (IPv4)   The version of the IP protocol upon which the majority of the TCP/IP internetworks are built.

IP version 6 (IPv6)   A newer version of the IP protocol to which all TCP/IP hosts might eventually migrate. IPv6 includes a new addressing structure that uses 128-bit IP addresses.

ipconfig   A command on many Microsoft PC operating systems that displays IP configuration information, including the IP address, subnet mask, default gateway, and DNS IP address.

latency   The time that passes while some event occurs. In networking, latency typically refers to the time between when something is sent in a network and when another device receives it.

Layer 1 devices   A networking device whose main function relates to OSI Layer 1. Ethernet hubs and repeaters are Layer 1 devices.

Layer 2 devices   A networking device whose main function relates to OSI Layer 2. Ethernet bridges and switches are Layer 2 devices.

Layer 3 devices   A networking device whose main function relates to OSI Layer 3. Routers are Layer 3 devices.

Layer 3 switch   A switch that performs wire-speed routing via dedicated ASICs.

learning state   An IEEE 802.1d STP state in which CAM entries are learned based on received frames. The switch does not forward frames in this state.

link   A generic term, often used for WANs but sometimes LANs, describing a transmission medium. Link state routing protocols utilize the state of the link (up or down) in their calculations.

link-state advertisement (LSA)   A basic building block of a link-state routing protocol that describes the local routing topology of a router and is distributed to all other routers in the area.

link-state database   A database consisting of all the learned OSPF LSAs for a particular OSPF process.

link-state routing protocol   A type of routing protocol algorithm in which the routing protocol advertises all the details of each link in the network, each router, and the state (up/down) of each link. The routers can then create a mathematical model of the network, calculate the best path to reach each subnet, and add routes to their routing tables.

link-state synchronization   The process of synchronizing the LSAs of all link-state routers in a given area.

listening state   An IEEE 802.1d STP state that is used as an interim state while a switch waits for its CAM entries to time out. The switch does not forward frames in this state.

local-area network (LAN)   A network created for devices that are in a small, limited geographic area, through which the company owning the LAN has the right to run cables. The network cables are relatively short, from a few tens of meters to a few kilometers in length.

MAC address table   On a bridge or switch, a table that lists all known MAC addresses, and the bridge/switch port out which the bridge/switch should forward frames sent to each MAC address.

max_age   A 20-second interval specified by IEEE 802.1d as the length of time reserved for purging stale entries in the CAM table.

maximum transmission unit (MTU)   The largest IP packet size allowed to be sent out a particular interface. Ethernet interfaces default to an MTU of 1500 because the data field of an Ethernet frame must be limited to 1500 bytes, and the IP packet sits inside the data field of the Ethernet frame.

Media Access Control (MAC)   The lower of the two sublayers of the IEEE standard for Ethernet. It is also the name of that sublayer, as defined by the IEEE 802.3 subcommittee.

Media Access Control (MAC) address   A 48-bit (12 hex digit) address, assigned to a NIC or other LAN interface when the NIC or interface is manufactured.

metric   With routing protocols, this is the objective measurement of how good a particular route is.

Metro Ethernet   The use of Ethernet as a MAN/WAN technology by which a service provided uses Ethernet between a customer site and the provider.

metropolitan-area network (MAN)   A network with a geographic size between a LAN and a WAN. Service providers typically use this to create a high-speed network in a major metropolitan area where many customers might want high-speed services between large sites around a city.

microsegmentation   A practice of putting a single end-user device off each switch port instead of connecting multiple devices via a hub attached to the switch port. This results in each collision domain consisting of a single end-user device and the one switch port, which in turn allows full-duplex operation.

mono spanning tree (MST)   An 802.1Q implementation of spanning tree in which only one instance of spanning tree is used for all VLANs.

multiaccess network   A network supporting more than two routers, such as an Ethernet network.

multicast frame   An Ethernet frame with a destination MAC address that has its high-order bit set to 1. These frames, by design, should be forwarded to all devices on the LAN that are configured to receive a copy of multicast frames sent to that specific multicast MAC address.

multicast packet   An IP packet sent to a destination IP address that begins with a number between 224 and 239, inclusively. The network should forward and copy multicast packets so that all IP hosts that are configured to receive a copy of multicast packets sent to a particular IP address receive a copy.

multilayer switch   A switch with dedicated ASICs that is designed to perform wire-speed switching at OSI layers greater than 2.

multiport bridge   A LAN switch. This term refers to bridges and switches using the same basic forwarding, filtering, address learning, and STP logic. However, switches have many physical ports or interfaces, whereas bridges typically have only a few ports.

multiport repeaters   Ethernet repeaters with more than two ports. Another name for hub.

name resolution   The process by which a computer sends a DNS request to a DNS server, with a name in the request, and the DNS server(s) reply with the IP address that corresponds to that name.

native VLAN   IEEE 802.1Q identifier value associated with a trunk port(The default is VLAN 1.) All untagged frames are assigned to the VLAN that is specified in the ID parameter.

neighbor table   A table that lists adjacent routers. This table is comparable to the adjacencies database that OSPF uses, and it serves the same purpose (to ensure bidirectional communication between each of the directly connected neighbors). Each protocol that EIGRP supports has a neighbor table.

Network Address Translation (NAT)   An IP feature that helped prevent IPv4 address depletion. NAT allows many hosts to use private IP addresses, while representing each TCP connection or UDP flow from multiple computers as if they all were from the same computer using a single public IP address.

network engineer   A person responsible for the planning and implementation of a network.

nonbackbone area   Any OSPF area other than the backbone area (area 0).

non-designated port   A port for a segment that is not directly connected to the root bridge that is normally in the blocking state to logically break the loop topology. When a port is in the blocking state, it is not forwarding traffic but can still receive traffic.

non-root bridge   Any bridge that is not the root bridge for a given instance of STP.

non-volatile RAM (NVRAM)   RAM that retains its contents when a unit is powered off.

Open Shortest Path First (OSPF)   Link-state, hierarchical IGP routing algorithm proposed as a successor to RIP in the Internet community. OSPF features include least-cost routing, multipath routing, and load balancing. Like IS-IS, OSPF depends on the Dijkstra algorithm to form a shortest-path tree relative on each router.

Organizationally Unique Identifier (OUI)   The first half of a MAC address. Manufacturers must ensure that the value of the OUI is one that the manufacturer has registered with the IEEE. This value is meant to identify the manufacturer of any Ethernet NIC or interface.

OSPF authentication   Each OSPF interface can present an authentication key that routers can use to send OSPF information to other routers on the segment. The authentication key, known as a password, is a shared secret between the routers. This key generates the authentication data in the OSPF packet header.

OSPF cost   100,000,000 divided by bandwidth (of an interface) in bps. For example, Fast Ethernet has an OSPF cost of 1.

OSPF hello protocol   The protocol used to establish neighbor relationships. Hello packets also act as keepalives to let routers know that other routers are still functional.

OSPF network type   OSPF routers determine which routers to become adjacent to based on the type of network to which they are connected. OSPF interfaces automatically recognize three network types: broadcast multiaccess, point-to-point, and nonbroadcast multiaccess.

Packet Tracer   A software tool from Cisco Systems, created for use by Cisco Networking Academy Program, that can be used to demonstrate and learn how the basics of the flow of traffic in networks work.

passive state   An EIGRP state for a route, reflecting the reachability of the route.

path cost   The shortest path to the root bridge based on cumulative link costs.

Per-VLAN Spanning Tree + (PVST+)   Cisco implementation of spanning tree whereby each VLAN has its own instance of spanning tree.

point-to-point link   With RSTP, a port operating in full-duplex mode is point-to-point. If you connect one port to another through a point-to-point link with RSTP and the local port becomes designated, it negotiates a rapid transition with the other port.

port-based memory buffering   Buffering mechanism whereby frames are stored in queues that are linked to specific incoming ports. A frame is only transmitted to the outgoing port after all the frames ahead of it in the queue are successfully transmitted.

PortFast   Optional IEEE 802.1d setting on Catalyst switches. With PortFast enabled, an end-user port automatically transitions from the blocking state to the forwarding state.

power-on self test (POST)   Series of tests that runs automatically to verify that the switch functions correctly. Often, system LEDs indicate the success or failure of POST.

prefix   In IP subnetting, a term referring to the portion of a set of IP addresses whose value must be identical for the addresses to be in the same subnet.

prefix length   The number of 1 bits in the subnet mask associated with a subnet—the length of the prefix.

process ID   Locally significant number between 1 and 65,535 that you select to identify the OSPF routing process.

propagation delay   The time required for energy to pass over a networking medium from one end to another. The time required varies based on the medium, with the speed typically varying between 50 percent and 90 percent of the speed of light in a vacuum.

protocol   Written specification that defines the way products should perform a certain task, typically in networking, and typically regarding logic or information as it is transmitted through a network. A standards body approves and accepts the specifications.

protocol data unit (PDU)   A generic term from OSI referring to the data, headers, and trailers about which a particular networking layer is concerned.

Protocol Type field   A field in a header, often a data link header, that identifies the type of network layer protocol header that is encapsulated inside a frame.

query packet   An EIGRP packet used to solicit specific information from one or all of its neighbors regarding a particular destination.

random-access memory (RAM)   Also known as read-write memory, RAM can have new data written to it and can have stored data read from it. RAM is the main working area, or temporary storage, that the CPU uses for most processing and operations. A drawback of RAM is that it requires electrical power to maintain data storage. If the computer is turned off or loses power, all data stored in RAM is lost unless the data was previously saved to disk. Memory boards with RAM chips plug into the motherboard.

Rapid Spanning Tree Protocol (RSTP)   Type of STP specified by IEEE 802.1w, which serves as an improvement to the original 802.1d standard. RSTP significantly reduces the time to reconverge the active topology of the network when changes to the physical topology or its configuration parameters occur. RSTP defines the additional RSTP port roles of alternate and backup, and it defines port states as discarding, learning, and forwarding.

RSTP port state   RSTP has a different set of port states from IEEE 802.1d. The RSTP port state controls the forwarding and learning processes and provides the values of discarding, learning, and forwarding.

read-only memory (ROM)   A type of computer memory in which data has been prerecorded. After data has been written onto a ROM chip, it can only be read, not removed. A version of ROM known as EEPROM (electronically erasable programmable read-only memory) can be written to. It is called Flash memory or firmware. The basic input/output system (BIOS) in most PCs is stored in EEPROM.

redundancy   In LANs, redundancy refers to a LAN design having more than one physical path between any two parts of the complete LAN. Redundant Ethernet LANs require the use of Spanning Tree Protocol (STP) to ensure that frames do not needlessly loop around the redundant parts of the LAN.

Reliable Transport Protocol (RTP)   Transport layer protocol that guarantees ordered delivery of EIGRP packets to all neighbors.

repeater   In Ethernet, a Layer 1 device that receives an electrical signal in one port, interprets the bits, and regenerates a clean signal that it sends out the other port of the repeater.

reply packet   An EIGRP packet used to respond to query packets. No reply packets result in a route going into active state.

root bridge   For a given instance of spanning tree, the root bridge is the bridge that has the lowest bridge ID.

root port   The port that has the lowest-cost path from the non-root bridge to the root bridge. Root ports are normally in the forwarding state.

route aggregation   The summarization of networks in which the summarized networks are classful networks or summaries of classful networks. Although it is similar to CIDR, the term aggregation is used more frequently in the context of summarizing networks with BGP.

route summarization   Consolidation of advertised network addresses that causes a single summary route to be advertised to upstream routers.

router   A network device, typically connected to a range of LAN and WAN interfaces, that forwards packets based on their destination IP addresses.

router-on-a-stick   A means of inter-VLAN routing that relies on an external router trunked to a Layer 2 switch.

routing   The process by which a router receives an incoming frame, discards the data link header and trailer, makes a forwarding decision based on the destination IP address, adds a new data link header and trailer based on the outgoing interface, and forwards the new frame out the outgoing interface.

Routing Information Protocol (RIP)   An old IP routing protocol that uses distance vector logic, hop count as the metric, with relatively slow convergence.

routing table   A list that a router holds in memory for the purpose of making decisions on how to forward packets.

routing updates   Messages sent by routers, as defined by each routing protocol, that include routing information of various kinds.

RSTP port role   RSTP specifies the following port roles:

- **root**—A forwarding port elected for the spanning-tree topology.

- **designated**—A forwarding port elected for every switched LAN segment.

- **alternate**—An alternate path to the root bridge, which is different from the path that the root port takes.

- **backup**—A backup path that provides a redundant (but less desirable) connection to a segment where another switch port already connects. Backup ports can exist only where two ports are connected in a loopback by a point-to-point link or bridge with two or more connections to a shared LAN segment.

- **disabled**—A port that has no role within the operation of spanning tree.

service provider   A somewhat generic term for any company that provides service to another, particularly some form of network connection. Examples include WAN service providers and Internet service providers.

shared bandwidth   Refers to devices sharing the same bandwidth because only one device can use a shared Ethernet media at a time.

shared memory buffer   Common memory buffer that all ports share where frames are deposited. The amount of buffer memory that a port requires is dynamically allocated. The frames in the buffer are linked dynamically to the destination port.

shield   Any cabling component that prevents unwanted interference from outside energy sources. Shields also help prevent wires inside the shield from interfering with transmissions on other cables.

shielded twisted-pair (STP)   A type of network cabling that includes twisted pair wires, with shielding around each pair of wires and another shield around all wires in the cable.

shortest path first (SPF) algorithm   Algorithm used to build a complex database of topology information. Efficiently computes the shortest path between nodes on a graph. In the case of networking, routers are the nodes and links are the edges of the graph.

Simple Mail Transfer Protocol (SMTP)   The process by which e-mail can be forwarded and then held for later retrieval by the intended recipient.

Simple Network Management Protocol (SNMP)   An application protocol typically not used by end users; instead, the network management software and actual networking devices use it to allow a network engineer to monitor and troubleshoot network problems.

slot time   The minimum time that a NIC or interface can take to send an entire frame. Slot time implies a minimum frame size.

small-form-factor pluggable (SFP)   A type of slot in Cisco routers and Catalyst switches that provides an alternative to the GBIC. The SFP slots are much smaller, requiring less real estate on the Cisco devices.

source MAC address   A field inside an Ethernet frame that lists the MAC address of the device that sent the frame.

spanning-tree algorithm (STA)   The underlying logic (algorithm) that STP uses.

Spanning Tree Protocol (STP)   A protocol, originally defined in IEEE 802.1d, that defines the way bridges and switches can dynamically determine how to allow a redundant LAN design while preventing frames from looping unnecessarily through the LAN.

standards   Written specifications that define the way products should perform a certain task. A standards body approves and accepts the specifications.

Start Frame Delimiter (SFD)   The eighth byte of an IEEE-standard Ethernet frame. It follows the IEEE-standard 7-byte preamble.

static route   An entry in an IP routing table that was created due to a network engineer typing the routing information into the router configuration.

store-and-forward switching   A method of internal processing by Cisco switches. The switch must receive the whole frame before it sends the first bit of the frame. *See also* cut-through switching and fragment-free switching.

STP topology   A subset of a LAN topology, specifically the ports that are in an STP forwarding state.

successor   An EIGRP route selected as the primary route to reach a destination. Successors are the entries kept in the routing table.

supernetting   Aggregation of IP network addresses advertised as a single classless network address. For example, given four Class C IP networks—192.0.8.0, 192.0.9.0, 192.0.10.0, and 192.0.11.0—each having the intrinsic network mask of 255.255.255.0, one can advertise the address 192.0.8.0 with a subnet mask of 255.255.252.0.

switch   In Ethernet, a Layer 2 device that receives an electrical signal in one port, interprets the bits, and makes a filtering or forwarding decision about the frame. If it forwards, it sends a regenerated signal. Switches typically have many physical ports, often RJ-45 jacks, whereas bridges traditionally have two ports.

switch virtual interface (SVI)   A logical representation of a VLAN as one interface to a routing or bridging function of a switch. It is essentially an evolution of the concept of bridge virtual interface (BVI) commonly used on Cisco routers in the 1990s.

switched bandwidth   A term that refers to LAN switches not having to share the bandwidth on one switch port with devices on other switch ports. A switch that has 24 1-Gbps interfaces has effectively 24 Gbps of switched bandwidth. *See also* shared bandwidth.

switched LAN   A LAN created by using LAN switches.

switching table   The table that a LAN switch uses for its forwarding/filtering decisions. The table holds a list of MAC addresses and the switch port out which the switch should forward frames so that they reach the right destination.

symmetric switching   Cases in which an Ethernet switch is forwarding a frame that enters the switch on an interface that uses one speed and exits the switch on an interface that uses the same speed. *See also* asymmetric switching.

Telecommunications Industry Association (TIA)   An electrical standards body that defines the standards for many networking cables, including most electrical and optical LAN cables.

Terabit (Tb)   1 trillion bits.

Terabits per second (Tbps)   A unit of measurement of the number of times 1,000,000,000,000 bits can be transmitted in 1 second. 1 Tbps = 1,000,000,000,000 bps.

Terabyte (TB)   1 trillion bytes.

Thicknet   A common term for 10BASE5 Ethernet, referring to 10BASE5 cabling being thicker than the coaxial cabling used for 10BASE2 (Thinnet).

Thinnet   A common term for 10BASE2 Ethernet, referring to 10BASE2 cabling being thinner than the coaxial cabling used for 10BASE5 (Thicknet).

throughput   The actual data transfer rate between two computers at some point in time. Throughput is impacted by the slowest speed link used for sending data between the two computers and myriad variables that might change during the course of a day.

Time To Live (TTL) field   A field in the IP header that prevents a packet from looping around an IP internetwork indefinitely. Routers decrement the TTL field each time they forward a packet. If they decrement the TTL to 0, the router discards the packet, preventing it from looping forever.

topological database   Set of all links learned from the flooding of LSAs (OSPF or IS-IS). Each router synchronizes its topological database with all other routers in the area. Also known as the link-state database.

topology table   Table that includes route entries for all destinations that the router has learned. Each EIGRP router maintains a topology table for each routed protocol that is configured.

Transmission Control Protocol/Internet Protocol (TCP/IP)   A network model defined by the IETF that has been implemented on most computers and network devices in the world.

trunk (or VLAN trunk)   In Ethernet LANs, an Ethernet link between two switches that allows traffic from multiple different VLANs to pass.

Type field   Another term for Protocol Type field. *See* Protocol Type field.

unicast MAC address   A MAC address that identifies a single NIC or interface.

unshielded twisted-pair (UTP)   A general type of cable that holds twisted pairs of copper wires and has little shielding.

uplink   In a campus LAN design, this is an Ethernet link connecting an access switch to a distribution switch.

variable-length subnet masks (VLSM)   A condition in which more than one subnet mask is used in different subnets of the same class A, B, or C network.

vertical cross-connect (VCC)   Interconnects the various IDFs to the MDF, normally with fiber-optic links.

virtual circuit   Ethernet switching increases the available bandwidth for a network by creating dedicated network segments (or point-to-point connections) and connecting them in a virtual network within the switch. This virtual network circuit exists only when two nodes need to communicate. This network is called a virtual circuit because it exists only when needed and is established within the switch.

virtual LAN (VLAN)   Group of devices on one or more LANs that can communicate as if they were attached to the same wire, when in fact they are located on several different LAN segments.

Virtual Private Networks (VPN)   The use of a public network, typically the Internet, to deliver packets that need to be treated as private. To do so, VPNs encrypt the packets before they pass over the Internet.

virtual terminal (VTY)   A command-line interface created on a networking device for a Telnet or Secure Shell session.

VLAN Management Policy Server (VMPS)   Catalyst switch that contains a database mapping MAC addresses to VLAN assignments. When a frame arrives on a dynamic port at the Catalyst access switch, the Catalyst switch queries the VMPS for the VLAN assignment based on the source MAC address of the arriving frame.

VLAN Trunking Protocol (VTP)   Cisco-created protocol meant to automate many VLAN configuration tasks so that configurations on a VTP server are propagated automatically to other switches in the VTP domain.

VTP domain   Set of Catalyst switches in a campus network with the same VTP name assigned to them.

VTP pruning   VTP technology that results in the prevention of unnecessary traffic on switch segments.

VTP server   A Cataylst switch on which configuration changes are propagated across links to all connected switches in the VTP domain.

wide-area network (WAN)   A network connecting devices in a wide geographic area that requires the use of transmission services from a WAN service provider. The service provider has the right of way to install cables over wide geographic areas.

Index

W-X-Y-Z

Register this Book for Exclusive Content

Gain access to the following benefits when you register *Switching Basics and Intermediate Routing CCNA 3 Companion Guide* on ciscopress.com.

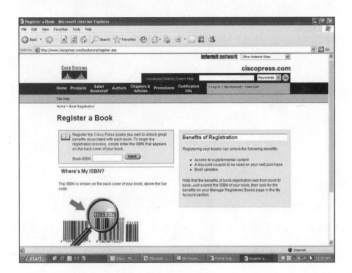

- PDF of chapter 4, "Dynamic Routing Protocols", from *Routing TCP/IP*, Volume I, Second Ed.

- PDF of chapter 3, "Information Technology: A Great Career", from *The IT Career Builder's Toolkit*

- Coupon code for **35% off** most Cisco Press titles

To register this book, go to **www.ciscopress.com/bookstore/register.asp** and enter the book's ISBN located on the back cover. You'll then be prompted to log in or join ciscopress.com to continue registration.

After you register the book, a link to the supplemental content will be listed on your My Registered Books page.

ciscopress.com

Learning is serious business.　**Invest wisely.**